GENDER CONSCIOUSNESS AND POLITICS

PERSPECTIVES ON GENDER

GENDER CONSCIOUSNESS AND POLITICS

Sue Tolleson Rinehart

Routledge
New York • London

Published in 1992 by
Routledge, an imprint of
Routledge, Chapman and Hall, Inc.
29 West 35 Street
New York, NY 10001

Published in Great Britain by
Routledge
11 New Fetter Lane
London EC4P 4EE

Library of Congress Cataloging in Publication Data

Rinehart, Sue Tolleson.
    Gender consciousness and politics / Sue Tolleson Rinehart.
        p.   cm.—(Perspectives on gender)
    Includes bibliographical references and index.
    ISBN 0-415-90684-9.—ISBN 0-415-90685-7 (pbk.)
    1. Women in politics—United States. 2. Feminist theory.
3. Women—United States—Socialization. 4. Political socialization—
United States. 5. Gender identity—United States.   I. Title.
II. Series: Perspectives on gender (New York, N.Y.)
HQ 1236.5.U6R56 1992
305.42′01—dc20   92-8240
                                                                            CIP

British Library Cataloguing in Publication Data Available on Request

CONTENTS

TABLES AND FIGURES

TABLES

FIGURES

ACKNOWLEDGMENTS

This work has preoccupied me for years, from its conception in some ephemeral questions while I was writing a dissertation—questions that, while they could not be addressed in that project, continued to haunt me—to its fragile gestation, first haltingly announced in a convention paper presented to the Annual Meeting of the Midwest Political Science Association in 1988. Although the thinking there was not yet complete and the empirical analysis benefited from criticism, colleagues nonetheless awarded the Midwest's Breckenridge Prize to that paper. That vote of confidence in my ideas was invaluable to me.

Others also have shown confidence in me, even when they were more than a little puzzled about what I was up to: my parents, Vern and Marie Tolleson, in the dark ages of the 1950s, started me off with very little confining traditional gender role socialization. They continued to encourage me when I was one of a tiny number of women at Georgia Tech trying to earn undergraduate degrees in an often hostile environment (I am thrilled to see so many more women there now), or when I romped and stomped as an exuberantly angry young feminist in the early 1970s, or when that anger led me to graduate school in political science. I thank them and my sisters, Peggy and Pam.

In graduate school, I, a woman who wanted to study gender, found no courses, almost no literature, and plenty of objections. But Jerry Perkins, Diane Fowlkes, and Tom Lauth, while they and I were at Georgia State, and then Roberta Sigel, Mike Delli Carpini, and others at Rutgers, especially the women at the Center for the American Woman and Politics, made many kinds of intellectual and emotional growth possible for me. In the years since, I have known

the joy that comes from feeling accepted and recognized by more of my colleagues, and I thank them all for befriending not only me but the scholarship of
gender politics. In particular, Clarke Cochran at Texas Tech University and Dick
Richardson and David Lowery at the University of North Carolina at Chapel Hill
were marvelously supportive department chairpersons, the last two adopting me
as a "foster colleague" in my sojourns as a visitor there. Indeed, I am grateful
to all the members of my "foster department" at UNC for their generosity to an
itinerant scholar, with special thanks to George Rabinowitz, Bill Keech, and
Stuart Elaine MacDonald.

The many women I have met and come to know in our profession have created
a beautiful, safe harbor in which I have sheltered over the years, and I hope I
have been able to do the same for them. Thank goodness for the Women's Caucus for Political Science, the Organized Section for Women and Politics Research, and Cathy Rudder and Sheilah Mann of the American Political Science
Association: they have all contributed immeasurably to women's development
as professionals and scholars in what otherwise would have been a mighty chilly
place. And to the women who staff the political science department offices at
Texas Tech and UNC, I say sisterhood is powerful!

Some friends have not been burdened with the manuscript itself but have suffered through it with me (and suffered me!) nonetheless: Jeanie Stanley, Kathleen
Harris, and Rick Battistoni keep me going in Texas, and Doris Elkin and Stuart
MacDonald perform the same service in Chapel Hill. Dorothy Stetson and Peggy
Conway supply me with affectionate support at meetings and conventions, by
letter (electronic or otherwise) and on the telephone. My love for them all is
only exceeded by my gratitude.

Jean Bethke Elshtain read and most kindly criticized an earlier version of
much of the historical and theoretical material in chapter five, for which I thank
her.

I made unmerciful demands on Virginia Sapiro, Roberta Sigel, and Kent Jennings: they have had much to read and criticize and admonish. Through a
lengthy period of thinking, writing, rewriting, through crises of belief in myself
and my ability to say anything worth saying, Gina, Roberta, and Kent have acted
not only as the most percipient of critics but as the most sustaining of mentors
and friends. I am sure that they will feel as relieved as I do that the book has
been born at last, after a pregnancy worthy of an elephant. The good in this
book I owe in very large measure to them, and to Lisa Freeman, my original
commissioning editor. I tried very hard to make the most of what they all gave
me; where I have failed to do it, it is my failure and not theirs. For this book,
and for so much else, I thank them from the bottom of my heart. I thank Max
Zutty and Ray Walker, my editor and production editor at Routledge, for easing
the last stages of bringing this book to light.

Scholars of gender in politics, history, philosophy, and literature have crafted a vibrant corpus amid disapprobation, disinterest, or contempt. I offer thanks for their courage and for their enormous contribution to the world's spirit, and to the life of the mind.

My husband, Cliff Rinehart, would much prefer it if I said only, "Hey. You. Thanks. You know who you are." While sympathizing with his fear of my unruly propensity to gush, to which this whole acknowledgment surely testifies, I can't go quite that far in self-restraint. I dedicate this book to him with love and gratitude.

Chapter 1

FEMINISM, ANALYSIS, AND THE SEARCH FOR MEANING

Yes, yes, if you please, no reference to examples in books. Men have had every advantage of us in telling their own story. Education has been theirs in so much higher a degree; the pen has been in their hands. I will not allow books to prove anything.

—Jane Austen, *Persuasion*, 1818

What had poor woman done, that she must be
Debarred from sense, and sacred poetry? . . .
As for you half-wits, you unthinking tribe,
We'll let you see, what e'er besides we do,
How artfully we copy some of you:
And if you're drawn to th' life, pray tell me then,
Why women should not write as well as men.
    —Aphra Behn, Epilogue to *Sir Patient Fancy*, 1678

What is the nature of woman? Jane Austen's gentle, and Aphra Behn's outraged, protests against masculine pronouncements on woman's proper sphere are available to us because Austen and Behn not only wrote, but strove mightily to publish their writing. In doing so they violated first one and then another of the canons of femininity. Jane Austen personally experienced little public outrage for the sad reason that she did not live to see most of her books in print, while those that did appear in her lifetime were modestly presented to the world as the work of "a lady." *Persuasion* was published a year after her death, and even then her name did not appear on the title page. The cloying eulogy, inserted as a preface by her brother Henry and revealing her identity at last, made her out to be a precious paradigm of modest feminine virtue quite different from the Jane we see in her own surviving letters (Austen, [1818] 1933). *That* Jane breezily confided to her niece Fanny, in speaking of an acquaintance, "He and I should not in the least agree of course, in our ideas of Novels and Heroines; pictures of perfection as you know make me sick and wicked" (Chapman, 1985: 198). Recent scholarship suggests that, indeed, Jane offered a spirited if diffuse feminist argument for those who could read between the lines of her novels (Kirkham, 1983). "Wonderful Aphra," as Antonia Fraser (1984: 333–335) buoyantly calls her, faced excoriation in her life and provoked such horrified offenses to delicate sensibilities in succeeding centuries that her work was all but lost to English literature until recently (Goreau, 1980).

Lest readers wonder why a book about politics would begin with literary figures, it is well to note at the outset that the debate on the nature of woman has been remarkably one-sided as it has come down to us. Indeed, it has hardly been a debate at all, since the voices raised in it have been almost exclusively male and almost completely in agreement. Our understanding of women's views on the question labors under the serious liability of women's once very restricted access to pen, paper, and the printing press. One of the greatest achievements of the contemporary Women's Movement has been the uncovering of those works of women that did survive in some permanent or public form. Through their discovery or reinterpretation, we learn that something like a modern feminist argument about men and women in public and private worlds has been made, and made with strikingly similar reasoning, for centuries. First among the demands these women have made is learning and literacy, for they always understood the severity of women's handicap when "men have had every advantage in telling their own story." Whether we listen to Aphra or Mary Astell, passionately advocating women's education in the seventeenth century (Fraser, 1984: 329–331; Kinnaird, 1983), or the reiteration of the advocacy in the eighteenth century by Mary Wollstonecraft ([1792] 1975), or in the nineteenth century by Elizabeth Cady Stanton ([1882] 1915) and Margaret Fuller (Blanchard, 1978: 218), or by a new chorus of women in the early twentieth century, we hear the same plea for women's intellectual development.

Why should women's education have been so impoverished and such a matter of dispute? This question is answered simply: received wisdom about the nature of woman included a belief in the undesirability, even to an assumption of the impossibility, of a fully intellectually active woman. To educate her is to equip her to become independent of rather than dependent on man, another subject rather than his object, active rather than passive, in short, to give her the means to strike out for an equality with men, whatever that equality may mean in a given time or culture. Such equality is frightening to many of both sexes. "Hence I am induced to believe, we are debar'd from the knowledge of humane learning lest our pregnant Wits should rival the towering conceits of our insulting Lords and Masters," wrote Mrs. Hannah Wolley in 1675 (Kinnaird, 1983: 28).

The question of *why* such a notion of woman's nature should have held such sway is not simple at all. It is almost irresistibly tempting to lay the issue at the door of male privilege. Patriarchy, no matter where one finds it, puts man ahead of, or at the head of, woman in every aspect of society's organization. In the family, in the marketplace, in the polis, traditional patriarchal orientations place women in a secondary position, more or less dependent on men, more or less restricted in their movement within or apart from their relationships with the men in their lives and the male world. Such an arrangement has been so beneficial to men, this view points out, that it has been defended against dissenting women by turning the tables and arguing that equality comes at the terrible price of women's forfeiture of their *superiority* to men. If women can be made to accept their secondary status, especially to the extent of embracing their chains, men gain compliant servants of their sexual, domestic, and emotional needs, while women, in exchange, lose those virtues that are the "sober offspring of reason" (Wollstonecraft, [1792] 1975: 125, 178–179). Masculinist society's benefits are all these things writ large. Women are brought not only to accept but to embrace their servitude by their incessant indoctrination into cult worship of their own femininity, as it has been defined for them by men. Potent Western examples of such socialization are the Victorian feminine ideal (Strouse, 1980; I return at length to this Victorian ideology of gender roles and its antecedents in chapter five) and Freudianism (Donovan, 1985; Elshtain, 1986: 96–100). John Stuart Mill demonstrated the logical limits of such a rigidly and artificially imposed "natural" femininity when he reminded his brethren that it is pointless to forbid a woman to do what *by her nature* she cannot do, and unjust to forbid her from doing what she can (Mill, [1869] 1970: 154).

No matter how satisfying the male privilege explanation of the evolution of relations between the sexes seems to be, it, at most, *begins* a genuinely two-sided debate rather than ending one. Among the questions it engenders are how such a view could have prevailed against women's own desires and intentions, how it might be eradicated, and with what it shall be replaced. All these questions, of course, take us right back into the maelstrom of the nature of woman and the extent and kind of its differences from the nature of man. Thus, all these questions have occupied feminist thinkers and have been the driving force behind practical attempts to change society, despite the fact that the question of whether the "nature" of the sexes is truly natural rather than conventional, or some amalgam of the two, probably never can be answered once and for all.

Nonetheless, male and female thinkers alike have struggled to establish the boundaries: where are men and women essentially alike, and where are they different? For feminists, and for those "masculinists" who have endeavored to justify and sustain the traditional order, the latter question is the limiting one.

Identifying genuine differences, and assessing their meaning, determines the common ground of similarity left to the sexes. But agreement on identification and meaning, of course, is precisely the problem. The present body of popular "how to" antifeminist advice, advocating "total womanhood" and the like, is but one representative of an extreme but usually unsophisticated picture of differences between the sexes. Although Steven Rinehart (1982), who provides an extensive review of these works, wonders why feminist thinkers have not expended more effort on rebutting them, feminists would no doubt agree that the effort to challenge established orthodoxy as it is represented in scholarship, art, and politics has been consuming enough without tackling these derivative postulations as well. Examples of resistance to a consideration of feminist formulations include Benjamin Barber's (1976) *Liberating Feminism,* employing a kind of reproductive false consciousness argument against feminism, although Barber's (1988) recent study of Hegel contributes thoughtfully to the ongoing conversation of the nature of relations between the sexes. One who has apparently not seen any reason to reconstruct his view is Allan Bloom; Bloom's (1979) introduction to his own translation of Jean-Jacques Rousseau's *Emile* takes a Rousseau-like preemptive slap at any feminist objection to Rousseau's extraordinary plan of education for women: criticism of Rousseau's benighted (if admittedly complicated) views of women is simply "an almost inevitable result of the bourgeoisification of the world [responsible for producing] the selfish Hobbesian individual, striving for self-preservation, comfort, and power after power" (p. 24). Case closed. And for Bloom (1987), the case has apparently remained so, for nearly a decade later, in his celebrated *Closing of the American Mind,* he dismisses feminism as a minor aspect of the sixties sexual revolution without acknowledging it as a system of thought as all but, again, rendering summary judgment on it. Other, sometimes puzzling, reactions include Hewlett's (1986) *A Lesser Life,* indicting women's economic and social plight but attributing the cause of women's problems to feminism.

As with theorizing, virtually any degree of stress on male-female differences has worked to the disadvantage of women in terms of public power, for the differences have almost always been seen as justification for assigning men and women to different spheres: men to the public arena, women to the private domain. The phrase "the personal is political," often on feminist lips in the early 1970s, however, warns us that the two spheres are not separate, that in fact the public arena has an enormous influence on the private domain, and that women, relegated to one and prohibited from free exercise in the other, are thus vulnerable. Women have also, from Elizabeth Cady Stanton to Eleanor Roosevelt to many contemporary feminist theorists, valorized the virtues of women's private, familial roles and have insisted that those virtues must be brought to the public arena.

It has required a feminist political perspective to make the vulnerability evident; the relegation of women and their children to the private domain was so complete that the almost total absence of public policy relevant to their concerns became a policy in default. Virginia Sapiro's (1986) essay on the gender bases of public policy demonstrates this in a general sense, and a specific examination of the history of maternal and infant health care policy makes it painfully clear (Tolleson Rinehart, 1987). But it has also required a feminist sensibility to reveal the existence of a historical continuity in the perspective: only recently has feminist scholarship endowed us with the knowledge that a Margaret Fuller or an Elizabeth Cady Stanton were moving toward conclusions that Sapiro and others would draw more than a century later. And, as for bringing private virtues to the public, the last decades of the twentieth century have seen "compassion issues," traditional "women's issues" of child welfare, health, and education, and issues of environmental quality and peace reach new heights in our collective consciousness.

The foregoing discussion would have been a very confusing introduction to any treatment of gender politics only a few years ago. Readers would have required, instead, a careful description of the status of women and their political rights from the struggle for suffrage to the mid-twentieth century. One result of gender politics scholarship to date is the fact that such a description, here, would only be redundant to the fine groundwork already laid (cf. Klein, 1984; Baxter and Lansing, 1983; and Darcy, Welch, and Clark, 1987). We can, instead, pause, step back, and consider what two decades of empirical work and a few centuries of feminist political thought have accomplished. The remainder of this chapter is devoted to that consideration; it is the fullest way to an understanding of the historical and present effects of women's gender consciousness on politics.

VARIATIONS OF THE THEME OF GENDER DIFFERENCES

Political Thought

The early "feminist" thought in the Western tradition has drawn on Enlightenment rationality and belief in human perfectibility, liberalism, transcendentalism, romanticism, and moral theory—strains, as Jean Bethke Elshtain (1986: 65) points out, not always comfortably compatible nor, as Cott (1987) makes so clear, even properly identifiable as "feminist" in the sense that we would understand it in the twentieth century. But in the sense that one strain—the plea for a recognition of woman's essential and complete personhood—has always been present, "feminist" is the term that will be used in these pages to describe evidence, wherever it appears, of women thinkers' advocacy for women.

Recently, Marxism and other socialist theories, psychoanalytic theory, and existentialism, as well as an argument for "maternal thinking" unique in the philosophical tradition, have also provided grist for feminist thought and new threads in the intricately textured tapestry of commentary on the relations between men and women (Donovan, 1985; Ruddick, 1980). The warp of original feminist philosophy is crossed by the woof of feminist intellectual history, reexamining the meaning of the role of women in the world view of male philosophers in the Western tradition (Okin, 1979; Saxonhouse, 1985, 1986).

The basic premises of feminist thought, whether they emanate from the individualist and egalitarian tradition of liberalism, the macroeconomic perspective of socialism, or the metaphysics of existentialism, resonate with the claim of woman's right to full participation in society. Although they differ over the justification for the claim, the nature of the participation, and the purpose to which participation is bent, they share an extremely developed consciousness of the importance of gender to women as individuals and to society as a whole. Much liberal feminist theory is labeled reformist in its prescriptions, since it appears merely to advocate the inclusion of women in extant political and economic structures; this, indeed, is the school of thought most evident in the women's movements of the nineteenth and twentieth centuries. A smaller body of thought, usually identified as radical feminism, prescribes a kind of revolutionary change. These includes Shulamith Firestone's call for a displacement of human reproduction processes onto mechanical, technological surrogates, and Mary Daly's advocacy of women's complete withdrawal from patriarchal society and even its language (Firestone, 1972; Daly, 1984). Hester Eisenstein (1983: 136) notes that Daly's withdrawal includes eschewing political struggle, but Daly and a handful of others whose thinking has led them to a conclusion in favor of separatism are a distinct minority in this regard. Virtually all feminist thought is intensely political, even when only implicitly so, but more often it is explicitly eager to promote women's entry into the political arena for the sake of participation both as a means and as an end in itself. Feminist thinkers, like their nonfeminist counterparts, are concerned with power, its acquisition, and its uses. But unlike many of their counterparts, they are also engaged by questions of the *transformation* of power, for few feminist thinkers, even among the reformist school, expect that empowered women would merely emulate men.

A particular interest in the transformation of power is common in feminist thought because, with some exceptions, differences between the sexes are acknowledged. The problem of whether the differences are the result of nature or nurture remains a thorny one. Indeed, Western feminism has taken a rather cyclical approach to the issue over the last two centuries. At times, rationalist, Enlightenment approaches have been preeminent, as with the arguments of Mary Wollstonecraft, which minimize any difference between the sexes not brought about by inadequate education and training, or with the perspective of some radical feminists, such as Firestone, who argue strenuously on the side of the social construction of all relevant differences (although Firestone's plan for a transference of reproductive function to *in vitro* technology may seem naive in the wake of recent and wrenching new dilemmas posed by that very technology). At a philosophical level, Firestone's reliance on technology makes the differences between the sexes appear so extreme, and women in need of such accommodation and remediacy, that hers would hardly seem like an argument for the "social" construction of gender after all.

At other times, woman's difference from man has been celebrated by feminist thinkers; the "moral superiority" granted to her by men, perhaps somewhat disingenuously, has also been vaunted by women as a powerful justification for wielding a more powerful hand in public as well as private affairs. This is evident in the transcendentalist thought of Margaret Fuller—woman must not " 'live too much in relations' becoming a 'stranger to the resources of [her] own nature' " (Blanchard, 1978: 218)—and is extremely prominent in the writings of Victorian-era feminists on both sides of the Atlantic, even when their arguments are otherwise starkly rational and utilitarian. Elizabeth Cady Stanton built her theory from just such an eclectic set of philosophies, as did the now nearly forgotten British analyst, Barbara Leigh Smith Bodichon (Herstein, 1985).

Given the cultural and political predispositions of middle-class Victorian milieux, it is not surprising that assumptions of woman's greater spirituality and moral sensitivity should have been woven into Victorian feminist thought, even to the extent of challenging the veracity of established religion's interpretation of the divine plan for relations between the sexes. Donovan (1985) provides us with an excellent exegesis of Sarah Grimké's critique of the church. Matilda Joslyn Gage ([1893] 1972) authored a forceful polemic against the political implications of religion's teaching about gender roles. At the same time, they understood, in terms anything but ethereal, that education and economic independence were absolutely essential to the empowerment of women, and they offered both hard analysis and visionary projections toward this end. Bodichon combined a hard-nosed legal analysis of women's status with an implicit theory of feminine friendship and community. Charlotte Perkins Gilman ([1915] 1979) went a step further, envisioning a feminine utopia, free of male aggressivity and competition.

Finally, they saw the helplessness bred from a socialization to dependence. Nowhere is this better expressed than in Elizabeth Cady Stanton's "Solitude of Self:"

> The strongest reason why we ask for woman a voice in the government under which she lives; in religion she is asked to believe; equality in social life, where she is the chief factor; a place in the trades and professions, where she may earn

her bread, is because of her birthright to self-sovereignty; because, as an individual, she must rely on herself. No matter how much women may prefer to lean, to
be protected and supported, nor how much men may desire to have them do so,
they must make the voyage of life alone. (Stanton, [1882] 1915: 2)

From the eclectic, intricate work of the Victorian feminist thinkers, then,
come two clear propositions: that women are endowed with all the necessary
qualities of full participation in all the world's arenas and require only education
and training for such an exercise of their powers, as is also true of men. But,
second, women would often put their power to different uses than have men;
their nurturance of and responsibility for the well-being of others would imbue
their political orientations with a desire for peace, for social welfare, and for
tolerance. This second proposition, indeed, was a core justification for the extension of the suffrage to women, and historical evidence does attest to the
claim's accuracy as a predictor of women's political behavior. Women in some
territories of the American West, granted local suffrage as early as 1869, quickly
used their votes to establish schools and others systems of community support
(Stratton, 1981: 264–267). Even without the vote, women had become the main-
stays of most voluntary societies concerned with social welfare (Scott, 1984:
259–284), and prior to New Deal programs, voluntary societies were usually
the only providers of aid. In this sense, women were inaugurating public policy
well before they were granted any formal position in the public sector (Tolleson
Rinehart, 1987), and their policy orientations were, from the earliest, distinguishable from those of men. Whether their concerns were a result of their gender role socialization or of innate gender differences was less important than the
clear demonstration of the capacity for an active public life signified in their
efforts.
    On the emergence of what is called the third wave of feminism (Rossi, 1973;
Cott, 1987, might implicitly agree) in the 1960s, much of this earlier thought
was reinvented. For one reason, at least, the duplication of effort was beneficial—it required the latest generation of gender conscious women to reason out
the philosophical and political problems for themselves. And, in another sense,
it was inevitable: the Women's Movement had to gain strength, visibility, and a
degree of acceptance before it could commission a search for women's history,
including their intellectual heritage. A review of late twentieth-century feminist
thought reveals the process. The earliest published work in the second wave
lacks a historical context; with fragile new roots in the shallow soil of the post–
World War II world, it begins with the premise of men's and women's essential
similarity, belittling differences between the sexes and demanding systemic
equality for women (Donovan, 1985; Jaggar and Rothenberg, 1984). It reminds
its readers very much of the passionate, angry ardor of a Mary Wollstonecraft,
herself rebutting her contemporaries in eighteenth-century England and France

rather than addressing historical conditions. Simone de Beauvoir ([1949] 1961), making the first large postwar contribution to feminist theory, wrote in the ahistorical context of existentialism: her arguments, though dazzling in and of themselves, could not profit from a consideration of women's status within changing cultures and epochs.

In just a few years, though, feminist theory has been enriched and diversified. The historical context has been developed, as feminist theorists have gained access to their intellectual history. More significant, perhaps, both for philosophy and for the practical construction of relations between the sexes, the possibility of important gender differences is no longer flatly denied. Feminists, of course, had a great stake in denying differences when difference so often meant, for women, relegation to an inferior position in sociopolitical terms. As some Movement goals were achieved, and some others were so stalled that feminism had even been proclaimed dead, feminist theory took on new life, gestating in the question of whether certain gender differences were not both real and valuable.

The argument is less concerned today with ascribing the differences to nature; that province is largely left to sociobiologists and other conservatives without a great deal of comment (for the sociobiologist's view of gender differences, see Wilson, 1978; and for the social conservative position, see Gilder, 1975). "Elinor agreed with it all," as Jane Austen said in *Sense and Sensibility,* "believing that he did not deserve the compliment of rational opposition." Indeed, the lack of any scientific support for sociobiological claims about the genetic or physiological origins of gender differences makes a clear refutation of them possible (Bleier, 1984) despite the fact, as Keller (1985) convincingly argues, that such claims are a part of a larger, gendered ideology of the doing of science.

Feminist theorists are also vulnerable to the temptation of ascribing difference to nature: the recent metaphysics of Mary Daly and some aspects of postmodern thought appear to conceive of a kind of natural woman distinct, even utterly alienated, from men (see Daly, 1984, and the discussion of Iragary and Kristeva in Donovan, 1985).

At the other extreme, Marxist and other feminists drawing principally on political economy for their reasoning continue to see gender differences only in macroeconomic terms, and women as the oppressed in the "sexual class system" (Eisenstein, 1984). But, in short, while most feminist thinkers see gender differences emerging from nurture rather than nature, the consequences of such differences are potentially great nonetheless. Nurture, after all, is indubitably critical to the shaping of an individual, and a vast body of evidence testifies to the depth and reach of gender role socialization (Maccoby, 1974; Gornick and Moran, 1971).

The salient point for us is that recent feminist theory explores the possibility that the differences simply mean difference, not inferiority. Women's difference from men, in fact, is brought forward once again as a justification for their full participation in politics, for their difference brings a necessary alternative perspective to the polis. Those who identify as "feminists" are not the only women to have articulated such a position; newly mobilized women elites of the post-suffrage era had done so before, as we shall see in the next chapter. Marxist feminists may do an injustice to their own arguments by relegating socialization to such a minor role. On the other hand, a celebration of woman's difference can run to almost mystical lengths, as I alluded to above in the case of Daly and the postmodernist thinkers. And when the differences are embodied in a concept such as "maternal thinking," the result can be a reaction to feminism's egalitarian goals rather than an expansion of them. There is also the danger that a conception of "woman," no matter how anchored in theories of gender role socialization or no matter how new and feminist it may seem, is as likely to be as stereotypical, as oblivious to numerous differences *among* women, as any previous depiction of the "fair sex" could have been. For black and other women of color in particular, this "woman" may seem to be a white woman only. Feminist scholarship has been struggling with women's diversity, but differences of race and ethnicity especially present extraordinary challenges (Lugones and Spelman, 1983). But the proposition that many results of traditional gender role socialization—nurturance, concern for others, tolerance, cooperation rather than competition, pacifism—are not only worthy in and of themselves but valuable to political culture and not to be minimized brings a new perspective to feminist theory at once evocative of the thinkers of the Victorian era and freshly contemporary.

Students of the subject, perhaps now comparatively free of the need to defend women's right to expand the scope of their lives beyond the rigidly enforced roles of the past, have returned to the questions of moral and political theory that engaged Grimké, Stanton, and others. Carol Gilligan (1982), for example, proposes that women's moral development was seen as lesser to men's not because it is so but because it is *different* and not captured in a Kohlbergian hierarchy of abstract justice. Her argument is that women's morality is of caring and of making the decision that will entail the least harm to others. Although her methods and theoretical perspective have been criticized, few contest the importance of her work to furthering the dialogue (Kerber et al., 1986).

The importance of reproductive function, an importance so great that it had to be denigrated by de Beauvoir and technologically obviated in Firestone's world view, is now the touchstone of considerable feminist theory—in the revisionist psychoanalytic perspective of Nancy Chodorow (1978) or in Jean Bethke Elshtain's (1986) plea for a more reflective feminist theory. Once again, it is well to remember that this cycle of denial and affirmation represents the degree to which women's differences from men, especially their reproductive differences, have been used as justifications for objectifying and limiting women. It is not surprising that "maternal thinking" could not enter the language of feminist theory until women's sociopolitical status was thought by the theorists, whose theory was also their political action, to be more secure in its hard-won new position. As the decade of the 1980s closed, that position looked rather less secure, and the feminist scholarship of the 1990s may take yet another turn on the spiral of difference.

The newly diverse political thought now characteristic of feminism still faces paradox. An uncompromising egalitarian position, dismissing most gender differences, seems necessary to any political struggle in liberal Western society, for duties and responsibilities have always been coupled with rights in the liberal tradition. The movements for suffrage, the Equal Rights Amendment, reproductive freedom, and an end to economic and employment discrimination have all grounded claims in the contention that women are no less able than men to assume the duties and responsibilities attendant on the rights they demand. Yet the very claim that there are no meaningful social or political differences between men and women consternated many potential supporters of the Women's Movement, as Jane Mansbridge (1986) argues. And such a claim seriously underestimated the extent to which feminism's apparent challenge to key traditional values would harm the prospects of its legitimation and acceptance (Kann, 1983a, 1985b). Feminism's present pausing and collecting of its thoughts, however, raises the aforementioned paradox of finding meaning in difference without slipping back into stereotypes of women's lives, a charge that some might lay at the door of Betty Friedan (1981). Thus the current challenge to feminist theory might seem to be, in Hester Eisenstein's words, "to incorporate the insights of a woman-centered analysis, without jettisoning the basic understanding of the social construction of gender, into a renewed commitment to the struggle for fundamental social change" (p. 141).

Empirical Analysis

Feminist thinkers have, of course, meant to speak to, of, and for women. Never, however, have more than a fraction of women read feminist political theory. And yet women have been political actors in the world. Women's actual behavior became the course of study of the feminist empiricists, who largely began their first wave of work concomitant with the third wave of feminism, since the nature of the empirical enterprise within social science was such that the work of Sophonisba Breckenridge (1933) stands almost alone as a scholarly result of the second great movement for women's rights.

The results of empirical analyses of gender politics are presented often in the chapters to come, and so they are not detailed at great length here. But while empirical work and normative feminist theory have often appeared to be virtually estranged from each other, at least in the sense that they have not usually appeared to refer to or draw on each other, the patterns of epistemological development in the two are very similar. Behavioral research, too, accompanied a burst of mass political activity. And, like their theorist colleagues, behavioral researchers have moved rapidly from challenging assumptions about women's politicization, to rebutting them, to beginning a new search for the causes of women's political attitudes and behavior. This movement, again like that of feminist theory, has entailed first denying the existence of any meaningful differences in men's and women's political capacities and then seeking meaning in different gender role socialization as the cause of apparent intersex attitudinal differences.

Despite Breckenridge's pathbreaking work, the question of gender differences was not seen as an important one for much of the twentieth century. The postwar behavioral revolution, truly revolutionary in its consequences for the methodology of political science, was nothing if not staidly conservative in its approach to the political behavior of women. The subfield of political socialization provides some of the best examples of the discipline's complacency regarding women; the earliest socialization literature is filled with hypotheses and data interpretations all biased in favor of finding little political interest or engagement among the female of the species (see, for example, Hess and Torney, 1967). The data gathered in these early days of the subfield do not now seem to support the kind of negative interpretation of women's political socialization with which they were so often presented—small differences between boys' and girls' images of the president, for example, were once taken to mean that girls were less politically "mature" (pp. 205–212), a judgment evocative of the Kohlbergian scale of moral development against which Gilligan formulated her theory of the "different voice." Robert Weissberg (1974) concluded that girls learn in early adolescence to abandon politics as a male enterprise, a conclusion that now looks as much like a prescription as a description of empirical reality. But while the results of gender differentiated political socialization can still be observed, especially among adolescents, we now examine it as a *variable* indicating the social construction of gender rather than an expression of things as they ought to be.

Our approach to the analysis of adult behavior has undergone a similar modification. The first few decades of postwar behavioral research used sex as a demographic variable, if it used it at all, and researchers apparently found few questions of gender roles and politics sufficiently interesting to stimulate sustained attention (Campbell, Converse, Miller, and Stokes, 1960; Key, 1966). Since women were expected to be underrepresented among political participants (Verba and Nie, 1972), little was made of evidence that they appeared to be so, even if appearances were deceiving (Bourque and Grossholtz, 1974). A number of scholars in the late 1970s and early 1980s ended this lacuna with detailed descriptions of women's political behavior at mass and elite levels (see, for example, Baxter and Lansing, 1983; and Diamond, 1977). At the same time, researchers occupied themselves with a search for causes of women's behavior and, particularly, with the causes of quantitative differences in that behavior as it compared to the behavior of men. Structural, situational, and socialization explanations for women's politicization were discerned and were pitted against one another as interest in gender politics grew (Sapiro, 1983; Klein, 1984; Welch, 1977). We learned that women were *not* an undifferentiated and largely apolitical mass but, like men, could be political creatures responding in various ways to their civic training and their environments within the particular constraints of their immediate contexts (Tolleson Rinehart, 1985). Such a statement seems almost tediously obvious now, of course, but given the dearth of attention that had been paid to women in the past, these findings began to establish women's place as subjects in the polis.

A student of the literature of political behavior could not have found evidence predicting a renascence of feminism in the 1960s, or any possibility of explanation for it. Political science's assumption of women's political passivity, and its consequent dismissal of gender as an important analytical touchstone, left the field unprepared for the remarkable level of women's political activity beginning in the 1970s. That activity reached a peak in 1980 when scholars and journalists, more watchful of women now, discovered the "gender gap."

The gender gap, a significant difference in men's and women's party, candidate, and policy preferences, catalyzed a number of things. It made gender politics studies fashionable in circles where the subject had gained little attention before, as scholars previously uninterested (at the very least) in women and politics suddenly wanted to be a part of this newest movement of the body politic. Among those who had already been tilling the field, though, it signified two more important developments. First, it helped to mark a transition in approach from *women* and politics to *gender* politics. The necessary restorative work of documenting women's political behavior having been done, scholars saw the necessity of thoroughly examining *intra*sex differences and, significantly, of treating sex differences *comparatively*.

The second, related development has taken empirical research in the same direction that feminist theory has gone, to a new consideration of significant underlying gender differences. As *quantitative* gender gaps in political behavior have virtually closed, *qualitative* gaps in political orientations have appeared, seeming at long last to justify suffragettes' claims that women would use their political enfranchisement not to echo the policy preferences of men but to bespeak their own. Findings of significant differences in the sexes' beliefs, whether in domains of foreign, domestic, or economic policy (first clearly documented in Frankovic, 1982), tantalize us with the suggestion that women *do* possess a real, empirically demonstrable "different voice." Genuine differences among women notwithstanding, gender gap research reveals that women's and men's approaches to politics are distinctive, and sometimes quite at odds.

Why should this be so? Does the gender gap represent not a distinction without a difference, or a fleeting political moment, but true variance in the sexes' fundamental orientations? Progress toward any sort of useful answer to such a question requires empirical researchers, like their theorist colleagues, to rejoin the dialogue on basic gender differences. In empirical research, this has taken the form of renewed inquiry into gender role socialization, with particular attention to context, situation, and the dynamic interaction of the individual with her environment. The effort has extended even to the study of feminists' socialization to feminism (Rossi, 1982). The inquiry, like that in feminist theory, also confronts the difficult task of balancing an assertion of men's and women's essential likeness in capacity to be political actors with a recognition that their *un*likeness may cause them to act for different reasons and toward different goals. The earlier behavioral research, after all, was no different from political philosophy in its unquestioning use of the "public man, private woman" ethos. To suggest that some aspects of that ethos—women's socialization to nurturance, for example—lead to real gender differences in political orientations, without seeming to imply that these different orientations are less "political" than "traditional" political concerns, is a challenging endeavor. Finding ways to operationalize and measure this perspective on gender politics is even more difficult.

THE RECURRING STRAIN OF GENDER CONSCIOUSNESS

Gender Consciousness and Feminism

Gender consciousness is the recognition that one's relation to the political world is shaped in important ways by the physical fact of one's sex, and feminism, regardless of the particular form it may take, is, at its root, a powerful manifestation of gender consciousness. Gender consciousness, like other forms of group consciousness, embodies an identification with similar others, positive affect toward them, and a feeling of interdependence with the group's fortunes. Like forms of consciousness rooted in race or class, gender consciousness may also carry a cognitive evaluation of the group's sociopolitical disadvantage, in absolute or relative terms, vis-à-vis other groups.

But gender consciousness is also potentially empowering, imbuing the gender conscious woman with a sense of the validity of her world view. Put simply, gender consciousness supports a perception of the relationship of gender roles to political roles that allows individual women to legitimate themselves. When gender consciousness politicizes women, stimulating them to articulate political attitudes harmonious with their own understanding of gender roles and political roles, it carries potential policy consequences. It prompts the assertion that "women's issues" such as education, health, and welfare, for example, are completely legitimate *political* questions.

The next chapter is devoted to a thorough discussion of the concept of gender consciousness, but before that we require a clear understanding of the *need* for the concept. First, it offers us a central, organizing construct as we seek to understand what people have made of the enduring question of the nature of woman. Those who have protested against the Western masculinist picture of private, passive, dependent, and nurturant woman might certainly be called feminist, although their versions of feminism can vary drastically one from the other. What they have shared is an acute consciousness of the importance of the world's view of gender. All of them have been sensitive, even if only implicitly, to the difference between *sex* roles, or the roles of actual physical reproduction, and *gender* roles, or those learned social roles that a culture chooses to derive from its understanding of the nature of biological reproduction (but simultaneously modifying the gender role codes it will apply to its different classes and races of women). All feminists possess gender consciousness.

But not all gender conscious women would call themselves feminists. One group of gender conscious nonfeminists comes from the ranks of politically active conservative women. Rebecca E. Klatch (1987) found two types of activists among the women of the New Right: social conservatives, most often moved to political action by their religious convictions and most engaged by issues of social morality, and laissez-faire conservatives, women who are relatively uninterested in social issues but are vitally interested in economic questions; their conservatism might be described as nineteenth-century liberalism. The latter group, concerned about individual liberty and economic freedom, seems sympathetic to a number of particular feminist goals, especially those regarding economic equity. And they seem quite aware of discrimination on the basis of sex. This group can easily be characterized as possessing gender consciousness. What may be surprising to many is the degree to which social conservatives can demonstrate something akin to gender consciousness, despite their unmistakable hostility to feminism. That hostility arises, in part, because of a deep distrust of men, a fear that men can use feminism as an excuse to shirk their responsibilities to their families—and this distrust is not entirely alien to a feminist critique (Klatch, 1987: 134–139; see also Rinehart, 1982). But it is also true that these social conservative women, as traditional as their values are, have come to believe that they have a valid, even essential point of view to bring to the polis. Luker (1984), in her study of prolife and prochoice activists, uncovered the same fervent political activity arising from passionate convictions about gender roles.

The traditional gender role divisions to which they subscribe, though, simply cannot accommodate public woman, and the measure of the challenge to traditional roles can be taken, paradoxically, in the competent defense of traditional gender roles made by women activists who are very public indeed.

Between avowed feminists and activist antifeminists lies the vast majority of women. The empirical research done to date suggests that many in this modal category may also be gender conscious. These are the women who are contributing to the gender gap, who articulate the policy preferences we detect to be at variance with the positions of most men. These are the women, furthermore, who respond to surveys by affirming that women and men should have equal roles and that women are just as politically capable as men. They don't identify themselves as feminists—only 1 percent of American women say they feel closest to *feminists* of all groups, and women claim to have only moderately warm feelings toward the Women's Movement, as measured in the 1984 American National Election Study data. But, although they do not choose to identify *as* feminists, large numbers of them are identifying *with* policy positions and goals that we could call feminist, and the traditionalists as well feel empowered to speak to the political world from their own experience of the meaning of gender roles.

The intensely felt gender consciousness of feminist activists no doubt has struck a loud chord to which many women respond, even if in lesser ways. But it is gender consciousness that is logically prior to, and necessary and sufficient for, feminism, and not the reverse, as discussion of "traditionalist" gender conscious women should make clear. Gender consciousness becomes a construct large enough to contain all variations of feminism, as well as an even larger range of women's political behavior that is perhaps only immanently feminist and some that is not cognitively structured on feminism at all.

BRIDGING BEHAVIOR AND THEORY

Feminist theory and empirical gender politics research have surely not been deliberately estranged, but it seems that they have had unfortunately narrow epistemological grounds, and almost no methodological grounds, in common. This is so despite the obvious, essential commonality of the two endeavors. Gender consciousness, as concept and construct, can be used to bridge the two. Because it is not dependent on any given kind of feminism, but can be seen as the necessary and sufficient condition for all of them, it opens an avenue of discourse within feminist political theory. The effort to operationalize it or, what is more likely, to find minimally reliable and valid indicators for it provides empirical research with an ongoing but unifying task. And the perspective of gender consciousness can make the work of both theorist and empiricist more accessible each to the other. Though some theorists would disdain any reference to behavioral research, feminist theorists are responsive to women's "real world" experiences, and that includes their political lives. Theorists need opportunities to measure their theories against the world, no matter what they do with the results, and behavioral scholars have long passed the point of documentation and description; the search for the causes and consequences of the behavior uncovered by gender politics research depends on a well-grounded theoretical perspective. Now, then, we can turn to the construction work: if consciousness requires one's identification with others, can women be thought of as a group?

Chapter 2

TRACING AN ELUSIVE CONCEPT

Here sleeps in Jesus united to Him by Faith and the Grace of a Christian Life all that was mortal of Mrs Ann Burges, once the tender and affectionate Wife of the Rev^d. Henry John Burges, of the Isle of Wight. She died 23 December 1771 in giving birth to an Infant Daughter, who rests in her Arms. She here waits the transporting moment when the Trump of God will call her forth to Glory, Honour & Immortality.

  Oh Death where is thy Sting?
  Oh Grave where is thy Victory?
          —tombstone in Bruton Parish churchyard, Williamsburg, Virginia

This inscription is as poignant a symbol, perhaps, as there can be of one of the most profound things uniting women. Its length and its language attest to the wild grief of the bereaved husband (and possibly to the affluence permitting him to leave such a mark of it). But its more telling message is that Ann Burges suffered the fate that, until quite recently and even then only in the Western world, all women had very real reason to fear: death in childbirth, or a premature death from the ravaging consequences of incessant childbearing.

  Not childbirth, or death in childbirth alone, but also societies' treatment of women's reproductive lives have been matters of salience to all women. History is replete with examples of attempts to exploit women's fecundity in system- or culture-serving ways. Fraser (1984) and Spruill ([1938] 1972) reveal that the unabashed bribing of women literally to go forth and multiply in new territories by seventeenth- and eighteenth-century powers in England and the colonies was actually seeking the reproduction of new laborers and colonizers, as well as the restraining, "civilizing" effect women were thought to have on new colonies.

Less obvious but equally manipulative aims were evident in current American and European pronatalist policies (Wattenberg, 1987; for a critical analysis of such orientations, see Blair, 1988). The terrifying consequences of such policies carried to the extreme are depicted in the fictional world of Margaret Atwood's (1986) *The Handmaid's Tale*. Present-day reality, however, can be frightening enough. Recent newspaper accounts of Indian states' experimentation with bans on prenatal sex testing, because the technology has been put to an unexpected use of identifying and aborting female fetuses, and accounts of female infanticide in response to the People's Republic of China's stringent birth control policies once more unveil the cruel paradox of value placed on females solely in proportion to their ability to produce males. Quite apart from the profound role of sexuality and reproduction in each person's life, reproduction on national scales—birth rates, fertility rates, infant mortality rates—has throughout history been a part of policymakers' thinking, perhaps affecting women most significantly when it is least explicitly articulated. Thus individual biological function and the social construction of gender converge to contribute to the determination of women's place in the polis.

While all women are no doubt daily aware of the physical epiphenomena of their sex roles, and share many of these physiological experiences with all other women, most probably do not give frequent thought to the kind of sociopolitical analysis of sex roles presented above. Nor, one suspects, do most men. What all people *are* aware of, however, at least in social terms, is gender. When two people meet, the sex of each is one of the first, if not the very first, things that the other takes note of. Indeed, social psychologists have been able to evaluate the degree of discomfiture we humans feel when we *cannot* immediately discern another's sex. But visual identification of primary sex characteristics is a problematic cue, to say the least, in most first meetings, and even secondary sex characteristics are subject to the disguises or alterations of fashion and cultural norms—the absence of facial hair, for example, is hardly a necessary and sufficient condition for concluding that the face we see is male or female. This is where gender becomes the handmaid of sex: in all cultures, gender roles are by definition sex-differentiated. Dress, the use of voice and gestures, and movement, as surely as behavior, are the results of individual internalizations of cues about gender roles supplied by the agents by whom one is surrounded from birth. So, too, are our concepts of "femininity" and "masculinity" formed. Almost all people know early in childhood that they are biologically male or female, and nearly as many arrive at adulthood "knowing" "masculine" or "feminine" comportment as well. Or so we assume.

But do we know so much? Are masculinity and femininity the same things as male and female gender roles? Whether they are or not, how do perceptions of each, or both, affect our expectations about ourselves, about others, and most important, about the nature of the political community and its actors? If, besides dress and behavior, gender role-playing includes constellations of political attitudes and dispositions, one for each sex, then gender is terribly important. And so is gender *consciousness*.

GENDER ROLE SOCIALIZATION AND POLITICAL SOCIALIZATION: REAL OR IMPLIED CONVERGENCE?

Traditional Assumptions and Ironclad Illusions

The publication of Herbert Hyman's *Political Socialization* in 1959 marked the birth of a remarkable subfield of research into the wellsprings of political behavior. But as fruitful as these forays into our knowledge of the development of the political self have been, the journeys began with a curious reluctance to do anything more than overlay long-standing beliefs about gender roles with the new language of politicization. A well-specified nexus was found, at least conceptually: as woman is passive and man is active, woman concerned with nurturance and man concerned with conquering the environment, woman emotional and man rational, so we have "political man" and woman citizen—but not political woman.

As I suggested in the first chapter, much of the research of the 1960s and 1970s was thus affected by powerful expectations that "political woman" was *not* to be found. Especially in the earlier writings on the importance of childhood socialization, much was made of the direct transference of sex-role behavior from the social to the political sphere, with family mediating both directly and indirectly in the transference. Examples from this literature are evocative. Jaros (1973: 82) attributed his finding of adult women's political passivity not to any structural or situational impediments but to the learning of particular roles, which "clearly extends back into childhood." Davies (1965) drew a direct connection between his findings of fathers' allegedly greater political influence over their children to the role of the father as the prime authority figure. Weissberg (1974: 116–117) attributed girls' reluctance to discuss partisan differences to their "general socialization to docility and niceness," and the inverse relationship of efficacy with age among girls to the assumption that "girls come to realize that getting things done politically is more suited to men despite their own feelings of competence and ability."

Since, for much of the century, the purpose of political socialization was thought to be the training of a system's young for "appropriate" citizen behavior, it is not difficult to see that views of "appropriate" gender role orientations would influence the limits we set on such political behavior. If, in this view, boys and girls are expected to learn the same things about the political system and a citizen's duties, they are expected to do quite different things with the knowledge, an expectation shared by system and researchers alike. An example of the effects such an expectation can have for interpretation of findings comes from the landmark childhood socialization studies of Hess and Torney (1967) and Easton and Dennis (1969). Both pairs of scholars analyzed the same data, from surveys of children in the second through eighth grades. Hess and Torney argued that boys gain and keep an edge in political sophistication and political awareness, but Easton and Dennis found sex differences to be small and insignificant.

Lest I appear to be pillorying scholars, holding them to a standard of critical judgment that would put them far ahead of their times and cultures, I should say that these gendered expectations would appear to affect all of us as we conduct our own informal assessments of our friends and family as political actors. Niemi (1974), in a delightfully telling use of the Youth-Parent Socialization Panel Study data, found that when adolescents guessed about their parents' political activities, they guessed that their fathers voted but were much less likely to ascribe such behavior to their mothers. Forty-six percent of the fathers in the study who called themselves highly politically interested were seen as such by their children. Highly politically interested mothers, on the other hand, were perceived to be interested by their children only 34 percent of the time.

It would seem, then, that scholars and those whom they study have alike been influenced by what Lipman-Blumen (1984) calls the "control myths" of women's passivity, nurturance, emotionalism—all the qualities thought to be indispensable to the female gender role, virtually equally indispensable to the maintenance of the private sphere, and thus incompatible with a public domain defined in rather heavily masculine terms. The "control myth" of women's selflessness, says Lipman-Blumen, has been used effectively to deflect women from working for their own rights and causes, across time and across cultures (1984: 181).

In times of crisis, however, role systems weaken. "Sociologically speaking, the criteria for participation in various roles change, with decreased emphasis on the formal characteristics of individuals or groups and increased recognition of their ability to achieve crisis-related goals. . . . Therefore, it is not particularly surprising to discover that crisis is a time when gender roles . . . are most likely to undergo change" (ibid.: 186).

The 1960s and 1970s were seen by many in the West as a chaotic period, with the feeling, vaguely uneasily or acutely, that cultures were careening from crisis to crisis. In the United States in particular, Vietnam and protests against American involvement there, the Civil Rights Movement, youths' radical departure from earlier patterns of behavior, perceptions of economic instability, and revelations of cupidity at the highest reaches of the political system blasted their way into the public consciousness. Under the circumstances it should come as no surprise that the public mentality often seemed that of survivors under siege. In the midst of this social and political tumult, the third wave (Rossi, 1973) of American feminism began to crest. Gender roles, as Lipman-Blumen (1984) argues, *did* begin to change. During the infancy of political socialization research, Dwayne Marvick (1965) had written with great sensitivity and foresight about the painful dissonance between being black and "becoming a citizen" as middle-class white children are expected to do. Robert Coles (1986) has gracefully expanded on children's diverse ways of bringing their cultural heritages to bear on their first confrontations with the political world. The potential conflict of traditional gender roles with the attitudes and behavior of genuinely politicized women was not so easily recognized. But some scholars, writing contemporaneously with those who clung to orthodox orientations, began to question orthodoxy.

Reconsidering Gender and Political Socialization

Richard Merelman (1971) found in his study of Los Angeles area adolescents that most sex differences in political orientations *favored* girls by the twelfth grade—girls were more efficacious and more cognizant than boys of the democratic "rules of the game" and of civic obligations. While their internal political competence rose with age, however, their political ambition, once rivaling that of boys, fell sharply in adolescence. This may have been the result of internalized disengagement with politics, or it may have reflected their growing judgment that there would be little external support for their politicization. Sigel and Hoskin (1981: 147–151) provided implicit support for the latter conclusion when they found that, far from being disengaged, high school girls in Pennsylvania in 1974 were more than twice as likely as boys to be simultaneously involved in school, community, and political affairs.

Yet simulations completed by college students in the 1970s showed that while hypothetical "candidates" were evaluated roughly equally, both young men and young women assumed that the male candidate would win office and that the woman office-seeker would lose (Sapiro, 1982). Even more disturbing was Bowman's (1984) finding that a physically attractive woman fared even worse among student voters in simulated elections—although handsomeness worked distinctly to the advantage of male candidates. Such findings introduced the possibility that women's apparent disengagement from politics results not from an internal disinclination born out of acceptance of a privatized role, but from growing awareness that the environment can be inhospitable to one's attempts to be political. Barriers formed of the structure of one's life can be difficult to overcome.

Among the earliest to delineate the structural barriers facing women even at the simplest levels of participation are Welch (1977), Jennings (1979), and

McGlen (1980). Each found that principal family caregiving responsibilities could act in concert with vestiges of formal discrimination to brake women's political activity. Welch found that effects were strongest among less educated and lower income women, precisely those who are least likely to have help in carrying out their caregiving. Stanley (1985) elucidated the bittersweet story behind those findings in her interviews with East Texas women too tired, too financially pressed, and too skeptical to expend their precariously poised energies for doubtful political returns. But when the interests of their families seemed clearly at stake, they responded with political activity. Jennings saw a similar underlying structure when he compared young mothers' national versus their local or school-district participation rates. McGlen found that even among the best educated and most highly motivated, the political activities most disruptive to one's family responsibilities were the soonest abandoned. In other words, as Sapiro (1983) has argued, gender roles that may be learned in adolescence are not structured, not really put to the test, until adult responsibilities are taken up. While politics may be seen as part of the adult male's responsibilities, the traditional responsibilities of the adult female may all but squeeze politics out of her life.

The ongoing work of Jennings and his colleagues, using a panel study of youth who were high school seniors in 1965 and their parents, has been particularly illuminative of the nexus of gender role socialization and politicization. Because the two generations were reinterviewed in 1973 and 1982, we are offered an unprecedented opportunity to witness their movement through some critical phases of the life cycle. Because members of each generation are blood kin to one another, we can observe, rather than merely speculate on, the transmission of political and gender orientations through the medium of the family. And because the daughters are a part of the first cohort to reach adulthood contemporaneously with the arrival on the scene of the latest incarnation of feminism, we are granted the benison of assessing their—as well as their mothers'—accommodations to demands for gender role change (for the complete examination of the filial generation in this regard, see Sapiro, 1983; my own analyses of the maternal generation are presented in later chapters).

Gender, in the earliest examinations of the youths and their parents, was a more significant demarcator of parental political involvement than it was for the adolescents: while mothers required some edge, such as higher education, in order to compete favorably with fathers in the accumulation of political resources, student sex differences were "usually trivial"; daughters, in fact, were generally more politically cosmopolitan than their fathers (Jennings and Niemi, 1974: 325–326, 307–309; see also Jennings and Niemi, 1968). The daughters, in short, were emerging from a comparatively gender-neutral school environment, where the emphasis on civic training would not have, overtly at any rate, excluded girls from participation in citizenship norms. And daughters resembled sons because these young women *didn't* resemble their mothers, at least in things political.

But while the ongoing study provided evidence for straightforward assumptions about the sources of politicization—that politically interested children are more likely to come from politically charged family environments, for example (Jennings and Niemi, 1981; Beck and Jennings, 1982)—more subtle dynamics were uncovered as well. Early on, Jennings and his associates had shown that, despite the mothers' own relatively resource-poor political lives, they were nonetheless the "bearers of the political culture" (Jennings and Niemi, 1971). Mothers' continual close contact with their children left a distinct political legacy even though, as Niemi later demonstrated, the children were not especially predisposed to see their mothers as political actors, and even though they and their society assumed that fathers were the source of political authority in the family.

The early finding of mothers' roles as their children's guides through the portals of citizenship explicated a truly ancient Western assumption about gender and the political division of labor. Plato, after all, was also bemused by a regime that could entrust the civic education of children to women and slaves, neither of whom were allowed a place in the polis themselves. The mothers in the Jennings study, of course, were accorded far greater rights than the matrons of Athens, and the daughters were about to enter an adulthood more politically privileged than that of perhaps any earlier generation of women. But in the most recent retrospective on the two generations, Beck and Jennings (1988) show that changes wrought by the Women's Movement have not affected everyone equally. By 1982, while father-son political agreement remained quite robust, mother-daughter agreement had continued to decline. Daughters did not abandon their mothers' political orientations because they came under the influence of their own husbands: on the contrary, married daughters resembled their mothers more closely than did unmarried daughters. Neither, however, could the gulf between mothers and daughters be attributed to daughters' wholesale rejection of traditional gender roles. Such a rejection was limited to those daughters who could, indeed, be thought of as privileged—those who were the best educated. My own analysis of the Jennings data reveals that some *mothers,* too, were abandoning traditional gender role perspectives from 1973 to 1982, and those mothers maintained much closer political ties to their daughters than did mothers who clung to traditional roles.

More will be said about the mothers and daughters of the panel socialization study in subsequent chapters. These data, along with other longitudinal studies like that of Bennington College students (Newcomb et al., 1967), however, provide us with virtually our only opportunities to ask empirical questions about gender roles and politics through the life course. The answers help to deepen and anchor conclusions arising from cross-sectional analyses of women's political behavior. From our infancy on, we are the recipients of endless, efficiently packaged messages about what our behavior and beliefs should be. Gradually, imperceptibly, we absorb many of the messages, and as we reach adulthood we must act in accordance with them, reject and replace them, or struggle to accommodate some combination of the two stances. For most women in the contemporary West, the last, uneasy position is no doubt the most frequent one. For women in the aggregate, that has meant a somewhat uneven increase in political activity in recent years.

Such aggregate trends in the mass must inevitably influence any "available" pool of women who are potential elites. Here, too, a number of studies have revealed the paradox of deeply involved and committed women who, no matter what the extent of their service, found it difficult even to imagine running for office themselves, despite the fact that in terms of any male calculation, they had paid their dues (Jennings and Thomas, 1968; Jennings and Farah, 1981; Fowlkes, Perkins, and Tolleson Rinehart, 1979; Sapiro and Farah, 1980). That, perhaps, is the outcome of internalized gender role socialization. But externalized, or cultural, expectations have even more serious consequences for elite activity than they do for simpler forms of participation. Motherhood poses some immediate problems: Mezey (1978) revealed them clearly when she found that the age of a candidate's children was strongly determinative of first entry into public office for women but not for men. Kirkpatrick (1974) similarly showed the importance to women officeholders of their husbands' support for their activities. The symbolic importance of motherhood has been such a limiting factor, according to Lynn and Flora (1977), that women national party elites tried to preempt criticism by justifying their activity as a *function* of concerned motherhood. And from the heady days of feminist exuberance in the 1970s to the present, little has changed. Despite genuine gains in the number of women officeholders and encouraging signs that political men are more disposed to assess the consequences for their families of their political ambitions, women officeholders in 1981 were still dramatically more likely than their male counterparts to rate spousal support and the ages of their children as very important factors in their decision to run for office (Carroll and Strimling, 1983; 25–29; 127–129). The needs of her family are also more determinative of a woman's *exit* from high office, as I have found in research on women in the U.S. cabinet.

Given prevalent gendered divisions of labor in society, the division would seem to create as much an external barrier as it does an internal role orientation. One generation's "socialization to expectations" about each sex's appropriate spheres surfaces in the next generation's occupational choices—and may even surface in the first generation's latter-day regrets about its own early choices (Eccles, 1987). Individual expectations are inseparable from society's: women are held accountable for their low ambition, when they may be doing no more than experiencing a very human reaction to blocked opportunities (Kanter, 1977: 159–161). When, on the other hand, society *expects* women political actors, as in places where there is a tradition of women holding office, it continues to *have* women political actors (Hill, 1981). When women challenge the most enduring of gender stereotypes by leaving the home for the marketplace, they have historically entered the political arena as well (Andersen, 1975).

The mortar between the bricks of structural barriers, then, is made of widespread adherence to traditional gender roles. As long as many men and women believe in the traditional role divisions, those who wish to challenge them must overcome not only their own interior uncertainty or ambivalence, but societal disapproval as well. The foregoing suggests, though, that the *interaction* between internal role structuring and external environment, between movement through an individual life and through the political world, is the crucible of women's political lives.

GENDER CONSCIOUSNESS

Eleanor Roosevelt's Paradox

Few have attempted to make genuinely rigorous arguments that women's ascription to a place outside the Western polis is a result of nature rather than nurture. Those who tried put themselves in the position of constructing such inverted or desperately strained reasoning that they were often driven to contradict themselves. Susan Moller Okin (1979), Arlene Saxonhouse (1985), and Shadia Drury (1987), for instance, have shown the limits of Aristotle's functionalist conclusions about the role of women in the city, not only for women themselves but for the completion of the idea of public virtue. Mary Wollstonecraft warred "not with [Rousseau's] ashes but with his opinions," as we have discussed in chapter one, but the fiercely condemnatory Rousseau with whom we are all familiar seems at war with his younger self, as he recalls a gentler, more optimistic youth who could envision companionship between the two sexes in full, mature flower (see the touching "Tenth Walk" in the *Reveries of the Solitary Walker*). Freud and his disciples, of course, provide the most formidable examples of the modern version of the argument, and its power to convince women that they unsex themselves when they find their fulfillment in other than their biological roles.

But the Victorian milieu that could culminate in Freud's articulation of the "problem" produced the "problem" first. What did women want? Our first answers are limited to the stories of women socially privileged enough not to be lost to history, but such a story can be found in the life of Alice James, the brilliant younger sister of William and Henry. Alice's diary shows a desperate struggle to suppress her intellect and immolate her personality at the altar of her father's wildly romanticized vision of womanhood, a struggle that is the most likely cause of her mysterious and lifelong invalidism (Strouse, 1980).

Aside from such striking examples as these, philosophers and empiricists have either left the nature-or-nurture question unaddressed—because of their own implicit acceptance of "natural" divisions, perhaps—or assumed the importance of education and training to each sex's accommodation to prescribed roles.

But when one takes the nurture side of this venerable dialogue, one is nonetheless confronted with the question of difference. Even assuming that the differences are learned and that contextual factors may account for the *quantity* of women's politicization, curiosity about the *quality* of political life remains. We have seen the ways in which the "equality of capacity but difference in ends" perspective has characterized thinking about women's entitlement to membership in the political community. Indeed, in one time and scholarly language or another, the perspective has emerged precisely from considerations of the nature of gender roles. And it is women's *own* perception of this paradox—equal but different—that is the source of gender consciousness. Whenever "uppity women" have demanded greater political rights so loudly that discussion of their activities percolates through the culture, more women, women like Alice James, and women about whom we will never know, have begun asking questions about the structure of their lives and about the contributions they make to the lives of others. We have recovered some of this fabric of questions in the English-speaking world from the seventeenth to the nineteenth centuries, and just recently, American scholars are discovering more threads in women's activities of the postsuffrage era. The threads of the woof were countless women's commitments to building on the suffrage victory, but the warp, as I shall show, is a consciousness of gender essentially unchanged for centuries.

Eleanor Roosevelt presented women with what Susan Ware (1981: 16) considers a paradox: "Women," Roosevelt said in 1940, "must become more conscious of themselves as women and of their ability to function as a group. At the same time they must try to wipe from men's consciousness the need to consider them as a group of women in their everyday activities, especially as workers in industry or in the professions." She continued, in the same *Good Housekeeping* article: "On the whole, during the last twenty years, government has been taking increasing cognizance of humanitarian questions, things that deal with the happiness of human beings, such as health, education, security. There is nothing, of course, to prove this is entirely because of the women's interest, and yet I think it is significant that this change has come about during the period when women have been exercising their franchise" (Ware, 1984: 56). Other women in the New Deal network, and in the political parties, shared Eleanor Roosevelt's ambivalence about "feminism," a term they reserved for the activities of the National Woman's Party, and there was considerable debate among political women over how best to proceed to achieve widely shared ends (Ware, 1981, 1984). Despite disagreements, it is clear, as Andersen (1988a) demonstrates, that women *saw themselves* as different kinds of political animals, in style, in end-seeking, and in their motives for participation. And, at the same time, women's increasing presence on the political scene made it concomitantly difficult to support past distinctions between woman/private and man/public or to treat "political woman" as an oxymoron.

The foregoing discussion may imply that I am linking gender consciousness to egalitarian, if not "feminist," perceptions of gender roles, and that is not entirely the case. I have tried to explain gender consciousness as a continuum, anchoring egalitarian orientations at only one of its ends. Nor is the point one of pondering a chicken-and-egg conundrum of whether a climate sympathetic to expansions in social policy finally yielded women the vote or whether newly mobilized women demanded and got broader social policies. Surely the two are recursive, catalytic of each other. The point *is* the way Eleanor Roosevelt and her compatriots among elite and mass women saw these relationships. In their minds, the apparently contradictory positions of, on the one hand, encouraging women's participation *as women* and, on the other, resisting attempts to single women out as a separate political group in need of remediation were not contradictory at all. The two tactics, practiced simultaneously, were simply the cornerstones of a strategy of ensuring acceptance of women's political participation generally and guaranteeing that women's "point of view" would be represented on the public agenda. The paradox is resolved if one views these orientations as a particular expression of gender consciousness. Eleanor Roosevelt's evolving position became one of faith in the political legitimacy of women's common interests and needs and in their individual competence to act in all socioeconomic and political arenas. Women qua women had a unique contribution to make, and should do so as a group—just as it had required group action to secure the right to make that contribution—but women must not be seen as so dependent on group membership for their political identification that their behavior as *individuals* is overlooked.

Consciousness as a Political Concept

Eleanor Roosevelt actually used the words "conscious" and "consciousness" to describe her conclusions about women's politicization, and she must have assumed fairly wide agreement on the meaning of the terms among her readers. But because "consciousness" has been a concept of considerable importance to political theory, and is of critical importance to the present work, a brief examination of its varied applications is useful to us as we explore the "gender consciousness" that has been formative of women's politicization.

No doubt Eleanor was not thinking of Hegelian or Marxian dialectics when she spoke of wiping "woman as group" from men's consciousness, and with apologies to scholars of Marx and Hegel, an intricate treatment of them is beyond the scope of my task. The First Lady was, however, speaking from within a Western culture influenced by the philosophy of modernity, and her prescription is evocative of some of its strains. The "consciousness" of modernity is the phenomenon of subject encountering itself in and of the world, and of confronting object. Beneath the veneer of abstract and universal language, was the idea of consciousness intended for male and female subjects alike? Hegel could comprehend love between men and women as a profoundly liberatory apex of consciousness, an emancipatory phoenix of spirit, a dialectic producing the sublation of the individuality of each to "what they are in common." But the end, for women, is profoundly discouraging. For while man proceeds from this dialectic to freedom's actualization, Hegel ultimately left woman not just incomplete but "incompletable," bound once and for all to the needs of the family, as historical necessity requires of her (Barber, 1988: 9, 15). Life, Marx answers Hegel in *The German Ideology,* is not determined by consciousness, but consciousness by life (Tucker, 1978: 154–155). That aphorism, joined to Marx's and Engel's lively condemnations of the depravity of reducing women to bourgeois commodities, appears to open the door once more to an ungendered conception of political consciousness. We can but conclude, though, that just as Marx had reason to believe that he was addressing an audience of men, he was more concerned with finding an anodyne against depravity for the sake of man's consciousness than he was with rescuing the consciousness of woman.

Simone de Beauvoir elucidates the impossibility of man becoming subject while he objectifies woman, and her argument provides an even clearer stake for *men* in cleansing philosophy of its gender biases than did that of Marx and Engels. But even more obviously, that she was compelled to write *The Second Sex* and that it stood for so long as a work of such uniqueness are testaments to the difficulty of claiming any use of "consciousness" for thinking about women.

As we swim up a few feet from the depths of this epistemological sea, our difficulties hardly lessen. Political psychology—in some sense, all modern political science—has lavished unceasing attention on "the group," from Arthur Bentley's *Process of Government* (1908) to the present. We may too often have stopped at the group as the unit of analysis, seldom penetrating to a study of its members (Garson, 1978), or worse, we may have assumed as Bentley did that identifying groups in politics was the "everything" of politics, ignoring the upper-class accent of the pluralist choir (Schattschneider, 1975: 34–35). Group membership has nonetheless been a continuing preoccupation of scholars of political behavior. At rare moments, we have encountered work on the nature of group bonds and group identification that truly illuminates the nature of the political self (Shils and Janowitz, 1948; Finifter, 1974), and while group *consciousness* as the animus of the connection between a group and its members is more implied than stated in many earlier works, delineations of it are explicitly sought in recent studies.

Shils and Janowitz showed that the intense group bonds of German combat units caused soldiers to withstand growing pressure to desert, even when individual survival seemed to demand it. Finifter found that political "deviants"—deviant only because they were black Republicans in union shops—made strenuous efforts to reconcile their political differences with the group by strengthening other, nonpolitical group ties. Hare (1973) observed Quakers for a year as they strove for the ultimate group consensus, the achievement of each member's deep individual commitment to the group's unanimous position on civil rights policy. Hirschman (1970) claimed that it is group loyalty that bars exit and raises "voice" in members who fear that their group is taking the wrong direction.

In these and countless other examples, groups and members' consciousness of belonging to them are formidable forces in attitude formation. Group members are clearly socialized by their experience of the group and just as clearly become socialization agents for others in the group. But these are also examples of "group" in the formal sense of the scholarly tradition. These groups share the common interests and goals, the group-specific norms and behaviors that separate "groups" from mere classes or categories of people (Golembiewski, 1978). They reveal the interdependence of interaction and sympathy, sympathy and action, and action and interaction that Homans (1950) urged us to observe and understand. This sense of interdependence and identification gives rise to the consciousness that scholars have recently been trying to delineate.

Could the working class, or black Americans, much less women, then, be a "group?" Could such large and crosscut classes of people share group consciousness? Conover (1984) found that "groups" as seemingly amorphous as "business people," "working people," and "the middle class" have distinguishable, and significantly different, political dispositions whenever objective group membership and subjective group identification interact to make the individual feel that the group's interests and her own are the same.

In these terms, Verba and Nie (1972: 160–61) argued for the existence of black consciousness and said that it explained blacks' overrepresentation in political participation relative to their socioeconomic status. They defined the consciousness in group terms: it emerged from blacks' awareness of their membership in a deprived group; cooperative activity in and in behalf of the group characterized black political behavior. Shingles (1981), in asking "but why not poor, disadvantaged *whites?*" answered that black consciousness requires a psychological link between high internal political efficacy and high political mistrust. Low trust triggers perceptions of the need to act, and high internal efficacy assures the ability to act. The activator of this psychological interaction, he concluded, is a transference of blame for one's status from individual fault to system malfeasance, a connection that poor white people do not make (pp. 89–90).

Neither Verba and Nie nor Shingles, unfortunately, examined gender differences among blacks. Shingles, in fact, went so far as to extend his argument to speculations of "red" or "brown" consciousness, but gender consciousness finds no place in his discussion, much less the possibility, among minority women, of black, brown, or red gender consciousness.

Defining Gender Consciousness

The concept of gender consciousness was introduced at the end of the first chapter, and a simple reiteration of a very complex construct is in order here. Gender consciousness is one's recognition that one's relationship to the political world is at least partly but nonetheless particularly shaped by being female or male. This recognition is followed by identification with others in the "group" of one's sex, positive affect toward the group, and a feeling of interdependence with the group's fortunes. It is suffused with *politics* when women's fortunes are assessed relative to those of other "groups" in society, women's particular contributions to politics and policy are weighed, and political orientations are constructed according to what the individual believes will be in the group's interest or expressive of the group's special point of view.

For an individual woman, gender consciousness awakens when she reinterprets the socialization process depicted in the foregoing pages: some catalytic event causes a woman to think that, perhaps, politics and other important activities are *not* "things better done by men"; that women too have contributions to make. Gender consciousness, in this sense, obviously encompasses different feminist approaches to women's claim on the public world. But it also encompasses "Eleanor's paradox" of women who would not consider themselves feminists but who do believe that women have a unique responsibility for seeing that what are now called the "compassion issues" hold a high position on the public agenda. And, as I discussed in chapter one, it also extends to those antifeminist or "traditional role" women who are active in *defense* of traditional role ascriptions, as were the women of Barcelona at the turn of the century (Kaplan, 1982). These women, united by a shared perception that state action put their responsibility for sustaining their homes at serious risk, took to the streets again and again. This also explains the behavior of the women of the Religious Right in the America of the 1980s (Luker, 1984; Klatch, 1987).

I have presented gender consciousness as a universal concept, universally available to women as a cognitive structure. And, indeed, I mean it to be so. But the largest, most searing challenge to its universality is race. Racial divisions remain as the potent result of such tragic wrongs in the history of the culture that Welch and Sigelman (1988) can find little evidence of a *black* gender gap, with consciousness of race so clearly still necessary. And Lugones and Spelman (1983) remind us that women of color have good reason to be wary of feminist "cultural imperialism."

Nonetheless, we are offered moving portrayals of black women's deep solidarity with one another, fictionally in Alice Walker's (1982) *The Color Purple,* in anthologies such as Barbara Smith's (1983) *Homegirls,* and historically in works such as *When and Where I Enter* (Giddings, 1984), as women simultaneously battle sexism and racism. White women, on the other hand, have often struggled to challenge racism, from the woman suffragists who emerged from abolitionist movements to the feminists who cut their political teeth in the antiracist movements of the New Left in the 1960s. And, as I have steadily maintained, *all* women have lived in cultures that have treated women singularly, because of their presumed reproductive, social, or economic "value" (or the lack of it) as judged by the ideology of the moment. Virtually *no* woman, regardless of color or class, has been seen by the male world surrounding her as citizen, in the fullest sense of the term, until she and other women have fought together for such recognition.

For these reasons, I shall examine differences between the races, where possible, in the spirit of letting the differences also speak for similarities. A recognition of the often devastating difference made by race in the condition of women should not obscure the power of perceptions of gender, also devastating in their potential to affect women's condition.

Finally, is there merit in a consideration of *male* gender consciousness? In some sense, anecdotes about men threatened by the end of all-male club memberships or by "reverse discrimination" seem to mimic something like "traditional role" gender consciousness among women. And men who are currently working to replace stereotypes about man as provider with acceptance of men as nurturers—"I am not a success object," as one button popular among some men in the early 1970s put it—seem to demonstrate a gender consciousness akin to the role-challenging consciousness of many feminists. But on the whole, male gender consciousness is less likely for definitional reasons: men, *as* men, do not assess their fortunes relative to those of other groups. Particularly if they are white, their fortunes are the yardstick against which other groups measure. And men, *as* men, have no need of articulating their group's special point of view, when that point of view is the system's. Men are subdivided and cross-pressured, as women are. Folk wisdom about "male bonding" is endemic, despite the importance placed on independence and competitiveness in Western male gender role socialization. While men may think of themselves as men, and no doubt do, during many of their waking moments, there is little reason to think that they see themselves as members of the "group of men," in political terms, rather than as individual males. Women, in contrast, have been addressed by the political system *as* a group—whether to restrict them or later to remove the restrictions—and thus have every reason to address themselves in group terms as well.

Saying "We"

This chapter began by pointing to the single most significant characteristic shared by all women, reproductive function, from which virtually all socially constructed understandings of gender have sprung. The power of the social construction of gender was illustrated via a discussion of the intersection of gender role and political socialization.

Women's own powerful uses of gendered political socialization—from the women of the New Religious Right, to women who practice "Eleanor's paradox," to the plethora of feminist formulations—were shown to be unified by the concept of gender consciousness.

But measurement of the concept, and its distribution among women, is yet another challenging stage of the journey, and a stage that must be completed before any clear empirical picture can emerge of the role of gender consciousness in shaping women's political attitudes and behavior. That completion is the task of the next two chapters.

Chapter 3

MEASURING WOMEN'S IDENTIFICATION WITH ONE ANOTHER

There is another greater and even more special reason for our coming which you will learn from our speeches: in fact we have come to vanquish from the world the same error into which you had fallen, so that from now on ladies and all valiant women may have a refuge and defense against the various assailants . . . the simple, noble ladies, following the example of suffering which God commands, have cheerfully suffered the great attacks which, both in the spoken and the written word, have been wrongfully and sinfully perpetrated against women by men who all the while appealed to God for the right to do so. . . . Thus, fair daughter, the prerogative has been bestowed on you to establish and build the City of Ladies.
—Christine de Pizan, *The Book of the City of Ladies,* 1405

Christine said that Lady Reason, accompanied by Lady Rectitude and Lady Justice, appeared before her and spoke the words above after Christine had concluded from her reading that "God formed a vile creature when He made woman, and I wondered how such a worthy artisan could have deigned to make such an abominable work which, from what [learned men from Aristotle to her own time] say, is the vessel as well as the refuge and abode of every evil and vice" (de Pizan, [1405] 1982: 5). But Christine's sympathies, despite the "evidence" of the printed word, were all with women, and the character and behavior of women that she herself had observed. Her solution, the founding of a city in the imagination, was in the tradition of Plato and Dante—but, as Lady Reason said, it was to be reserved for and peopled with women, and its purpose was that of sanctuary. Extraordinary Christine, who became what we might today

call a professional journalist when widowhood at the age of twenty-five compelled her to put her remarkable education and talents to the service of supporting her small children, used this imaginary sanctuary both as an expression of
her identification with women and as a rebuttal of the characterization of women
at large in literate Western culture. Since some twenty-five manuscripts of the
work, most prepared in her lifetime and under her supervision, circulated
through Europe (Introduction, p. xliv), she may have influenced some men's
attitudes or, no less a consideration, provided solace for women who could gain
access to a manuscript and, thereby, entry into the City.

Christine's work is not, of course, subject to any simple twentieth-century
feminist labeling, but her intellectual and emotional bonds to other women are
nonetheless unmistakable. Her participation in the common plight and glory of
being a woman is the participation I have called the beginning of gender consciousness, whether of the role-challenging or traditional role-acceptance variety. Christine's work, in fact, illustrates both, for while she insisted that women
were possessed of noble qualities, qualities that men basely repudiated, she also
accepted a view of women—as patient, maternal, and self-abnegating—that we
would call "traditional" gender role ideology today (but that is also evoked
among feminist "maternal thinkers"). Thus, as Gottlieb (1985) makes clear, we
would commit the "sin of anachronism" if we were to assume that Christine
advocated something like a contemporary feminist agenda: the world of the
fifteenth century, after all, is not the world in which we live. Yet Gottlieb em-
phasizes Christine's solidarity with women and her concern to uphold women's
virtues against the calumny of men. In that sense, Christine de Pizan was a
feminist.

But while Christine's identification with women leaps off the pages of her
book, such identification among the masses of Western women today is a challenge for quantification and analysis. Have modern women sought refuge not in
an imaginary City of Ladies but in a sense of their connections to one another?
Insofar as they have, the tasks before us are to find a valid way of measuring
those connections, to seek evidence of the transformation of identification into
consciousness, and to illuminate the operation of consciousness on women's
political life.

WOMEN'S MEMBERSHIP IN THE "GROUP" OF WOMEN

This chapter begins our empirical analysis of gender consciousness by present-
ing the results of measuring women's group closeness with the indicators in the
American National Election Studies of 1972, 1976, 1980, 1984, and 1988. This

exploration of women's closeness to other women, or women's *group* identification, is the first step toward finding valid and reliable ways of ascertaining gender consciousness. In chapter four, group identification is combined with orientations toward women's role; the result allows us to explore women's identification, as measured by group closeness, in a more revealing way, by uncovering women's bonds to one another within a framework ranging from traditional, private constructions of women's roles to more egalitarian, public constructions of those roles. But the reader is warned that gender consciousness itself will not be seen in the way that we usually expect to see concepts operationalized as variables, nor, indeed, should it be thought of as a variable "thing" to be related to other measured "things." It seems clear that gender consciousness is a process more than it is an object, an organizing scheme for attitudes rather than an attitude itself. Thus gender consciousness will not appear here as a variable: it is, instead, to be seen in the *relationship* between identification, as far as we can measure it, and various political objects, attitudes toward which are shaped by women's identification as women.

Before we can begin exploring those relationships, we must define women's gender identification. Women's identification with one another—the sense of a common bond, of shared status—is fundamental to any truly *political* notion of consciousness, but identification is also deeply problematic. We have seen that Eleanor Roosevelt, despite a long and difficult struggle toward acknowledgment of herself as a feminist, could speak quite readily of a consciousness among women. She thought, moreover, that that consciousness was not only significant to *individual* women's politicization but, when one awakened consciousness joined others, would have its cumulative effect on the public agenda.

This belief, couched in the language of different eras or theoretical frameworks, has also been the assumption of most contemporary scholars of gender politics. If only implicitly, we have expected that women's "consciousness" (even before we had probed the phenomenon deeply enough to understand that it was, indeed, "consciousness" that we were trying to plumb) would function both individually and systematically—and, in complementary fashion, that it would arise from an intricate interplay of factors both internal and external to the individual.

But this, precisely, reveals the great challenge to our understanding of gender (and gendered) politics, just as our ability to meet it should signify the power of this perspective to inform our comprehension of political life generally. For women are not a bounded "group" in any classical sense; women are, of course, roughly half the membership of all other demographic groupings. This is obviously why sex, when treated as a dichotomous indicator, provides such partial explanations of political attitudes or behavior. The second edition of a popular public opinion textbook said in 1980, for example, that "differences in the political attitudes of men and women are so slight that they deserve only brief mention," although the authors did allude to women's apparent propensity to be more "tender minded" than men on what we would today call the compassion issues (Erikson, Luttbeg, and Tedin, 1980: 186). Some of these attitudes, such as women's supposedly more dovish orientations toward international relations, have been documented for quite a while (Hero, 1968).

Yet the division of people by sex does yield partial explanations. Even this most rudimentary indicator of gender role socialization shows the degree to which, sometimes, women have "cheerfully suffered the great attacks" (in acquiescing to the limited political role prescribed for them) or, sometimes, "ladies and all valiant women [have sought] a refuge and defense" (in asserting their own definition of their political prerogatives). Thus we have seen gender gaps in voting turnout, favoring men, close. And we have seen the gap in turnout give way to gaps in policy preferences, "favoring" women. By favoring women I mean that they have been relatively united across these preferences and, now that their turnout equals or surpasses that of men, they are deemed an electoral force to be reckoned with, and candidates and parties through the 1980s have adjusted their agendas accordingly. It was a simple division of the mass into female and male that first characterized scholars', journalists', and political elites' analysis of the "gender gap" (Frankovic, 1982, 1985; Baxter and Lansing, 1983; Shapiro and Majahan, 1986; Kenski, 1988), in part because this division alone generates clues to the power of gendered political socialization and the potential power of a resocialization to political life.

Still, as Nancy Cott (1987: 9) has so perceptively argued, women's identification with other women, their "willingness to say 'we,' " may come about most readily when women do not also see themselves as members of other oppressed or disadvantaged groups. Women who are black or poor may not only mean other women, or even mean women at all, when they say "we." In political terms, this problem of cross-pressuring is the root cause of charges from numerous quarters that the contemporary Women's Movement is a white middle-class movement. In an even larger sense, the potency of cross-pressuring calls the universality of women's identification with one another into question; Patricia Hill Collins (1990), for example, shows most powerfully the ways in which perceptions of white women's complicity in racism are a terrible obstacle to black women's identification with them.

I have already tried to suggest that thinking about gender consciousness is best done without excessive reliance on the "woman as victim" perspective. The view of women as an oppressed class is in its own way as crude an attempt to explain the meaning of gender differences as is the division of citizens into biological males and females. Both ignore the delicate but profound interactions of individual personalities with history and environment. The construct of oppression, nonetheless, has its uses here. Class—not just in simple economic terms but as microculture—may reinforce patterns and traditions that make traditional gender role structures most cognitively consonant with one's world view or it may create a climate supportive of significant revisions of traditional roles. One need only compare Luker's (1984) depiction of poorly educated and/or working class antiabortion activists on the one hand to feminist academicians writing on variations of "maternal thinking" on the other to see the astonishing difference that something as supposedly universal as motherhood makes to the different cognitive frameworks of different women.

And race surely must be more urgent than class in its effects. Women of different races have been divided, and have divided themselves, from one another more frequently than they have been able to bridge that divide. Even in the Women's Movement, which, regardless of different ideological strains within it, still makes a broad appeal on behalf of the "group" of all women, apologias and accusations about the treatment of race differences are legion.

Within each of the demographic of racial or cultural groups, however, women have been "other," the object of men and many of their actions, and almost every extant culture or subculture has been to some extent patriarchal. Women's potential ability to recognize this, the potential for gender consciousness, has existed virtually throughout Western history, as I hope the chapter epigraphs in this volume make clear. For some, the recognition has burst through in some historically appropriate version of Jane O'Reilly's "click," and that has led to some historically located kind of feminism, and that feminism has often been articulated in clearly political terms. I return to this point at some length in chapter five. But for others, it has meant a vigorous demand on the state to protect women's *traditional* roles from the faithlessness of the men on whom the fulfillment of those roles depends. We can recall the historical example of peasant women in Barcelona before World War I (Kaplan, 1982) or see it in Nazi women's behavior in the decade before World War II erupted (Koonz, 1976). The most extreme American example of mobilized traditional consciousness can be found in the Women of the Ku Klux Klan in the 1920s, a mass movement that capitalized on women's recent enfranchisement by appealing not only to racist nationalism but to "a specific, gendered notion of the preservation of family life and women's rights" (Blee, 1991: 58). At least part of the appeal of the WKKK to some women was its trumpeting of the threat to women and children when men abandoned "traditional family values." More recently, this view helps us explain the behavior of women in New Right political movements. Here, too, we can find a mistrust of men, and doubts about their willingness to adhere to the traditional role of provider. From this perspective, women with traditional role ideologies may be as aware of women's vulnerability as any feminist would be, even if the two groups would attach different meanings to the vulnerability and different remedies for it (Klatch, 1987).

What complex of factors brings about either kind of collective thinking? Or, more important, what galvanizes identification? Identification, albeit generative of consciousness, must be catalyzed before it is transformed into individual and group political development. The catalytic process itself is probably the concept most resistant to quantification of any with which we are dealing. We are more likely to see its consequences than to see it, since "it" is almost certain to be the individual's own unique revised interpretation of her experiences and her position in the world. But pausing here to reflect on theories about groups in politics prepares us for the foray into empirical tests of women's identification with one another, just as some considerations of political learning in adulthood help us, in the next chapter, to understand the different syntheses of group identification with individuals' particular constructions of gender roles.

Group Identification and Politics

The concept "group" has been relied on to enrich our understanding of politics and has been seen as an especially important part of informal political processes, not only to explain political behavior in the relatively open context of Western societies, but to explain patterns of alignment in closed or developing systems as well. Although Arthur Bentley (1908) was denigrated by his contemporaries for insisting that the group was "everything" of politics—partly because of the formal, constitutional paradigm holding his fellow scholars in its grip—a later generation of political scientists, enamored of behavioralism, seemed to agree with his assessment. Citizen behavior was more and more described in interest group terms, as legalistic modes of inquiry were all but supplanted by those of pluralism. Sidney Verba (1961: 18) went so far as to proclaim the "rediscovery of the primary group," vital, Verba said, to industrial states' ability to assure the appropriate socialization, affective development, and attitudinal flexibility of their citizenries. But from Bentley to Verba to the present, the group itself has been treated as the unit of analysis in most studies of group influences in politics. Whether by its proponents or by its critics, discussion of representation and interest articulation have rarely penetrated into the group (Garson, 1978). Treating the group as the unit of analysis would, naturally, be an important stage in a multilevel analysis of interactions within the group, between the group and its members, and between the group and the larger political system. The problem is that the last-named stage alone has been the focus of most behavioral research.

The unit-of-analysis problem is compounded, particularly in research on political behavior, by the fact that group membership has usually been determined objectively: the researcher's own decision about an individual's membership in a given group has often been the beginning and end of inquiry into the bonds between a group and its members. The combination of problems produced by examining the group, not its members, and assuming that the group is composed of those objectively, rather than subjectively or self-identified, takes the group concept in political science a good distance from its use in psychology and social psychology. The nature of the distance is meaningful to any discussion of group consciousness, since the consciousness we seek to identify is not so much that of the group as of its members, and identification with the group in question requires subjective identification as a necessary if not sufficient condition for consciousness. For both reasons, group consciousness is not easily got at via our usual behavioral analyses. (A somewhat different but most useful critique of behavioral failures to understand group identification can be found in Dennis, 1987.)

Social psychological definitions of groups depend heavily on not only subjective identification of members with the group, but fairly intense intragroup interaction on the part of the group's members. The first five decades of social psychological group research, in fact, were almost utterly preoccupied with intragroup phenomena: the facilitation of common tasks, the development of group norms, the emergence of group leadership and its qualitative type, the group's ability to confront and solve problems, and the effect of group-member interaction on the formation of individuals' attitudes (Hare, 1976; and for a classic early example of such research, see Allport, 1920). All these concerns have their counterparts in political scientists' interest in the sources of political behavior. And in particular settings, research of an almost purely social psychological kind has been conducted. Danelski (1979), Janis (1972), and Golembiewski (1978), for example, have elucidated the effect of group-member interactions on judicial, foreign policy, and bureaucratic decision making, respectively.

In each of these examples, members' subjective identification with the observed group is unquestionable, as is the high level of members' communication with one another, and our view of the interaction of the group with its members clearly yields a deeper understanding of group decisions than would a study of either the group or its individual members alone. But these political groups unambiguously meet the social psychological definition. Other "groups" in which we are interested—especially when we are thinking of group consciousness—do not. Social psychologists would call race or sex a category, not a group (see, for example, Homans, 1950). The "group" of all women is too large, too diverse, too lacking a sense of shared group identity or interest to be a group in any true sense, they would say.

Two decades after Verba "rediscovered" the primary group, however, the group was rediscovered once more: in the years since what was lost was again found, the group has been newly appreciated precisely for its role in shaping political affect and political cognition. In other words, it has been seen just as social psychologists have traditionally seen it, although political scientists and their colleagues in other disciplines might continue to argue over whether it is a group or a category that has been found. Pamela Johnston Conover (1988c) provides a lucid, concise review of the perspectives of this literature, from reference group theory to intergroup conflict, before using it to show evidence of group awareness among women—evidence of the consequences of just the kind of shared group identity so central to classic definitions to the group.

In Conover's work, as in the work of others, objective group membership is still the starting point, and objective membership by sex or by race has piqued the most scholarly curiosity of late. The vastness of the "categories" of race and sex notwithstanding, there are plausible "group" goals and behaviors and sympathies to be hypothesized about with regard to each. Race has been by far the most prominent target of this current research orientation, and it is also most likely to be talked about in terms of consciousness rather than mere group identification (Verba and Nie, 1972; Shingles, 1981), because the possibility of something like black consciousness is so abundantly clear, and so (albeit indirectly) supported by myriad evidence, even if the evidence derived from *explicit* measures of subjective identification with the group has been infrequent. The heritage of black people's identification with one another is a richly textured and voluminous record, and their treatment by the political system on the *basis* of classification in a racial group, and that alone, has required an enormous share of the political system's energy, first to maintain such an apparatus of discriminatory treatment and then to begin dismantling it. Under such circumstances, the potential for a politicized black consciousness seems overwhelming.

Are Women a Group?

Feminist scholars have presumed, and with good reason, that feminist sensibilities supply the same kind of stimulus to the development of gender consciousness although, to belabor a point, this particular kind of gender consciousness is actually only one end of what might be a spectrum. The point is that, as with black people, women *can* see themselves in group terms: a larger group than any classical social psychological definition would permit, no doubt, but with the sense of group identification and interdependent group fortunes that we have thought make groups so meaningful to political orientation and behavior. As I said earlier, women's reproductive functions have been invoked for centuries as the largest place where women's commonality inheres. Supporters of and opponents to the proposed Equal Rights Amendment supply us with more explicit indications of gender identity. Each side encompassed women acting *in* more formally organized groups, but more important, both were making their appeals *in behalf* of the "group of all women," not just the women in their groups, and even though the appeals were antithetical to one another (Boles, 1979; Mansbridge, 1986). We find more recent examples in the activities of abortion rights activists (Staggenborg, 1991) and also among antiabortion groups, even though women in the latter groups are more likely to be the troops following male leaders (Luker, 1984). It is difficult to question the existence of real gender consciousness in either kind of activist, one a consciousness grounded in protection of traditional roles and the other grounded in a challenge to the validity of those same roles. Whether, despite their vehement differences over these two emblematic policy questions, their consciousness might induce them to share preferences on other policies is one of the questions I shall be addressing.

Gender politics scholars would wish, however, to find some more systematic means of locating consciousness than a reinterpretation of extant accounts of women's political behavior permits. Thus far, the consciousness we think we have measured is at best subjective group identification at the level of the individual and at least objective group membership at the aggregate level. But most of the as yet small body of research focusing on this aspect of gender takes a highly aggregative stance, drawing its perspectives from stratum and reference group theories even when it attempts to ascertain individual level group identification. There is one notable exception to this pattern, and it is discussed below. First, however, it is useful to review the techniques employed to date.

To take the latter case, that of objective identification, first, some (e.g., Sears et al., 1984) have tried to operationalize gender as a cognitive schema by using objectively determined sex associated with various symbolic policy orientations as surrogates. Conover (1987) has also used objective sex as the basis of a variety of identifications, and has examined both feminist identification and the "ingroup/outgroup" perspective of men and women to show the role of group identification and group sympathy in shaping policy orientations (Conover, 1988b, 1988c). Ethel Klein (1984) correlated periods of cultural role strain and patterns of behavior and opinion with documented policy initiatives to reveal the ebbs and flows of feminist consciousness through the twentieth century, a breathtaking synthesis of mass orientations and system response that nonetheless remained at the level of the aggregate.

The most systematic attempts to focus on gender as a source of *subjective* group identification, in fact, still draw their theoretical perspectives from the aggregate approaches of sociological stratum and reference group theory. Patricia Gurin and her colleagues first examined gender in a study of the comparative consciousness of race, class, sex, and age groups (Gurin, Miller and Gurin, 1980). They presented four components of consciousness: group identification, or a psychological feeling of belonging to a particular stratum; polar affect, or the preference for members of the ingroup and a corresponding dislike of outgroup members; polar power, or the expression of satisfaction or dissatisfaction of the group's status, power, and resources relative to those of the outgroup; and individual or system blame, the respondent's attribution of responsibility for the group's fortunes. Their analysis used the group closeness questions in the 1972 American National Election Study data to establish subjective identification, and contrasted group identifiers' positions on a range of orientations reflecting the remaining three components of consciousness. Not surprisingly, given such a focus on consciousness as the manifestation of thinking in ingroup/outgroup and

subordinate/dominant terms, Gurin and her co-workers found gender consciousness to be significantly less obvious among women than race consciousness is
among blacks. In 1981, they replicated their construction of consciousness in
data from both 1972 and 1976, this time to assess its relationship to political
behavior. They found that the interaction of their four components explained
voting turnout and other forms of political behavior better than predictions based
on socioeconomic status alone, but once again they concluded that gender consciousness is less evident than race consciousness (Miller, Gurin, Gurin, and
Malanchuk, 1981).

Later, Gurin speculated thoughtfully about the structural conditions limiting
the development of women's gender consciousness, especially in contrast to that
based on race. She argued that gender inequality, while persistent, is not as
marked as race inequality, and noted that *perceptions* of inequality are harder to
sustain when the inequality does not seem extreme. Women also find that their
economic fates are virtually inextricably entwined with those of men, and
women and men also share value systems, not only as husbands and wives, but
as brothers and sisters. Finally, she argued, the most serious obstacle to women's
gender consciousness is the structure of their relations with other women and
with men: stratum and reference group theories assume that consciousness is
partly a product of much contact within the ingroup and far less frequent interaction with outgroup members. Women, of course, are rarely positioned in such
a way that they have little contact with the "outgroup" of men. She concluded
that while women's gender consciousness had increased during the 1970s, especially as a reflection of women's evaluation of their relative power, it hadn't
increased by much—and men had, over the same period, relinquished many of
the attitudes that helped to perpetuate gender inequalities and the consciousness
that such inequities might stimulate (Gurin, 1985).

Arthur Miller, in a departure from his work with Gurin, tried once more to
pin the concept down—but not successfully—by segmenting women's subjective group identification according to their affective responses to the Women's
Liberation Movement (Miller et al., 1986). He and his colleagues were, quite
appropriately, attempting to show the relationship between group identification
and group consciousness that has so thoroughly occupied us here and may have
been trying to use the Women's Movement as a multidimensional surrogate for
the polar affect, polar power, and system blame components of the earlier work.

But the division of group identifiers according to their positive or negative
evaluation of the "Women's Liberation Movement" (as it has been called in the
American National Election Study data) errs in two ways. First, it forces us to
accept a huge and questionable leap from group identification to emotional
warmth toward a political movement; only those who both identify with women
and feel such emotional warmth are labeled gender conscious—if it *is* meant to
summarize the remaining components of consciousness, the validity of the as-

sumed relationship requires scrutiny. Which "movement" are respondents thinking of, and what do they think the "movement" means to their own lives? Second, this formulation makes it impossible to identify any *nonfeminist* form of consciousness. These two problems are illustrated below.

Consciousness is fundamentally cognitive, not affective, and it is a process, not an endorsement. Those who *are* gender conscious might certainly form attitudes toward the Women's Movement (although we would still be obligated to ascertain just what in the movement women were responding to, exactly), but such attitudes should be seen as a possible result of consciousness, and not gender consciousness itself. To put it another way, a gender conscious woman would see the Women's Movement as a *means* (or block) to the overarching policy ends her consciousness constrains her to take—but she might not. Consider the following scenario: a highly gender conscious woman becomes thoroughly exasperated with the political ineptness of the National Organization for Women, as some of Mansbridge's (1986) pro-ERA activists in Illinois did. But her assumption, almost certainly correct, is that the Women's Movement is often seen as synonymous with NOW, the largest and most visible movement organization. Her "affect" toward the Women's Liberation Movement, then, is actually a complex cognitive evaluation of the movement as a means to her ends: the Movement is not the end toward which her consciousness is bent, but merely a potential vehicle of its expression—or an obstacle to it, if she believes that its foremost formal organization is ineffective. Thus, while it is clearly important to look at the relationship between gender identity and the Women's Movement, we should not make the conceptual error of doing so because we think support for the Movement is the best single indicator of consciousness.

In any case, even if warmth or animosity toward the Women's Liberation Movement *were* a limpid reflection of the presence or absence of gender consciousness, the Miller et al. formulation ignores the traditional role form of gender consciousness that animosity might possibly reflect. Gurin, in 1985, frankly admitted that she posited consciousness as a collective strategy for change and, thus, feminist. Miller et al. simply assume that this is so. Failure to recognize the possibility of the traditional role form of consciousness is one of the consequences of our genuine difficulty in reaching conceptual agreement on the meaning of gender consciousness, especially when our thinking is so dependent on notions of sociological strata and reference groups, notions that were meant to describe groups far more bounded and structurally homogeneous than the "group of all women" could ever be.

Does Group Membership Mean Group Consciousness?

These conceptual and analytical difficulties arise in part from a very understandable limitation of perspective. All scholars interested in consciousness are looking for evidence of a truly political phenomenon, and it is hard to think of such a politicized consciousness without thinking as well of feminism, especially when race consciousness has supplied a template for so much of the current thinking about gender. Race consciousness, though, does not extend across the kind of spectrum that I have posited for gender consciousness: it is virtually impossible to think that some black people seek their political identity in a return to traditional black/white role divisions when those divisions once meant literal black enslavement. Such a reactionary belief would certainly not seem to be the motivation of black neoconservative thinkers, the group most obviously different in its orientation from many blacks' support of the Civil Rights Movement (a movement that is also less subject to questions of who and what it is than is true of feminism).

Some women, in contrast, can quite conceivably seek their entire identities within traditional roles that seem secondary in every domain to the roles of men; firm arguments for women's subordinate status have been extracted from the Judeo-Christian and Islamic religious traditions, for example. Commitment to such fundamentalist religious beliefs can resonate powerfully with the belief that man is the head of woman in all things. But women who hold such beliefs, while acknowledging men's "superiority," may still argue that women have a unique and uniquely valuable part to play.

The helpful exception to recent thinking about gender consciousness that I alluded to above is the work of Roberta Sigel, and it is most illuminative of a number of these problems of conceptualization. In particular, it helps us to illustrate women's consciousness *not* as a result of women's recognition of themselves as a sociological stratum or their recognition of men as an "outgroup," those perspectives of such limited utility to women as they think about their lives and to scholars as they think about women. Rather, she returns the idea of gender *consciousness* to its roots in women's beliefs about the construction of gender *roles*. In earlier analyses of telephone interviews with four hundred randomly selected New Jersey adults (Sigel and Welchel, 1986a, 1986b), she uncovered significant awareness of discrimination against women as well as strong resentment over it; she dubbed the interaction of the two components women's "minority consciousness," a nomer evocative of the stratum-based work I have just discussed, despite the fundamental differences of perspective between that work and hers. But while this minority consciousness was significantly present, it is not overwhelming: she detected it in only 38 percent of the sample of women.

Why should this figure be so low? Inventively considering work done in the 1950s by McKee and Sheriffs that had revealed a discrepancy between women's ideal self-concept (containing considerable preferences for qualities deemed masculine) and actual self-image (constructed according to assumptions about what men/society expected to see in women's behavior), Sigel concluded that role *ambivalence* interferes with women's push toward full equality with men. This ambivalence arises from the conflict of what one may aspire to be with what the reality of one's life seems to allow (Sigel, 1988). Evidence supporting her ambivalence thesis comes from the richly detailed observations of fifty women in the sample who were asked to participate in focus groups. The focus groups, like the telephone survey, revealed, again and again, women's belief that men "aren't bothered" by women's relatively disadvantaged status, in fact preferred it, and that sympathy for women's plight would come only from other women, not from men. Regardless of the accuracy of women's assessments about men, it is women's perceptions that orchestrate their synthesis of internal belief with external constraint, and it is these perceptions that also lead to a divided self-image.

Ambivalence also requires coping strategies, and Sigel identified two: "double duty" and "not me." The "double duty" strategy allows a woman to assume that, because she won't be *given* the treatment she wants and deserves, she must simply work harder, alone and self-reliant. "Not me" is a strategy permitting a woman to acknowledge systemic discrimination while considering herself a lucky exception, *individually* less subject to the constraints she nonetheless believes *all* women face. Both strategies for coping with ambivalence would limit the development of politicized consciousness. Sigel's portrait of ambivalence and its sources illustrates the degree to which, although men may be targets of considerable anger on the part of women, men simply cannot be seen by most women as an "outgroup," but it also illustrates the way that women's identification with one another is based on shared roles—especially fundamental and all-pervasive gender roles—and not on socioeconomic status.

Sigel found that women in the focus groups were far less likely than they had been in the telephone survey to evince either coping strategy and far more likely to acknowledge disappointment in their own personal treatment, while strongly maintaining their earlier opinions about systemic discrimination. Sigel speculates that this change in patterns of attribution arose from "group contagion" in the focus group setting, and I believe that she is right. But far from viewing such group contagion as a methodological problem, I think that the group contagion she witnessed is truly a case of having captured a moment of women's identification with one another.

Sigel concludes by pointing out that an increase in women's personal strength, even in their bonds to one another, is not necessarily an increase in their political strength, especially in collective terms. That is surely so; indeed, the gender role socialization, or at least individual perceptions of it, that is the wellspring of gender consciousness may also mitigate against women working in apparently self-interested ways *for* themselves. I, however, unlike others who have been struggling to locate and measure gender consciousness, have defined consciousness as something bent toward more than women's individual political empowerment: it reaches beyond empowerment to the desire that "women's" substantive political goals are firmly secured on the public agenda. Because of this broader, less apparently self-interested goal, even women who have "traditional role" consciousness could seek enough political power to achieve it, as the women of the New Right have done.

We are cautioned, then, not to try to define women's consciousness in the old terms of stratum or reference group, nor do we wish to restrict gender consciousness to support for feminism. Our point of departure, however, is still women's identification with one another. First and foremost, the potential for women's subjective identification with other women must be shown to be virtually universal, as potentially encompassing of all women as objective assignment by sex would be. By this I do not mean that we cannot proceed *unless* all women identify with women, but I do mean that the propensity to identity cannot be restricted to certain kinds of women alone, whether by "kinds of women" we mean those of a particular class or race *or* of a particular political predisposition.

And yet by talking of women's identification with one another as something "potentially universal," I am well aware that such thinking is prey to the troubling dilemmas of political philosophy and feminist theory, or feminist reconstruction of other theory, discussed at such length in the first two chapters. My analysis is no less free of the implications of "difference," and the rejoinder that almost *no* thinking in a gendered world has been free of those implications hardly excuses a consideration of them. As "difference" has been used to justify boundaries around women's sociopolitical domains, so "difference" has also been used by women themselves to justify women's special claim to a share in the life of the polis. From nineteenth-century suffragettes and Eleanor Roosevelt struggling with the apparent paradox of women's equality of capacity yet difference in ends, to traditional women's political mobilization to preserve traditional roles, to some almost eerie contemporary feminist theorizings about an innate feminine spirit, we hear changes rung on women's "difference." While the enormous power of gender role socialization relieves us of any need to base a claim of "difference" in nature, however, even socialization explanations seem to insist that intrasex differences are often less than those between the sexes, and such insistence can lead us in dangerous directions. To put it another way, earlier behavioral research based on a limited grasp of gender role socialization looks pitifully inadequate today because of its blithe dismissal of women as *not* political. We would be equally wrong to make converse but no less superficial assertions that women are *uniquely* and uniformly so. It is important, then, to stress the "potential" in "potentially universal" and to accept cognizance of these dilemmas as an astringent but beneficent restraint on any grand conclusions.

WOMEN'S GENDER IDENTIFICATION, 1972–1988

After recounting such formidable theoretical and methodological problems, only the hardy will press on. The best extant survey data permitting us to tap women's subjective gender identification have been the American National Election Studies, for they use the same indicator—the group closeness items—over time, while they also offer us a wide variety of items measuring political behavior and attitudes. In these surveys, respondents are shown a list of groups (16 in 1972 and 1976, on which "women" appeared 12th; 18 in 1980, when women were still 12th on the list; 19 in 1984, with women in the 14th position; and 15 in 1988, when women fell 11th on the list) and are asked to say "which (or which letter) of these groups you feel particularly close to—people who are most like you in their ideas and interests and feelings about things." Respondents are not limited in the number of groups to which they say they are close. After group closeness has been ascertained, respondents are asked which, of all the groups, they feel *closest* to. These are the measures used by Gurin and her colleagues, and I employ them as well. The data are from complete pre- and postelection waves of interviews in 1972, 1976 (weighted to produce a properly representative cross-section from the original 72–74–76 panel study and respondents newly selected in 1976), 1980, 1984, and 1988. The total number of cases for women in each year is 1252, 1412, 794, 1074, and 1168, respectively. After cases with missing data on the group closeness items are excluded, the number of cases remaining for analysis in each year is 1242 in 1972, 1339 in 1976, 787 in 1980, 1068 in 1984, and 986 in 1988.

In each case, the vast majority of respondents is white, and most of the remaining cases come from black women. Other nonwhite women, usually American Indian, Asian, or Pacific Islanders, were added to the black total. This was done for two reasons: first, I simply did not wish to lose any cases, and even the number of black women alone is usually too small for sound statistical comparisons by race. But second, and more important, criticisms about feminism, the Women's Movement, and studies of gender consciousness are frequently based in the assumption that it is a "white" phenomenon. If that is so, then women who are members of other racial minorities, in addition to black women, may also reject the Women's Movement, or the idea of "women's" consciousness, as so far outside their racial experience that it does not comport with their experience as women. For that reason, the reaction of white women should be compared to *all* women of color. Such a choice, of course, ignores the vast differences between racial minorities—between an African American and Japanese American woman, for example—but even the label "white" hardly denotes homogeneity. Many people of Hispanic descent consider themselves white, for instance, while some consider themselves black, and still others consider themselves to belong to a separate racial group. And the Women of the Ku Klux Klan defined "white" as Protestant, not as Jewish or Catholic (Blee, 1991). The meaning of race, in short, is terribly important, and terribly difficult to capture in a behavioral analysis. Nonetheless, because it is important to examine whether gender consciousness appears to be a "white" phenomenon, the decision was made to examine white women versus women of color, most of whom are black, wherever analysis by race was possible. In 1972, there were 154 women of color in the portion of the sample for whom there are data on gender identification. In 1976, the sample included 178 women of color, and for subsequent years the numbers are 105 in 1980, 154 in 1984, and 182 in 1988.

There has been considerable debate about whether the group closeness items tap little more than social affect and about their meaning generally. The question about group closeness, though, does seem to embody a number of the elements of gender identification as I have defined it—"people who are most like you in their ideas and interests and feelings about things" does seem like a genuine sense of identification. But the possibly varying reactions to it on the part of respondents remain an open question, and the best way to proceed is to scrutinize the patterns of identification that it yields. In particular, keeping Gurin's discussion of the structural limits on women's identification in mind, we need to examine its prevalence within a variety of demographic, lifespace, and socialization contexts.

It is important, however, not to think of these contexts as something to be "controlled for." Herbert Hyman's (1955: 254–257) invaluable warning is pertinent here:

> [T]he concept of spuriousness cannot *logically* be intended to apply to antecedent conditions which are associated with that particular independent variable as part of a developmental sequence. Implicitly, the notion of an uncontrolled factor which was operating so as to produce a spurious finding involves the image of something *extrinsic* to the . . . apparent cause. Developmental sequences, by contrast, involve the image of a series of entities which are *intrinsically* united. . . . Consequently, to institute procedures of control is to remove so-to-speak some of the very cause that one wishes to study.

For our purposes, this means that we are not attempting to "control" socioeconomic factors away, although it is to be hoped that such differences among women will have little effect on their propensity to identify with one another. And yet gender identification and gender consciousness must be stimulated by something—some event or pattern of events or feature(s) of one's environment—that causes one to begin thinking in gender identified, gender conscious terms. Thus we might expect that aspects of one's position in life or in society might provide especially fertile ground for the growth of consciousness. On the whole, then, the integrity of both concepts demands that they be relatively free of dependence on such things as socioeconomic status or race, but perhaps more readily expressed in some life courses than in others.

The strength of women's gender identification can be arrayed, using the group closeness items, quite simply: 0 = not close to women; 1 = close to women; and 2 = closest to women of all groups. This array, henceforth called "gender identification," is the primary independent variable for the rest of the analysis. It is combined with role ideology, ranging from closeness within traditional role frameworks to closeness within "role challenging" frameworks in the next chapter. First, though, we explore women's patterns of group identification *generally*, and then we zero in on women's gender identification.

Women's Group Closeness

Over our five time points, 25 groups were offered to respondents for their evaluation, 13 of them in all five years. Perhaps the most striking feature of women's response to these groups in society is that they seem to identify with the kinds of groups that orthodox gender role socialization *would*, indeed, direct them toward. In Table 3.1, the responses of white women are the first entry for each group, and the responses of women of color follow, in order to see at the outset whether what we have is the "white" phenomenon discussed above. The table shows that white women are less likely than are white men to feel close to liberals in 1972 and 1976, and they are less likely to identify with conservatives in all five years. Black and other minority women are somewhat less likely to differ in such identification from their male peers, although it should be noted here that for all group reactions, the difficulty of achieving statistical significance from relatively few cases means that the appearance of greater similarity between minority women and men is stronger than the reality: the intersex differences in both races are usually parallel. Women are closer to young people and the elderly, groups whose care has been women's charge, and they were somewhat more likely to identify with their religions in 1972 and 1976, a finding that also comports with societal expectations about women as keepers of the faith (Tolleson Rinehart and Perkins, 1989). But in the face of claims of enormous membership by political groups of the religious right, it should be noted that women of any race were not attracted to "evangelists" in 1980 or 1984 and felt even less positively disposed to "Christian fundamentalists" or "Evangelical groups active in politics" in 1988.

A change in the *wording* of the items provides us with a second notable finding, by actually suggesting that women do respond to group labels in strong cognitive terms. Women were much, much less likely to feel close to "businessmen" and "workingmen" than were men in 1972 and 1976. But when the language was made gender neutral in 1980—"businessmen and businesswomen," "workingmen and workingwomen"—intersex differences diminished sharply.

TABLE 3.1　PERCENTAGE OF WOMEN WHO FEEL CLOSE TO GROUPS, 1972–1988, BY RACE

Groups	1972	1976	1980	1984	1988
Poor people (white)	21.7	27.8[b]	31.6	38.4	32.8[b]
(nonwhite)	59.2	67.9	75.2	59.5	66.1
Liberals	8.3[a]	8.6[a]	9.0	17.4	10.4
	15.9	16.1	13.2[a]	24.1	11.3[a]
Southerners	15.5	16.2	16.5	21.4	(NA)
	10.2	27.4	21.5	29.7	(NA)
Hispanics	(NA)	(NA)	5.4	13.0	(NA)
	(NA)	(NA)	14.0	15.9	(NA)
Catholics	19.9	21.6[b]	(NA)	(NA)	(NA)
	13.4	14.7	(NA)	(NA)	(NA)
Older people/Elderly[c]	44.6[b]	52.9[b]	52.1[b]	54.9[b]	49.3[b]
	54.1	58.7[b]	60.3	55.4	57.0
Protestants	32.8[b]	35.1[b]	(NA)	(NA)	(NA)
	23.6	26.3	(NA)	(NA)	(NA)
Blacks	6.8	5.3	8.1	17.4	8.4
	72.0	66.1	69.4	63.1	67.0
Jews	6.9	7.8	(NA)	(NA)	(NA)
	6.4	6.6	(NA)	(NA)	(NA)
Labor unions	(NA)	(NA)	8.6[a]	13.2	8.0[a]
	(NA)	(NA)	21.5	21.0	13.4[a]
Environmentalists	(NA)	(NA)	35.0[b]	40.7[a]	(NA)
	(NA)	(NA)	29.8	33.8	(NA)
Businessmen/and -women/ /Businesspeople[c]	12.2[a]	14.1[a]	23.9	37.9	23.6[a]
	4.5[a]	4.2[a]	15.7	31.3	15.1
Young people	44.6	48.6[b]	46.1[b]	55.5[b]	41.4[b]
	45.9	52.6	51.2	51.3	51.6
Conservatives	14.8[a]	18.0[a]	20.4[a]	32.4[a]	20.3[a]
	3.2	5.3[a]	5.8	27.7	7.5
Workingmen/ and -women/ Working people[c]	35.4[a]	46.9[a]	53.5	61.8	70.9
	25.5[a]	42.6[a]	52.1	51.8	69.9
Farmers	25.5	30.8	34.5	38.6[a]	(NA)
	12.1[a]	20.5	24.8	33.3	(NA)
Whites	42.5	49.6[b]	42.6	56.4	42.5
	14.0	18.7	20.7	37.9	20.4
Evangelists	(NA)	(NA)	5.4	13.2	
	(NA)	(NA)	5.8	23.1	
Christian Fundamentalists					13.9
					22.0
Evangelical groups active in politics					5.1
					4.8
Middle class	57.2	69.7[b]	58.8	68.9	70.8
	21.0	36.6	35.5	53.8	43.0
Big business	(NA)	(NA)	4.9[b]	(NA)	(NA)
	(NA)	(NA)	5.0	(NA)	(NA)

TABLE 3.I (*continued*)

Groups	1972	1976	1980	1984	1988
Feminists	(NA)	(NA)	(NA)	16.7	8.9[b]
	(NA)	(NA)	(NA)	17.9	12.4
Men	(NA)	(NA)	(NA)	27.3[a]	(NA)
	(NA)	(NA)	(NA)	24.6[a]	(NA)
(Men close to men)				47.0	
				38.8	
Women	42.8[b]	57.6[b]	48.4[b]	58.4[b]	52.7[b]
	47.1[b]	51.3[b]	53.7[b]	54.9[b]	57.0[b]
(Men close to women)	17.5	19.8	16.9	40.4	17.4
	29.2	22.2	32.2	41.4	25.0

SOURCE: American National Election Studies, 1972, 1976, 1980, 1984, 1988.
[a]$p < .05$ *less* likely than men of same race to identify with the group.
[b]$p < .05$ *more* likely than men of same race to identify with the group.
[c]"Older people" was changed from 1980 on to "Elderly." "Businessmen" was changed in 1980 and 1984 to "Businessmen and Businesswomen," and changed again in 1988 to "Business people." "Workingmen" was changed in 1980 and 1984 to "Workingmen and Workingwomen," and changed again in 1988 to "Working people."

The wording was changed again in 1988, to "business people" and "working people," and while women once again were somewhat cooler to "business people," than were men, their warmth toward "working people," a group in which they could feel included, continued to be much higher than their affect toward "workingmen." This pattern of a changed response to changed language held even for minority women, where the small number of cases required huge intersex differences for statistical significance. Women's professed warmth toward the "business" group was double, triple, or more in gender-inclusive language than it had been toward the gendered "businessmen" in the 1970s, and they identified twice as often with "working people" as they had done with "workingmen." This cannot be attributed to the general propensity to identify with more groups over time, since men also identified with more groups in the 1980s than they had in the 1970s. The simple conclusion is that women took the gendered language at face value, assuming that "-men" meant actual men, but changed their responses when they were given an inclusive alternative. This is also evident in white women's rejection of "big business" in 1980, the only year that group was offered to respondents for their evaluation. It may also be inferred from women's cooler reactions to labor unions, most of which are predominantly male in membership and overwhelmingly male in leadership.

With the exception of white women's tendency to identify with other whites and the middle class in 1976, the remaining pattern is straightforward: women don't identify with groups widely associated with the white male status quo, and they do identify with groups thought to be special targets of women's concern.

Our particular concern, women's identification with women, reveals the most unambiguous findings of all. Large numbers of women feel close to other women, and women of all races are always more likely to identify with women than are men. In 1984, when "men" was added to the list of groups, women were far less likely to feel close to men than men were to feel close to women. "Men," unfortunately for a fascinating potential analysis, was one of many groups dropped from the list in the 1988 election study, and so this interesting intersex comparison cannot be continued. The patterns of group identification taken all together provide reason for confidence that the measure is, indeed, tapping a genuine subjective identification.

The distribution of gender identification presented in Table 3.2 shows that while *closeness* to women is substantially increasing, gender identification as the *closest* identification has been relatively stable over time: the apparent slight erosion in 1984 may be almost completely attributable to the addition of "feminists" to the list in that year. Virtually all who were closest to feminists were also close to women, although we cannot be certain that they would have chosen women as the closest group had they not had this new alternative. In any case, "closest" identification levels had returned to previous levels by 1988. Race differences are all but nonexistent in four of the years; in 1976, black women evince more close identification, but white women are more likely to take the closest identification, no doubt for the obvious reason that race must be the most severe of women's cross-pressured identifications.

At this point one might think once again of men and their gender identity, and something can be said about the 1984 data. Something, but not much. No men were closest to their own sex of all groups, and only 1.5 percent of men were close to men without also being close to women—the comparable proportion for women is a strong 35.0 percent. Men's "gender identity" was exhaustively analyzed, and nothing systematic in it could be found; nor could it be found to explain anything about men's political behavior. With regret, then, we will not be able to pursue any lines of inquiry into men's gender consciousness, tantalizing recent media accounts of men in groups, beating drums, reciting poetry, and bonding notwithstanding (but for a significant new anthropological consideration of masculinity, see Gilmore, 1990). When I examined the orientations of men who are close to *women*, however, I found the same patterns of socially integrated, socially conscious, sympathetic behaviors identified by Conover (1988a).

Social integration also seems to be an important outcome of women's identification with one another, as we see in Table 3.3. Women who are close to women have sympathy for other groups as well, and while respondents generally seem to be becoming more gregarious over time, perhaps explaining the otherwise inexplicable leap in men's closeness to women in 1984, women lacking gender identification consistently lag behind other women in the number of their

TABLE 3.2   THE STRENGTH OF WOMEN'S GENDER IDENTIFICATION, 1972–1988: PERCENTAGE IN EACH CATEGORY, FOR ALL WOMEN AND BY RACE

Closeness	1972	1976***	1980	1984	1988
A. All women					
not close	56.3	40.8	42.8	31.6	47.1
close	34.5	48.6	47.3	61.7	42.9
closest	9.2	10.6	9.9	6.7	10.0
B. White women					
not close	56.9	40.1	43.4	31.3	47.8
close	33.9	48.1	45.7	61.2	42.2
closest	9.2	11.8	10.9	7.5	10.1
C. Women of color					
not close	51.9	45.2	38.4	32.6	44.0
close	39.0	52.0	57.6	65.2	46.2
closest	9.1	2.8	4.0	2.3	9.9

SOURCE: American National Election Studies, 1972, 1976, 1980, 1984, 1988.
***Differences between races significant at $p < .01$.

group memberships. While we cannot imply causation here, it seems more likely that women's gender identification prompts them to think in "group" terms than that group orientations prompt gender identification.

It is to be lamented that the group closeness items are not accompanied by open-ended queries about what one means when she says she is close to women. In the absence of such a direct measure, however, we can still conclude that women are as likely to identify with women as they are with *any* social group: gender identity competes with virtually any other significant social cleavage— only race overshadows it, and even in that case, black women's identification with blacks appears to be stable over time, while their identification with women grows.

Demographic Influences?

Women who identified themselves as working class were marginally less likely also to identify with women in 1972, and the same pattern—mostly attributable to differences among white women—appears in 1976. But by 1980, class differences in gender identification are no longer meaningful (if they are ever so in America, where the plurality of people think they are middle class). But this suggests something implicit in Table 3.4 and indeed all the findings: the effect of time. The sixteen-year period anchored by the elections of 1972 and 1988 was eventful for women; the passage of time and events and what they mean for individual cognition are processes to be kept in mind as we examine the life positions and developmental sequences that might influence gender identification.

Family income also appears to make a difference in 1976 and more obviously

TABLE 3.3   WOMEN'S PROPENSITY TO FEEL CLOSE TO GROUPS IN SOCIETY BY CATEGORY OF GENDER IDENTIFICATION, 1972–1988

Mean number of groups	1972	1976	1980	1984	1988
not close***	2.9	3.5	4.3	4.0	3.3
close	6.8	6.7	7.4	9.9	4.6
closest	4.1	4.7	6.2	7.8	3.9

SOURCE: American National Election Studies, 1972, 1976, 1980, 1984, 1988.
Note: Maximum number of groups, including women, is 16 in 1972 and 1976, 18 in 1980, 19 in 1984, and 15 in 1988.
***Differences in number of groups to whom respondent felt close by gender identification is significant at $p < .01$ in each of the five years.

in 1984 and 1988: could it be that by the end of the conservative 1980s, the general climate was less fostering of gender identification? What is much more significant than family income, though, is the respondent's own income, quite a discriminator from 1976 on. This makes a good deal of sense when we think of gender identification as a cognitive process. Women with their own income, whether they live alone, head a household, or contribute to a household's income, have every reason to think about the economic climate for women generally and to think that their fortunes and those of other women are interdependent in this regard. One can call to mind the participants in Sigel's focus groups for examples of the very real, direct significance that larger economic and employment patterns can have for an individual woman's life. The comparison of respondents' family incomes to women's own income, in the absence of other considerations, suggests that women's *independent* economic condition is not, on the whole, bright.

An analysis of the region of the United Sates in which respondents were living revealed almost nothing; political scientists' penchant for dividing the United States into "south" and "nonsouth" does not avail us of anything here, and the analysis is not shown. Despite genuine differences in regional cultures, or perhaps because of the homogenizing effects of mass media, women's propensity to identify with other women does not significantly vary by place of residence. Similarly, intraregional differences by race are minor.

The Influence of Indicators of Lifespace

One's age appears always to be an influence on one's identification, with younger women more likely to evince gender closeness. But an "if young, then close" syllogism masks far more interesting possibilities in the nexus of period, generation, and maturation. The "second wave" of feminism produced tremendous activity on the part of women in a number of spheres. While I agree with Alice Rossi (1973) that the turn-of-the-century movement was a true second wave, separate from the nineteenth-century movement, I carry it further than the

TABLE 3.4   DEMOGRAPHIC POSITION ACROSS CATEGORIES OF GENDER IDENTIFICATION, 1972–1988

Characteristic	1972	1976	1980	1984	1988
A. Subjective social class: % middle and higher					
not close	44.4**	50.3***	46.4	46.4	47.5
close	47.6	51.2	50.2	51.5	48.9
closest	57.2	51.8	59.2	57.0	52.8
B. Mean family income (in thousands of dollars)					
not close	7.5	9.6***	12.7	14.4**	16.0***
close	8.2	10.6	13.4	15.6	17.6
closest	9.2	11.4	14.7	18.4	21.0
C. Mean individual income (in thousands of dollars)					
not close	(NA)	3.7***	5.5***	9.4***	9.9***
close	(NA)	4.4	6.5	10.0	11.1
closest	(NA)	5.3	7.9	10.9	11.1

SOURCE: American National Election Studies, 1972, 1976, 1980, 1984, 1988.
**Differences by category of identification significant at $p < .05$.
***Differences by category of identification significant at $p < .01$.

achievement of suffrage, where she believes it ended. The excellent research in women's history, such as that I have relied on for descriptions of women's behavior in the New Deal era, justifies a claim that the second wave extended to at least the outbreak of World War II. The "third wave" of Women's Movement activity, of course, came of age concomitantly with the fabled baby boomers. For these reasons it seems important, and is certainly intriguing, to look at the patterns of identification in two "generations" of women, broadly defined: those who were born before 1920, and those who were born between 1946 and 1964, in the multivariate analysis to come. At present, a simpler presentation of age and marital status suffices to make the point. Some of one generation would be the mothers of some of the other, in literal as well as figurative terms, but each generation was offered a unique environment in which to consider the meaning of being a woman (for an elegant discussion of the problem of distinguishing among generation, cohort, and period effects, see Delli Carpini, 1989).

The aging of both generations over the sixteen-year period means that cohort replacement took place, with "baby boomers" overwhelming "second wavers" by the mid-1980s in sheer numbers alone—the mean age of each group, in each year, appears to be similar, but the 40-year-olds in 1972, whose early formative experiences occurred between the world wars, are replaced by 40-year-olds in 1988, whose early socialization occurred in the late 1940s and 1950s. If we skip for a moment to Table 3.6, the cohort analysis presented there shows that it was "second wave" women, born before 1920, who were the identifiers in the 1970s. Most of the baby boomers were still too young, in the early 1970s at least, to have had cognizance of the real structures of adult gender roles (see Sapiro, 1983). By the 1980s, they were where their mothers had been earlier: seasoned adults, with ample opportunities to reflect on gender roles in their own lives and in society. As women who had been middle-aged in the 1970s grew older, in contrast, their patterns of identification became somewhat less stable. The "baby boom" and "second wave" generational cohorts make conceptual sense, but they also cover quite long periods of time. The oldest and youngest baby boomers, for example, would have had vastly different experiences of the war in Vietnam and the civil rights and women's movements of the 1960s. I have tried to capture that possibility of difference by using an interaction term (age $\times$ the generational dummies) in the multivariate analysis that concludes this chapter. In the meantime, though, the much narrower cohorts displayed in Table 3.6 seem to tell us that both maturation and the "nature of the times" are at work, but that this interaction occurs across generations.

Returning to Table 3.5, the influence of marital status might be the influence of, in Gurin's terms, living with a member of the outgroup. In fact, that is precisely why it is marital status and not the presence of small children in the home in which we should be interested. Although the influence of motherhood as a brake on women's political participation has often been investigated, there is no good theoretical reason why motherhood itself would influence gender identification one way or the other, although one's beliefs about motherhood might be influential. Marriage, in contrast, could do so. Unmarried women might more readily seek identification with other women. But while the differences presented in Table 3.5 are significant from 1976 on, they are so because being married is overwhelmingly modal for *all* categories of identification, and this statistical significance is the same whether we analyze in terms of the proportion of the close who are married or the proportion of the married who are close. In this table, the former is displayed: of all women who were not close to other women in 1972, 60.5 percent were married, 20.1 percent were widowed, and so forth. Since so many women marry, the distribution of the residual difference suggests only that widowhood dampens, and being unmarried fosters, closeness to women.

The Adult Socialization Environment

The figures in Table 3.7 are presented as an illustration of women's collective educational advances in the last half of the century; their purpose is to provide a broader context for the educational attainments of our respondents. The environment surrounding higher education may provide stimuli and a supportive climate for thinking about gender roles, but as the aggregate data so clearly show, this has been widely available to women only recently. Older women, unless they were uniquely privileged, would not have been as likely to have access to edu-

TABLE 3.5 LIFESPACE POSITION ACROSS CATEGORIES OF GENDER IDENTIFICATION, 1972–1988

Characteristic	1972	1976	1980	1984	1988
A. Mean age					
not close	46.0***	48.1***	46.8***	48.7***	48.7***
close	45.5	43.5	43.6	43.1	43.4
closest	39.3	39.2	38.0	36.3	42.3
B. % who are . . .					
. . . married					
not close	60.5	59.0***	61.1***	52.8***	51.9***
close	61.4	59.2	51.5	52.3	51.2
closest	70.8	54.2	47.4	52.9	49.5
. . . widowed					
not close	20.1	23.3	17.8	20.5	19.2
close	19.7	15.2	16.4	15.3	12.1
closest	6.2	16.2	10.3	1.4	9.1
. . . divorced/separated					
not close	9.9	11.7	11.9	13.4	17.7
close	7.0	13.7	15.3	15.1	19.9
closest	8.8	12.7	18.0	24.3	26.3
. . . never married					
not close	9.6	6.0	9.2	13.4	11.2
close	11.0	11.8	16.9	17.3	16.8
closest	15.0	16.9	24.4	21.5	15.2

SOURCE: American National Election Studies, 1972, 1976, 1980, 1984, 1988.
***Differences within characteristic by identification significant at p < .01.

TABLE 3.6 GENERATIONAL OR PERIOD EFFECT? PERCENTAGE OF WOMEN IN EACH AGE COHORT WITH CLOSE OR CLOSEST GENDER IDENTIFICATION, 1972–1988

Age	1972	1976	1980	1984	1988
18–21ª	59.3	27.3	74.5	58.7	55.6
22–25		33.8			
26–29			62.2		
30–33				75.5	
34–37	48.5	46.9	65.1	67.6	66.1
38–41		38.1			
42–45			60.0		
46–49				58.2	
50–53	65.6	40.5	53.3	76.9	40.4
54–57		55.8			
58–61			45.3		
62–65				60.0	
66–69	64.8	52.1	47.7	67.4	40.7

SOURCE: American National Election Studies, 1972, 1976, 1980, 1984, 1988.
ªA very small number of 17-year-olds present in 1972, 1976, 1984, and 1988 is excluded from each year's calculations.

TABLE 3.7   WOMEN'S SHARE OF EARNED DEGREES CONFERRED, BY LEVEL OF DEGREE

Degree	1950	1960	1970	1980	1985
Bachelor's[a]	24.0	35.2	41.5	47.3	49.5
Master's	29.3	32.0	39.7	49.3	50.0
Doctoral	9.1	10.2	13.4	29.7	34.0

SOURCE: Percentages calculated by the author from actual numbers in thousands in Table No. 254, "Earned Degrees Conferred, by Level of Degree: 1950 to 1985," *Statistical Abstracts of the United States,* 108 ed., U.S. Commerce Department, Census Bureau (Washington, D.C.: GPO, 1988). [a]Includes first professional degrees.

cation and, perhaps more important, the encouraging climate in which higher education takes place. The information in Tables 3.8 and 3.9 certainly suggests higher education's beneficent effects on gender identification, but once again we should recall the influence of time and events. Educated women are simply more likely to identify with women than are their less schooled sisters, but by 1988, high school graduates were nearly as likely to identify with women as were those with graduate training in 1972. Among college graduates and postgraduates, it becomes increasingly difficult in the late 1980s to find women who do *not* identify with other women.

Housewives would not necessarily be more isolated or have fewer opportunities for interaction with other women than would women in the workplace. On the contrary, housewives are uniquely positioned to have "traditional role" gender consciousness, particularly if they felt themselves to be under assault from a women's movement that did not value their roles. Alternatively, a life contained by the home might be a narrow one, limiting the development of internal political resources and group orientations (Sapiro, 1983; Gurin, 1985). Table 3.8 shows that housewives' patterns of gender closeness are similar to those of all women, but also reveals that they are always less likely than others to identify with women and more likely *not* to feel close. This augurs poorly for housewives' contribution to "traditional role" identification, since they more seldom identify with women at all (as can be seen at a glance in Table 3.10).

Similarly, there is no single clear hypothesis about job segregation, the phenomenon of a woman working in employment predominantly occupied by men (see the Appendix for a discussion of the creation of the job segregation variable). Housewives were assigned a score of 100, because my interest was more in whether women "do things women usually do" than in the particular job itself. If *segregation* in one's daily activities is the quality we seek, then an exclusion of housewives seems inappropriate. But segregation is potentially misleading in other ways: secretaries, highly segregated by the nature of their occupation, may nonetheless spend their workdays surrounded by men (as do most secretaries in academic departments). Thus, as we review the findings, we must reflect on

TABLE 3.8 SOCIALIZATION ENVIRONMENT ACROSS CATEGORIES OF GENDER IDENTIFICATION, 1972–1988

Characteristic	1972	1976	1980	1984	1988
A. Mean years' education					
not close	10.9***	10.9***	11.7***	11.7***	12.1***
close	11.3	12.1	12.4	12.6	12.6
closest	12.2	13.0	13.4	13.7	13.3
B. Housewives' identification					
not close	57.7	47.8	52.3	40.1	51.3
close	32.9	44.3	39.3	55.5	39.7
closest	9.5	7.9	8.4	4.5	9.0
C. Mean job segregation					
not close	70.8	78.1**	80.3**	74.5***	71.2
close	67.7	74.1	71.9	69.7	72.0
closest	69.8	72.3	74.0	69.4	73.4
D. % with wage-earning mothers					
not close	11.4	35.6	41.7*	43.1*	37.5***
close	14.0	41.2	43.5	49.0	48.5
closest	12.3	39.9	56.6	54.9	59.6

SOURCE: American National Election Studies, 1972, 1976, 1980, 1984, 1988. Source for computation of job segregation: Table No. 677, "Occupations of the Work-Experienced Labor Force, By Sex 1970 and 1980," *Statistical Abstracts of the United States 1987,* U.S. Commerce Department, Census Bureau (Washington, D.C.: GPO) (for 1972–1984); Table No. 645, "Employed Civilians, by Occupation, Sex, Race and Hispanic Origin: 1988," *Statistical Abstracts of the United States 1990,* U.S. Commerce Department, Census Bureau (Washington, D.C.: GPO). Housewives (assigned a score of 100) are included in these job segregation figures. See Appendix for more information on the creation of job segregation scores.
*Differences by identification significant at $p < .10$.
**Differences by identification significant at $p < .05$.
***Differences by identification significant at $p < .01$.

TABLE 3.9 EDUCATION AS ENVIRONMENT: PERCENTAGE OF WOMEN IN EACH EDUCATIONAL GROUP WHO IDENTIFY CLOSELY OR MOST CLOSELY WITH WOMEN, 1972–1988

Years of education	1972***	1976***	1980***	1984***	1988***
< 12	36.8	41.4	46.2	55.9	43.0
12	42.7	61.9	78.2	66.2	59.2
13–15	50.5	67.3	64.7	76.2	80.1
16	61.5	74.8	63.3	77.7	92.9
> 16	62.5	77.6	80.7	80.5	94.2

SOURCE: American National Election Studies, 1972, 1976, 1980, 1984, 1988.
Note: Formal schooling is in academic institutions only; nonacademic training is included with last year of formal schooling.
***Differences significant at $p < .01$.

TABLE 3.10   PERCENTAGE DIFFERENCE IN HOUSEWIVES' AND ALL WOMEN'S GENDER IDENTIFICATION, 1972–1988

Housewives—all[a]	1972	1976	1980	1984	1988
not close	+ 1.4	+ 7.0	+ 9.7	+ 8.5	+ 4.2
close	− 1.6	− 4.3	− 8.0	− 6.2	+ 3.2
closest	+ 0.3	− 2.7	− 1.5	− 2.2	− 1.0

SOURCE: American National Election Studies, 1972, 1976, 1980, 1984, 1988.

Note: Numbers may not total zero because of different rounding of percentages in the separate groups. *N*s of cases for housewives are 1972 = 583, or 46.9% of the total; 1976 = 501, or 37.4% of the total; 1980 = 214, or 27.2% of the total; 1984 = 247, or 23.1% of the total, and 1988 = 231, or 23.6% of the total.

[a]A minus sign indicates that housewives are less likely to possess the quality than are all women; a positive sign means that housewives are more likely than all women to possess the quality. For example, in all years, housewives are more likely than all women to say that they do not feel close to women, and from 1976 to 1988, housewives are less likely than all women to say that they are closest to women.

whether the nature of the job itself—its role socialization cues—or the physical work environment—complete with its *own* set of possibly competing cues—is the formative factor in which we are interested. While a single, constructed variable such as I have created cannot capture the full flavor of working life, it is suggestive.

Job segregation alone obscures another important consideration: job segregation is curvilinearly related to education. Skilled heavy industrial workers and physicians, for instance, are in predominantly male occupations, but the difference between them in formal schooling may be immense. In any case, it is difficult to choose between the competing hypotheses of women in male environments having particular cognitive and emotional needs to identify with women, or women in highly segregated occupations developing powerful gender identification, as could be true of nurses. The presence of housewives with scores of 100 may muddy things a bit, but the information in Table 3.8 suggests sotto voce that the first hypothesis is more useful from the mid-1970s to the mid-1980s, and tells us less in 1972 or 1988, the two anchors of our sixteen-year period.

Whether women had mothers who were employed outside the home is in part an artifact of shifting labor patterns; the closer we come to the present, the more likely our respondents were to report having had wage-earning mothers. This trend is not overwhelming until 1988, as it shouldn't be, given that it is recent and our respondents are adults. Otherwise, a mother's employment outside the home may furnish her daughter with a broader gender role model—rarely, of course, in terms of the glamorous image of a Claire Huxtable on television's "Cosby Show," but there is certainly the opportunity to show her daughter a measure of feminine economic independence and competence; the evidence that such intergenerational socialization occurs is clearest in 1988. If we think back to Sigel's reconsideration of the McKee and Sheriffs work on role conflict, we might argue that a mother who filled more roles could, by example, relieve a daughter of some of the ambivalence about women's roles and, perhaps, women themselves. My earlier research on a small group panel study found such a process at work (Tolleson Rinehart, 1985). But race and class differences must be noted here. Economic forces have operated much differently, particularly for black women. Many more women of color in all categories of gender identification had had working mothers from 1972 on. But by 1984, the interaction of this component of childhood socialization and adult identification with women seems gently to reveal itself, as it had somewhat sporadically for the whole sample from 1980.

A LAST LOOK

Would any of these possible influences emerge in a controlled multivariate context? This is the final question to be addressed to the "potentially universal" nature of gender identification. We have already seen hints that age might interact with education, or education with the nature of one's employment. Identification, and consciousness, as I have suggested, could only be the result of subtle interactions between attitudes and orientations, internal to the individual and the result of lifelong thought and intellectual digestion, with structural aspects quite external to the individual. Any statistical technique would be less than perfectly adapted to revealing such a delicate, complex process. And yet these measures can give us a glimpse into gender identification.

Thus, gender identification was regressed on all the indicators of socioeconomic position and lifespace in addition to three interaction terms. One is the aforementioned interaction between job segregation and education, and the other two control for the very broad spread of ages in our two "generations" by reflecting *intra*generational age, since, in both cases, the "generations" in question are broad enough—roughly 18 years—that different period effects might have intervened within one generation, as I have already mentioned. Although we can regress gender identification on the same indicators for the women of color in the sample, results are highly suspect because of the technical problem of using so many variables to explain so few cases. This regrettable omission is partly ameliorated by providing two sets of results, one for all women and one for white women alone. Differences in the two equations, had they been notable, might have implied something about the different influences of the contexts of race.

The results of the regressions presented in Table 3.11, however, tell a con-

TABLE 3.11   SIGNIFICANT FACTORS DETERMINING WOMEN'S GENDER IDENTIFICATION, 1972–1988

Characteristic	1972	1976	1980	1984	1988
A. All women		•			
Close to other groups	.380	.298	.334	.469	.286
Years of education	.078	.152			
Marital status		.108	.147		
Subjective social class		−.077			
Job segregation					.102
Having a wage-earning mother					.130
Constant	.079	−.026	.091	.233	−.864
R^2	.167	.158	.210	.288	.152
adj. R^2	.158	.149	.189	.277	.133
B. White women only					
Close to other groups	.383	.281	.318	.462	.311
Marital status	.085	.134	.157		
Years of education		.135			
"Baby boomer"	−.781				
Baby boom × age	.714				
Job segregation					.110
Ed. × job segregation					−.106
Having a wage-earning mother					.121
Constant	.047	.097	.348	.147	−.889
R^2	.179	.154	.203	.285	.170
adj. R^2	.169	.143	.179	.272	.147

SOURCE: American National Election Studies, 1972, 1976, 1980, 1984, 1988. Entries are standardized regression coefficients (Betas).

Note: "Significance" refers not only to the fact that unstandardized regression coefficients are significant as determined by t-tests, but also that B > 2 (Std. Error B).

vincing if partial story of the significance of interactions between internal and external forces on the formation of gender identification. Few individual indicators had overwhelming impact, but all of them combined explained from about 15 percent to over 25 percent of the variance in women's closeness to women. The one phenomenon common to each year is the propensity to be close to other groups. This indicator of social integration does not make gender identification an artifact (we do not have a case of being close to all kinds of groups, and tossing women in while we're at it); gender identification and the number of groups to whom respondents feel close are only very moderately associated. The structure of women's other identifications shown earlier in the chapter suggests, instead, that gender identification coexists with being able to think about groups in politics. This, theoretically, is as it should be: women cannot identify with other women, and they certainly cannot progress to a fully political gender consciousness, if they are not "willing to say 'we.' "

Women's gender identification is not restricted by race or class or education; it is not the purview of the single or professional woman or the baby boomer.

Some points in the life course and some environments are more facilitative of its development than others, but none is strongly determinative. One thing that has mattered is time. Women have had a decade and a half of encouragement to think of themselves in such terms, and identification has grown steadily over those years. Now we can ask how women have structured their identification within the framework of their beliefs about gender roles.

Chapter 4

THE INTERSECTION OF GENDER IDENTIFICATION AND GENDER ROLE IDEOLOGY

Considering the length of time that women have been dependent, is it surprising that some of them hug their chains, and fawn like the spaniel?
— Mary Wollstonecraft, *A Vindication of the Rights of Woman*, 1792

I guess I would look at it differently if I were a woman who had to go out and work and had to support myself. I would be more anxious for the rights they claim they do not have. I'd look at it a different way.
— Moral Majority activist quoted in Andersen (1988b: 239)

Through the ages, men have disparaged women's capacity even to befriend one another, much less act in solidarity for all women's welfare. We have seen that, in truth, countless women *have* identified with one another most closely. Historically, in each of the women's movements to arise in the West, women have been able to overcome considerable obstacles in order to bond together and to achieve a change in women's status. Suffragettes won the vote; Progressives at the turn of the twentieth century won a precarious placement for the health and welfare of mothers and children on the public agenda. Although the struggle for real change in gender roles continues, contemporary liberal feminists have secured for women some basic economic reforms and legal protections. All the while, women have felt increasingly free to acknowledge not only their identification with, but their friendship for, other women.

Yet gender role ideology represents a profound source of division for women, as it has never been to quite the same extent for men. For belief in "traditional " gender role ideology, with its central dictum of women's privatization, on the one hand, and belief in men's and women's equality, on the other, are fiercely opposed to each other. I do not mean that they are opposed in the simplest political sense of becoming two "sides" or positions, although, in practical policy terms, that is often what results. I mean instead that acceptance of or challenges to gender role ideology places truly terminal values—values that shape women's very beliefs about what it means to be a woman—into opposition with one another (similar questioning about the cultural imperatives of "manhood" is only now receiving much attention). Even such profound divisions of women as those by race or economic status or political geography are less central to the individual, and less global in scope, than the potential division of women by gender role ideology.

The "traditional" gender role ideology and its variations, to be found almost everywhere one looks, bears as its central dictum the privatization of women, their restriction to the domestic sphere. This may extend to the utter obedience of women to men, whether they are fathers, husbands, sons, or members of the elite, inherent in Confucianism. Or it may demand the restriction of women's actual physical movement, as was true in ancient Greece and is true in contemporary fundamentalist Islamic culture. The most frightening consequences of the secondary value placed on women are seen in recent demographic findings that fully 100 million women who should be present on the planet are not, because of sex-selective abortions, female infanticide, differential medical treatment for boys and girls, and such sources of murder as dowry burnings (Kristoff, 1991).

Nor are Western cultures immune from placing women in subservient roles or from tolerance of violence against them (Nice, 1988). The Western manifestation of traditional gender role ideologies, captured in the phrase "women's place is in the home," persists despite recent widespread modifications in mass beliefs about men's and women's equality of capacity. Its most pernicious meanings are found now, as they were in Mary Wollstonecraft's time, in the sexual objectification of women and the violence against women that such objectification brings. It can be seen slyly at work in contemporary sociobiologists' assumptions that women are genetically driven to compete for the protection of the fittest males, and therefore are neither trustworthy as individuals, because no wiles are beneath them in their pursuit of protection for themselves and their young, nor capable of bonding with one another, since they are genetically driven to compete with other women for men. (This ideology, if not its justification in "science," was shared by Rousseau, and it is this to which Mary Wollstonecraft was responding in the epigraph to this chapter. I consider Wollstonecraft more closely in chapter five. Sperling [1991] provides an intriguing feminist attempt to "rescue" sociobiology from misogyny.)

Acceptance or rejection of traditional gender role ideology divides women for two reasons. First, those who accept the status quo and have internalized its values would not embrace challenges to it and, indeed, may feel threatened by them. Feminist criticism of women's traditional roles can all too easily seem to be a criticism of the women who have adopted them; they were certainly construed this way by both antifeminists and the media establishment in the 1980s (Faludi, 1991). Women for whom the role of wife is not only a demographic or status category, but the core of belief about what being a woman means, risk having to question the very validity of their lives if they entertain a feminist challenge to the definition of those roles. The Moral Majority activist quoted in the epigraph of this chapter demonstrates awareness of at least part of the challenging nature of women's divisions over gender role ideology. Kristin Luker (1984) and Rebecca Klatch (1987) found the same value conflict in their studies of antifeminist women, conflict so much more poignant a mobilizing force than the varied motivations of the mostly male leaders of those movements. The depth of the conflict—not just over policy, but over personal identity—is one reason why we can conclude that Staggenborg (1991) is correct when she assumes that conflict over abortion will continue to escalate. But she explains the upward spiraling of mobilization and countermobilization around the issue in the aggregate, structural language terms of social movements. It is well to remember that abortion could not be such an enduring source of cleavage were it not that it touches deeply personal and intimately connected values—about gender and also about where gender beliefs are located within moral and religious frameworks. We shall see some of the connections among moral and religious beliefs, abortion, and gender consciousness in the following pages.

The second reason that gender role ideology is so potentially divisive is women's status as a "group" or, more particularly, a group most of whose members have intimate and ongoing conflict with the "outgroup" of men. Here we must expand a bit on what we considered in chapter three, for this is not only a straightforward problem of group loyalty, although that is involved. For the "traditional" or privatized woman, a constrained gender belief system would normally demand primary allegiance to one's mate, and not to other women; the "traditional" from of gender consciousness would arise most usually when such women found that the compact between men and women to which they had agreed had been violated, or when they saw that women's unique roles made them uniquely responsible for a public question, such as community morality or the well-being of children. We have already seen examples of this.

But even for women who might otherwise have feminist gender consciousness, there is the problem of whether one's intimate relationships can be separated from one's abstract beliefs about gender or whether the principle should force a change in the intimate relationship. As a young feminist activist in the early 1970s, I was told by a friend and compatriot that I was hopelessly compromised because I "lived with the enemy"—because I was married. She liked my husband, and she and I continued to be friends and allies. But in her eyes, my gender consciousness would always be a little suspect, just as my husband's feminism, though admirable, would never be completely trusted. Today, her reservations would be less adequately expressed by the term "heterosexism." I say "less adequately," because her worry about where loyalties can lie was not only a statement about the systemic oppression of lesbians, no matter how grim that oppression is. It was also a question about cross-pressuring, competing ties. Within quite racially or ethnically homogeneous groups, as the demographers interviewed in the *New York Times* article have so startlingly reminded us, some women have advertently or inadvertently chosen their culture's gender ideology over the lives of other women, even when those "women" are in fact their own small daughters.

In racially diverse societies, the cross-pressuring is more painful still. In societies where one group has historically oppressed another group, how can women in each group cross the barriers to trust or align with one another? Women of color such as Barbara Smith (1983), Paula Giddings (1984), bell hooks (1989), and Patricia Hill Collins (1990) all show the anguish of black and other minority women who, in order to identify as feminists, must simultaneously confront the sexism of men of color and the racism of the culture in which their white "sisters" reside. In short, as I have already said, women have bonds other than their bonds to women: to their race, to the cultures of their home places, to their sociodemographic environment. To break, or at least weaken, these in order to reach out to other women is challenging enough. But for heterosexual women to overcome the powerful ties of intimacy with men, especially when the whole culture has told them that these are the ties that matter most, is a quandary indeed.

Thus we see that gender consciousness is a matter not only of gender identification, but of role ideology as well. Consciousness may take the "traditional" form under the conditions I have already presented, and indeed, the *combination* of identification with other women and traditional gender role beliefs may well mobilize women to act against the status quo in some cases and sometimes even make them the allies of women with egalitarian consciousness. (A most unusual combination of traditional and egalitarian consciousnesses can be seen in Elizabeth Joseph's feminist defense of polygamy in the Op-Ed pages of the *New York Times* [1991].) Women's own belief in the value of traditional roles and the women who fill them has stimulated countless efforts in the realms of education and public health. American temperance activists in the nineteenth century, for example, were primarily motivated by their knowledge of what drinking did to the women and children dependent on intemperate men. While the Women's Christian Temperance Union eventually supported suffrage, most of its membership was not "feminist," and many sought the vote for women in order to protect traditional values of home and family against their perceptions of a depraved polis. They did, however, identify with other women. Without gender identification, women of traditional beliefs are merely the holders of a conservative gender ideology, supportive of the status quo and potentially hostile to other women; they may even be mobilized by what they see as threatening not only to their own roles but to the economic interests of their husbands (Chafetz and Dworkin, 1987).

Women with egalitarian gender ideologies would seem to find gender identification much easier, and in fact that is the case. But here, too, not all women who have egalitarian beliefs are gender conscious, just as not all gender identified women are egalitarian. Scholars explicate numerous kinds of feminism, as I have done in these pages. But for most Western women, most of the time, feminism is likely to be the feminism of liberal individualism, of a belief in equal rights. That need not be accompanied by a strong identification with other women; it may be a question of individual self-interest, or, as appears to be the case among feminist men, it may be a not wholly distinguishable part of an overarching schema of rights and justice. Such women may have a *feminist* consciousness, but it is not the broad gender consciousness I have defined. What we need is a way to examine these permutations of gender identification and gender role ideology.

BELIEFS ABOUT GENDER ROLES

We can make such an examination by analysis of responses to the "equal roles" question present in the National Election Studies of 1972, 1976, 1980, 1984, and 1988. Its wording has been unchanged in the years that it has been asked: "Recently there has been a lot of talk about women's rights. Some people," the surveys say, "feel that women should have an equal role with men in running business, industry, and politics. Others feel that women's place is in the home. . . . Where would you place yourself on this [seven-point] scale [where one equals men and women as equals, and seven is women's place is in the home], or haven't you thought much about this?" The data in Figure 4.1 present a considerably broader distribution of responses to this question than we might expect, given that the plurality in favor of the "equal roles" choice has grown in recent years. But the proportion of people choosing the most extreme egalitarian position has varied through the 1980s, and for the population as a whole, there was a mild retreat from egalitarianism during the Reagan years, from which we may be rebounding now. Responses also vary according to many contexts of socialization, such as education. These patterns of change and continuity suggest that we can be fairly confident about the indicator's ability to reflect a diversity of beliefs, despite the real possibility that at least some responses are the result of "social desirability."

Figure 4.1. Percentage with egalitarian position on equal roles, 1972 - 1988

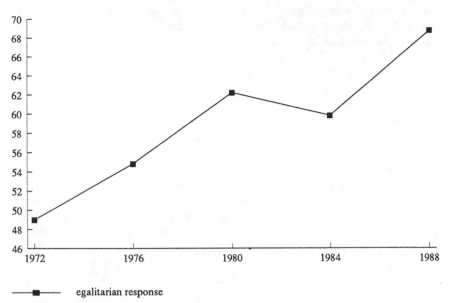

──────■────── egalitarian response

SOURCE: American National Election Studies, 1972 - 1988; whole sample

Because the question *does* vary, across time and across different subpopulations in different life circumstances, and because it varies in ways that we would expect given what we know of gender role socialization, it would seem to be doing the job for which it was designed. Claire Knoche Fulenwider's (1980: 48–56) rigorous analysis of the indicator in 1972 and 1976 also shows that, for all people but those of the lowest cognitive abilities, their position on the equal roles question is thoroughly integrated with other dimensions of their political orientations. The long view we can get, over the sixteen years elapsing between the elections of 1972 and 1988, is also important to our understanding of the development of gender consciousness.

This same question was asked in the 1973 and 1982 waves of the Jennings Youth-Parent Socialization Panel Study. Sapiro (1983) has, of course, provided us with a very thorough examination of the women in the filial generation, and their beliefs about equal roles in 1973, as they were taking up the roles and responsibilities of adulthood, are pivotal in her analysis. It was this work, in fact, that introduced the term "privatized" into the working vocabulary of scholarship on the political psychology of gender. The socialization data, however, offer us another opportunity to make a foray into the cognitive processes underlying gender ideologies. Jennings and his collaborators, on asking their respondents to answer the equal roles question again in 1982, asked them also to recall what they had believed in 1973 and to volunteer reasons for whatever change in their views the respondents believed had taken place in the interim.

Markus (1986) explored the correspondence of stated policy preferences and respondents' later recall of them for a number of questions, including that of equal roles. He concluded (p. 21) that "remembrances correspond poorly to opinions as originally expressed . . . respondents readily supplied 'explanations' for their self-perceived attitude history, even when those perceptions directly contradicted observed opinion change." For Markus, poor correspondence of actual to recalled opinions does not result from measurement error. He blames our own flimsy processes of political cognition instead. If most of our policy attitudes have weak cognitive underpinnings—if they have neither deep roots nor firm connections to one another—then they can shift and change. If or when they do, we may make revisions in our "cognitive autobiographies," for the sake of present consistency, that "render the changes invisible" (ibid.).

But beliefs about equal roles, Markus found, do not conform to this general trend. Both youths and their parents become more liberal or egalitarian over time in their beliefs about gender roles, in contrast to conservative shifts on most other policy questions. More important for our purposes, respondents more reliably recalled their 1973 positions in 1982 on gender roles than on other attitudes. Respondents' greater accuracy in recalling earlier positions, and in explaining change when it occurred, prompted Markus to temper his otherwise pessimistic view of the quality of political cognition. Beliefs about gender roles demonstrated that for "those persons whose policy preferences are integral to their views of themselves, cues about prior policy attitudes will be cognitively available and recall of such attitudes will be reliable" (p. 41).

Figure 4.2 offers a comparison of observed and recalled positions on the equal roles question among the women of the parental generation. We see there that women thought they had been slightly more decided—firmly choosing one side or the other—and slightly more egalitarian in their 1973 views than their 1973 responses suggest they had been. But they also underestimated the extent of the change they had undergone. Thirty-two percent of the women in the parental generation *thought* they had not changed their views at all; we observe that 32.4 percent of the sample did not appear to alter their attitudes (recall that genuine measurement error may account for some respondents' return to the same position they held in 1973). The change we can observe is about twice in magnitude what respondents had guessed. Among those who did seem to experience a change in beliefs, 76.7 percent perceived more change than we are able to measure, although they correctly recalled the direction of change (only 5 percent were mistaken about direction). For the vast majority of women who thought they had changed their attitudes over time, the difference between "real" and

Figure 4.2. Women's actual and recalled equal roles positions, 1973 and 1982

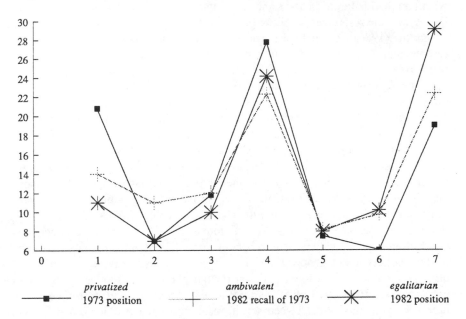

	privatized	ambivalent	egalitarian
━━■━━	1973 position	┈┈┼┈┈ 1982 recall of 1973	━✳━ 1982 position

SOURCE: Youth-Parent Socialization Panel Study data provided by M. Kent Jennings

"perceived" change was only approximately one point out of the seven-point scale. Slightly over 10 percent of those who changed seemed to know perfectly accurately both how much they changed and in which direction.

Most women were correct in thinking that the direction of their change in attitudes was toward egalitarianism. Over half of the women espousing the privatized orientation in 1973 *thought,* in 1982, that they had been at least ambivalent, if not egalitarian, nine years earlier. An even larger proportion of them had shifted toward egalitarianism by 1982. Far fewer of the women who had been egalitarian in 1973 remembered themselves to have been otherwise; nor were their original attitudes as susceptible to modification. They knew, in short, about where their attitudes had been in 1973, they maintained a good deal of consistency over the period between surveys, and if they changed, they understood why.

Just over half the women who were privatized in 1973 had shifted toward egalitarian beliefs in 1982—and were more likely to project their current beliefs backward in time, engaging in some "revision of their cognitive autobiographies." Many respondents shifted their perception of the earlier beliefs to conform more closely to what they now believed; they were less likely to recall themselves as having been ambivalent, or "somewhere in the middle," than they were in 1973, or even in 1982, but otherwise they were likely to assume a degree of internal consistency. As Niemi (1974) and Markus (1986) have both argued, inaccurate recall reflects not just simple error, but the desire for cognitive consistency as well. A belief in one's own consistency, or in the rationality of one's reasons for change, helps one knit one's attitudes into a neat, serviceable structure. Kristi Andersen (1988b) has drawn similar conclusions from her study of conservative, "pro-family" women active in the Ohio Moral Majority: attitudes like those toward women's roles can become the core of a cognitive schema that allows one to apprehend, filter, and connect new ideas to existing ones. But this process also involves the construction of beliefs that are helpful and rational to the individual who considers why and how she may have changed her views.

Many respondents in the parental generation of the Jennings study, especially those taking egalitarian views to begin with, neither changed much in actuality nor thought they had done so over the period. But Jennings and his colleagues were able to elicit reasons for a change in view from about a quarter of the respondents. These 173 comments are most instructive: they reveal that attitudes toward gender roles are not held lightly, are changed thoughtfully, and are the products of close observation of one's life and environment. Twenty-two percent of the proferred reasons for change refer either to position in the life cycle—aging or the empty nest, for example—or to the "nature of the times," usually referring to changes in the economy, employment, society, and the like. A quarter of the responses are reflective of changing cognition: "I'm wiser now; I know more now; I have learned things; I have had different experiences." Forty percent of the remarks might be deemed explicitly pro-woman: "Women have proved that they can do more; women have proven themselves; women need to work." Another 6.4 percent of the remarks make unspecific references to women or the Women's Movement. Only 6.4 percent of the reasons explain a retreat from earlier egalitarianism: "Things have gone too far; family life is worse now." The vast majority of the comments, in short, make eminent sense. They reflect a respondent's own changing life circumstances and her observations of the world around her. What we seem to have found here is not random or spurious change, but the "true" change on which all theories of human cognitive development and political learning depend—even when a precisely correct memory of the magnitude of change does not always follow.

The mothers in the Youth-Parent Socialization Panel Study are not a representative sample of all American women, of course, since their inclusion was an epiphenomenon of the selection of their children into the study. But given these women's reflectiveness, the diversity of their views, and the rational reasons for changes in those views when change occurred, they provide us with strong evidence for the centrality of gender role beliefs to other, especially political, sets of beliefs. Their responses also illustrate reciprocity in the ongoing development of politicization. By this I mean that the women of the maternal generation not only influence events and other people in their environments, but respond to them as well. Reciprocity means, for example, that mothers socialize their children, but as those children grow, mothers may receive nearly as many socialization cues from them as they give to them. I find it difficult to think of a better place for such reciprocity to occur than in mother-daughter discussions of women's roles. Let us look at some pairing of mothers and daughters in the Youth-Parent Socialization Panel Study and in other research.

Arland Thornton and his colleagues have also established a picture of change toward egalitarianism in sex role attitudes, and were able to elucidate some of the contextual sources of the change over time, among a sample of Detroit area women who gave birth in July 1961 and who were questioned about their attitudes at intervals from then until 1980 (Thornton and Freedman, 1979; Thornton, Alwin, and Camburn, 1983). They found in 1980 that mothers' sex role attitudes had had a net effect over time on the attitudes of their children. Sigel and Reynolds (1979–1980), surveying mother-daughter pairs from among alumnae of Douglass College (the women's college at Rutgers University), and their daughters who were also Douglass students, found that although the daughters were more likely to espouse feminism, there was a good deal of mother-daughter agreement. While they found evidence that the flow of socialization streamed from parent to child, they also saw evidence of daughters socializing their mothers, usually toward more egalitarian outlooks. My analysis of mother-daughter pairs in the Youth-Parent Socialization Panel Study makes it clear that the best intergenerational congruence occurs in pairs where the mothers were egalitarian in 1973. But overall, the *mothers* came into closer agreement on this issue with their *daughters* over time, another caveat against a too-casual assumption that the flow of socialization is always from parent to child, even though it is also true that, from the beginning, politically attentive and egalitarian mothers were more likely to raise daughters who, in adulthood, remained in closer agreement with their mothers (Tolleson Rinehart, 1989). In a small panel study of college-aged and mature community women who participated in a community leadership program, I had firsthand opportunities to witness women undergoing—and discussing—changes in a number of beliefs as a consequence of their changing views about gender roles (Tolleson Rinehart, 1985). Though not consanguine mother-daughter pairs, the community women and college students certainly offered one another reciprocal, intergenerational cues.

The results from the Youth-Parent Socialization Panel Study and these other analyses increase our confidence in the utility of the equal roles indicator of gender role ideology and of "true" attitude change, although all the studies seem to suggest that it is much more difficult to change from egalitarianism to privatization than the reverse, or perhaps even to sustain a privatized gender ideology in a changing world. It goes without saying, though, that the question's emphasis on privatization versus egalitarianism probably fails to capture different *kinds* of feminist beliefs; there are far fewer alternative constructions of the traditional role prescription toward which a similar concern might be bent. But the question is not meant—and is not used here—to differentiate among feminist ideologies. It is meant, instead, simply to query beliefs about men's and women's proper roles—a most central aspect of any feminist belief, certainly, but not an ideology by itself. Second, it is used to sketch a portrait of mass beliefs over time: it will assuredly give us no more than snapshots, but they are nonetheless valuable clues to the meaning of political processes at large. It is a common denominator: when one is *forced* to choose among the responses, even if they are not as articulate or complex or visionary as one's own spontaneous answer might be, what will the choice be? That choice—between home and wider world—says something about one's construction of gender. The face validity of this question is still substantively important.

The equal roles question helps us "unfold" gender identification, allowing us to examine the orientations of women who identify with other women but hold a traditional gender role ideology, those who identify with other women and hold egalitarian beliefs, and those women who are not gender identified or who are ambivalent about gender roles. And we shall examine this "unfolded gender identification" in terms of the same range of demographic, lifespace, and socialization contexts employed in chapter three.

The equal roles question, like any attempt to capture a complex structure of beliefs in simple terms, opposes the private—woman's place is in the home—to the public—men and women should have equal roles in society. In doing so, the indicator obscures the degree to which the two resonate with each other, the extent to which "the personal is political" in the sense that conditions of society impinge on one's private, and perhaps especially one's family, life, while the growing recognition of needs emerging from collective experiences of "private" conditions often becomes the impetus behind demands for social policy. The equal roles question, in this case, is not different from orthodox Western political theory or much recent feminist theory. Both see this kind of polarization in the structure of the political world (for a critique of the limitations of this kind of perspective, no matter the ends to which it is put, see Bookman and Morgen, 1988). Indeed, an inchoate awareness of the artificiality of the dichotomy is a good candidate for explanation of the political behavior of women at both ends of *my* artificially polarized array of beliefs: "traditional" nonfeminist and feminist women alike work for public policies, albeit different ones, that will enhance the fulfillment of private responsibilities—to children, to one another, and to the community. Moreover, both make the argument that those private responsibilities are the elemental fibers in the public fabric, even if their prescriptions for ideal public and private lives may differ in the extreme. Our job here is to keep those reverberations in mind, to assess the direction from which each kind of consciousness comes, and to secure a glimpse of the contexts that make them possible.

PROBING GENDER IDENTIFICATION

Women's Closeness to One Another and Their Beliefs About Gender Roles

Even in 1972, a plurality of women evinced egalitarian views about gender roles, and the closer women have felt to other women, the stronger their egalitarianism, as we see in Table 4.1. By the 1980s, the numbers of women who are gender identified and yet privatized in their role orientations has dwindled. At the same time, women's admission of role *ambivalence* is holding steady or increasing as time passes, especially among women who do not identify with other women. By 1988, even among the identified, role ambivalence appeared to characterize something less than one-fifth of women in the samples. We are constrained in our ability to draw conclusions about individual patterns of change over time, but we can speculate that ambivalence seems to be the result of a modification in views on the part of some privatized women, rather than a wholesale retreat from egalitarianism. This seems rational: women with the *most* privatized orientations, after all, would have had the most difficult time continuing to reconcile their views with a changing culture, unless they remained insulated by their own particularly strong, reinforcing immediate environments. If one enters the paid workplace solely for financial reasons and not from any impetus toward equality, for example, one is still entering an environment ripe with opportunities to consider whether sex, or beliefs about the sexes, is not the basis of much questionable treatment of women there.

But we can also raise the possibility that widespread perceptions of the *meaning* of "equal roles" has deepened and become more sophisticated since 1972. Where once it may have meant "equal work for equal pay," or sanguine, naive expectations about husbands "helping out" at home, doubtless more people now understand "equality" to mean a problematic and very serious reevaluation of *all* gender roles. A more complex view of the consequences (or even the definition) of "equal roles" is bound to provoke some ambivalent reactions. Increasing sophistication in this case is analogous to changes in attitudes toward, let us say, "big government." Nie, Verba, and Petrocik (1976: 125–128) posited that changes in such attitudes might be explained by people's conclusion that "big government" came to mean not only beneficent, reformist government, but the "big government" of Vietnam and Nixon's Enemies List. Their hypothesis has

TABLE 4.1 GENDER IDENTIFICATION AND BELIEFS ABOUT WOMEN'S ROLES, 1972–1988

Identification	1972***	1976***	1980***	1984***	1988***
A. % of those *not close* who are . . .					
most privatized	22.8	19.4	10.3	10.1	7.9
privatized	11.4	14.5	14.8	12.1	11.2
ambivalent	21.8	25.0	25.5	30.3	17.9
egalitarian	12.9	14.3	26.2	21.9	19.6
most egalitarian	31.1	26.8	23.2	25.6	43.4
B. % of those *close* who are . . .					
most privatized	20.7	10.2	5.6	5.9	6.3
privatized	10.6	11.5	11.3	11.6	6.8
ambivalent	20.5	18.3	15.5	22.3	13.3
egalitarian	14.7	21.4	29.1	20.8	27.6
most egalitarian	33.5	36.7	38.4	39.4	46.0
C. % of those *closest* who are . . .					
most privatized	10.8	7.3	2.7	0.0	1.1
privatized	9.0	9.2	2.6	4.3	5.5
ambivalent	16.2	17.6	5.3	15.7	14.1
egalitarian	17.1	24.2	20.0	28.5	21.8
most egalitarian	46.8	41.8	69.3	51.4	57.6

SOURCE: American National Election Studies, 1972, 1976, 1980, 1984, 1988.
***Differences significant at p < .01.

been challenged (see, for instance, Smith, 1989) as an explanation of shifts in opinions of "big government," but their reasoning has considerable appeal to seekers of insight into something as central to people's lives as gender roles, especially when the popular culture all around us sends such very ambivalent cues. "Equality" may look harder to achieve than ever.

The figures in Table 4.1 do not emerge from normal distributions of either gender identification or gender role ideology. As we have already seen, those for whom "women" is the *closest* identification make up a much smaller group than either the groups who feel close to women or those who do not. We also know that the balance now favors egalitarianism on the question of gender role beliefs. For reasons of analytical soundness, then, I collapse the "close" and "closest" categories into one group, the "identified," and call the remaining women, who are not close to other women, the "individualists." I have also collapsed the seven-point scale of the equal roles question into three parts: the "privatized" (those falling on any of the three points on the "women's place is in the home" side of the scale), the "ambivalent" (those choosing the exact midpoint of the scale), and the "egalitarian" (those falling on any of the three points of the "women and men should have equal roles" side).

Having done this, I can combine the categories of gender identification and gender role ideology into an array reflecting these two necessary aspects of gender consciousness. We might think of the array as occupying a space defined by the x-axis of ideology and the y-axis of identification, something like this,

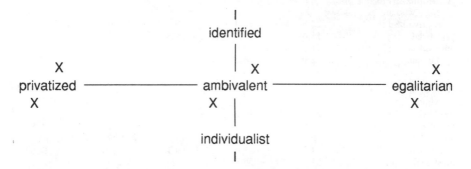

where the points above the x-axis, moving from left to right, represent the identified privatized, identified ambivalent, and identified egalitarian women, respectively. The points falling below the x-axis, correspondingly, represent the individualist privatized, individualist ambivalent, and individualist egalitarian women, respectively. Extant research has generated findings that associate liberalism and egalitarianism; for this reason, we might have put egalitarianism on the *physical* as well as the ideological left. But Western minds are also trained to expect a progression (at least as it is depicted on the printed page) from "less" of the quality on the left to "more" on the right, and thus "less feminism"/ privatization falls to the left on the x-axis. Similarly, identification is placed above individualism along the vertical or y-axis. We need not trouble overmuch about these devices if we can agree on the construct I have tried to establish.

Note also that in our conceptual space, the two sets of women are not parallel to each other above and below the x-axis. I have presented the diagram this way to suggest the degree to which gender identification "shifts" a variety of attitudes that might otherwise be predicted by gender role ideology. Once again, let us consider the ways we expect gender consciousness to affect politization, in order to cement our expectations about how the analytical construct of consciousness depicted above will behave. From past research, we would expect that movement along the x-axis role of ideology from more privatized to more egalitarian would correspond at least fairly closely to movement from more "conservative" to more "liberal" on various policy preferences; this assumption reflects the linear, right-left conceptualization of ideological constraint that so thoroughly influences modern theories of mass political behavior. But scholarship ranging from analyses of gender gaps in policy preferences and voting behavior, to the influence of gender role socialization on political socialization, to feminist theory argues that the construction of gender *itself* influences political cognition in important ways. If I reason rightly, then we need not make a forced choice between the "either/or" of liberal versus conservative or the "either/or" of a mechanistic assumption that a gender gap divides all women from all men in their preferences. Instead, we seek explanations for other political preferences in the degree to which a woman has traditional role consciousness, egalitarian consciousness, or no clear gender consciousness. Consciousness of either traditional or egalitarian form should prompt a given woman to hold different attitudes than she would if she had no consciousness. Thus, a traditional role consciousness would direct a woman to prefer some policies that an equally "traditional" but individualist woman would shun. For the latter woman, some cognitive framework other than gender consciousness must do the work of organizing her attitudes.

Similarly, although both identified and individualist women with egalitarian gender role ideologies would be expected to support obviously feminist questions, consciousness would make the difference on other issues. While an egalitarian individualist may well think only in terms of whether a question of equal rights and ungendered justice is involved, her philosophy does not oblige her to assume that men and women have any meaningful differences. Indeed, her philosophy may *obviate* such an assumption. Her conclusions on policy questions, then, would more likely be based on evaluations of structural fairness: if she deems such fairness to be present in a given case, little further consideration of gender is required. If fairness is not present, then the absence of fairness itself becomes the only question of moment. She wishes for complete gender equity in the workplace or in public office, for example, because it is right and just and not necessarily because she believes women have a particular point of view to bring to the workplace or the legislature. (The starkly simple representation of this classical liberal feminist outlook probably belies the complexity of most women's practical evaluations of the world. The most orthodox liberal does not fail to recognize that, because of socialization patterns and the unbalanced distribution of resources, women may differ from men in significant ways. But the belief that in the aftermath of a gender-just society, women's and men's differences would be quite small, remains a tenable proposition.)

Identified women with *either* privatized or egalitarian role ideologies, however, do think in group terms. They would be more likely than individualists not only to think of what would benefit the group of all women, but to consider what unique perspective the group of all women can contribute to any given policy position. Their solidarity with other women, the comfort and sustenance that their group identification brings them, also brings a motivating, mobilizing element to their *behavior* that individualist women would not experience in quite the same way. Identified women, even if they are privatized, are willing to say "we."

We see in Tables 4.2 and 4.3 that, by the 1980s, the plurality of women had

TABLE 4.2   DISTRIBUTIONS ACROSS GENDER IDENTIFICATION/ROLE IDEOLOGY CATEGORIES, 1972–1988

	1972	1976	1980	1984	1988
% who are . . .					
individualist/privatized	19.0	13.1	10.6	6.7	8.8
identified/privatized	12.9	12.8	8.6	11.2	6.4
individualist/ambivalent	12.1	9.7	10.7	9.2	8.2
identified/ambivalent	8.7	11.1	8.0	15.1	7.3
individualist/egalitarian	24.4	15.9	20.7	14.4	28.9
identified/egalitarian	22.9	37.5	41.4	43.4	40.4
Ns of cases[a]	1183	1214	739	981	934

SOURCE: American National Election Studies, 1972, 1976, 1980, 1984, 1988.
[a]These are the numbers of cases in all subsequent analyses.

TABLE 4.3   DISTRIBUTIONS ACROSS CATEGORIES OF GENDER IDENTIFICATION/ROLE IDEOLOGY FOR WHITE WOMEN AND WOMEN OF COLOR, 1972–1988

Category	1972	1976*	1980	1984	1988
individualist/privatized					
% of white women	19.4	13.3	10.6	6.7	9.0
% of women of color	16.0	11.8	10.3	7.0	7.9
identified/privatized					
% of white women	12.5	12.6	7.8	11.1	6.2
% of women of color	15.3	13.8	14.4	12.0	7.3
individualist/ambivalent					
% of white women	12.1	10.1	11.2	9.7	8.6
% of women of color	11.8	6.4	7.2	6.3	6.7
identified/ambivalent					
% of white women	9.2	11.7	8.4	14.8	7.4
% of women of color	4.9	6.7	5.2	16.9	6.7
individualist/egalitarian					
% of white women	24.3	14.9	20.9	13.7	29.6
% of women of color	25.7	22.9	19.6	18.3	25.6
identified/egalitarian					
% of white women	22.4	37.4	41.1	44.1	39.2
% of women of color	26.4	38.4	43.3	39.4	45.7

SOURCE: American National Election Studies, 1972, 1976, 1980, 1984, 1988.
See chapter three for a discussion of combining black and other women of color.
*Difference in distribution by race significant at $p < .10$.

become identified egalitarians. We also see almost no differences by race; indeed, recent scholarship by African-American feminist theorists suggests that the standpoints of women of color, and their personally grounded ways of "knowing," make them particularly likely to hold the kind of gender conscious identification about which we have been thinking (Collins, 1989, 1990; Giddings, 1984; but see also hooks, 1989, for a discussion of divisions among black women that correspond at least in part to the gender-based divisions among

white women). For all women, the category most sharply declining as a preference since the 1970s is that of the privatized individualist, the antifeminist backlash of the 1980s notwithstanding. But though their numbers have dwindled,
privatized women still compel us to examine the role played by gender ideology
in their politicization.

The numbers displayed in Table 4.4 serve as another cross-check on the validity of our measure of gender identification, as well as showing yet more point-
edly that differences among women are not based on role ideology alone. In
1976, 1984, and 1988, "women" was included on a list of groups in society
toward which respondents were asked to say how warmly or coolly they felt by
picking a number on a symbolic "feeling thermometer," with numbers below 50
suggesting affective chilliness and numbers above 50 suggesting increasing emotional warmth. Individual response-set patterns may confound our ability to
draw general conclusions from some feeling thermometer questions (cf. Wilcox,
Sigelman, and Cook, 1989), but we should certainly expect that the mean feeling thermometer readings of warmth toward "women" for each category of consciousness would correspond to respondents' closeness to women.

We do find such correspondence in the table. Identified women generally feel
significantly warmer toward women than their individualist peers. The identified
egalitarians positively sizzle in their mean scores. But despite sound theoretical
assumptions that privatized women's very privatization, by making home and
family their principal domain, might mitigate somewhat against collective thinking, identified privatized women, like their egalitarian counterparts, feel warmer
toward women than do privatized individualists.

Gender Identification, Gender Ideology, and Attitudes About Women

Each election-year survey has contained some variety of questions about women
or things thought to be especially significant to women's sociopolitical position.
One way to explore the political meaning of identification/role ideology is to ask
women to assess women's influence over sociopolitical institutions. In 1972 and
1976, respondents were asked to judge whether a number of groups in society
had too little, too much, or just about the right amount of influence "in American
life and politics." Table 4.5 shows the pattern of "shifting" I discussed above
when women of different identifications and ideologies are asked to discern
women's influence. The identified are significantly *less* likely to think women
have too much, and significantly *more* likely to think women have too little,
influence than do most individualists—the egalitarian individualists are a bit of
an exception in 1972, but not a surprising one, given their gender role ideologies. Once again, the identified egalitarians outstrip their antipodal counterparts,
but both sets of identified women would seem to prefer that women have a

TABLE 4.4   MEAN FEELING THERMOMETER SCORES FOR "WOMEN," BY CATEGORY OF GENDER CONSCIOUSNESS, 1976, 1984, 1988

Category	1976***	1984***	1988***
Individualist/privatized	74.26	70.41	71.08
Identified/privatized	82.07	71.08	80.76
Individualist/ambiva-lent	76.13	68.35	70.13
Identified/ambivalent	79.03	71.17	80.31
Individualist/egalitarian	75.07	77.45	76.71
Identified/egalitarian	82.76	82.20	85.33

SOURCE: American National Election Studies, 1976, 1984, 1988.
***Differences in feeling thermometer scores by category of identification/role ideology are significant at p < .01.

greater social and political say, an appropriate manifestation of their strong identification with other women coupled to a strong gender ideology. Both groups would think that women have particularly important perspectives on public policy to offer.

It should also be noted that these findings occur during a time when the *whole* sample, including men, seemed to resent highly visible groups, and the resentment reached levels by 1976 that we might almost call churlish. In both years, in the whole samples, poor people and workingmen receive considerable sympathy, and the middle class is seen as pretty well disenfranchised. But liberals, labor unions, blacks, big business, and particularly protesters (in 1972) are overwhelmingly judged to have more influence than they deserve. With such an apparent collective distaste for "the noisy ones," as Meg Greenfield once called feminist activists while trying to explain this same phenomenon of resentment, these findings suggest two things. First, most women may have been separating "women" from "feminists," another group seen as having unfair shares of influence—a suspicion strengthened by the "feeling thermometer" reactions to the Women's Liberation Movement presented below. Second, despite aversion to the feminist label, large numbers of women *do* think in terms of women's *group* influence on society and politics and are not happy about the smallness of their portion. The evidence that this is a manifestation of collective, and not simply ideological or feminist, thinking, is amply present in the identified egalitarians' far greater dissatisfaction with things than seems to be true of their individualist sisters.

When we examine the association of gender consciousness with feelings toward the Women's Liberation Movement, however individual women might define it, we can reasonably expect a straightforward linear relationship, for here the operative consideration is gender role ideology—and even identified privatized women ought to be more hostile to the Movement than ambivalent women, and certainly more hostile to it than are egalitarians. Individualists might endorse the Movement, seeing the possibility of improvement in their own condition as a consequence of the Movement's activities, or they may find it distaste-

TABLE 4.5 PERCEPTIONS OF WOMEN'S INFLUENCE IN AMERICAN LIFE AND POLITICS, BY CATEGORY OF IDENTIFICATION/ROLE IDEOLOGY, 1972 AND 1976

	1972***	1976***
% saying women have . . .		
A. . . . too *much* influence		
individualist/privatized	14.0	14.2
identified/privatized	8.1	11.6
individualist/ambivalent	6.6	9.5
identified/ambivalent	3.7	5.8
individualist/egalitarian	3.7	5.8
identified/egalitarian	1.9	1.4
B. . . . too *little* influence		
individualist/privatized	17.5	26.4
identified/privatized	32.6	30.5
individualist/ambivalent	25.0	23.1
identified/ambivalent	32.7	32.3
individualist/egalitarian	37.8	33.8
identified/egalitarian	57.6	62.6

SOURCE: American National Election Studies, 1972, 1976.
***Differences significant at p < .01.

ful, or they may simply disregard it. The egalitarian identified are obviously the group most likely to embrace the Women's Movement. And so they seem to do (Table 4.6), with consistently warm mean scores. Privatized women express commensurate coldness, and those with neither identification nor a clear gender ideology are also relatively indeterminate about the Women's Movement.

Respondents' reactions to the proposed Equal Rights Amendment, that incendiary attempt to extend constitutional legitimacy to egalitarian views of gender roles, fall clearly into place according to gender role ideology, but identified women of any ideological stripe support the amendment more frequently than do their individualist counterparts (Table 4.7). We also see, however, the evidence of a cultural sea change. In 1976, both presidential candidates and their wives supported the ERA, as did the majority of the public, with no one knowing then that the ratification effort had already peaked and would soon falter. Thus opposition to it, in its heyday, was muted. By 1980, the climate had changed, ERA opponents had become thoroughly and successfully organized, and the Religious Right appeared to be a juggernautian force in American politics, with all that that implied for further discussion of gender roles and women's rights (see Boles, 1979; Mansbridge, 1986; and Wald, 1987). The climate is reflected in the strength of opposition to the ERA among those with a privatized gender ideology.

Geraldine Ferraro's vice-presidential candidacy in 1984 gives us yet another opportunity to test the relationship between gender consciousness and general

**TABLE 4.6 MEAN FEELING THERMOMETER SCORES FOR THE WOMEN'S
LIBERATION MOVEMENT OR FEMINISTS, 1972–1988, AND FOR GERALDINE
FERRARO, 1984, BY CATEGORY OF IDENTIFICATION/ROLE IDEOLOGY**

	1972***	1976***	1980***	1984***	1988***
A. Women's Movement					
individualist/privatized	32.83	34.87	39.78	42.55	36.86
identified/privatized	39.75	45.72	46.44	42.89	45.49
individualist/ambivalent	33.75	43.98	39.67	49.36	45.70
identified/ambivalent	45.38	49.21	46.38	57.49	52.66
individualist/egalitarian	49.49	56.52	55.29	62.96	53.53
identified/egalitarian	58.18	64.35	65.56	65.40	59.42
B. Geraldine Ferraro					
individualist/privatized				47.98	
identified/privatized				45.53	
individualist/ambivalent				44.32	
identified/ambivalent				55.26	
individualist/egalitarian				57.90	
identified/egalitarian				66.14	

SOURCE: American National Election Studies, 1972, 1976, 1980, 1984, 1988.
Note: In 1988, the "women's liberation movement" was replaced by "feminists."
*** Differences for Women's Movement and Ferraro feeling thermometer scores are significant at p
  $< .01$.

**TABLE 4.7 PERCENTAGE OF APPROVAL OF THE EQUAL RIGHTS AMENDMENT,
BY CATEGORY OF IDENTIFICATION/ROLE IDEOLOGY, 1976 AND 1980**

Category	1976***	1980***
Individualist/privatized	58.3	33.9
Identified/privatized	62.5	43.9
Individualist/ambivalent	75.4	41.4
Identified/ambivalent	78.2	45.1
Individualist/egalitarian	91.2	68.9
Identified/egalitarian	92.1	80.1

SOURCE: American National Election Studies, 1976, 1980.
***Differences in ERA approval significant at p $< .01$.

orientations toward women's political roles. Like reactions to the Women's
Movement and the Equal Rights Amendment, the "feeling thermometer" reaction to Ferraro, also presented in Table 4.6, correlates moderately strongly with
category of consciousness: ambivalent and egalitarian women who identify with
other women feel warmer toward Ferraro than do their individualist counterparts. Her most fervent partisans come, as we would expect, from the ranks of
the egalitarian identified, for whom the sight of a woman on one of the major
parties' tickets must have been a moving one, as it certainly was to this author.
Identification does not ameliorate privatization in this case, perhaps because of
Ferraro's overt feminism.

Reactions to Geraldine Ferraro, as to the Women's Movement or the Equal
Rights Amendment, emerge rather notably as a result of one's propensity to feel

a part of the "group" of all women and whether one believes that the group should fulfill essentially private or more public roles. One's identification with other women is part affect—one feels emotional warmth toward other women—and in larger part cognition—one wishes to see this group's influence increase. A convincing demonstration of the centrality of consciousness can be found in the fact that controlling for partisanship does not weaken the relationship between identification and egalitarianism and support for Ferraro: not Democratic women, but simply women, responded positively to her candidacy (the zero-order correlation between consciousness and Ferraro feeling thermometer scores equals .252 [p < .00]; controlling for Democratic party identification reduces the relationship minimally, to r = .240 [p < .00]).

Another aspect of the manifestation of gender consciousness demands our attention. That aspect reveals the transmutation of identification into consciousness, via the classic argument that conscious groups must make their demands on government. Here we can query the degree to which women assert their belief in civil society's obligation to *them*. We have seen identified women express their warmth for other women and, depending on their gender ideology, the espousal or rejection of symbolic policies and individuals. But what of a generalized sense that the government bears a responsibility to women, to protect and enhance women's place in the polis? These are, after all, the rights and privileges that have been coupled invariably to the duties of citizenship in the history of Western political thought.

Two questions in the 1984 election study permit an approach to this kind of consideration, and fortuitously, they do so in a way that also introduces an element of collective thinking. "Some people," respondents were asked in 1984, "feel that the government in Washington should make every effort to improve the social and economic position of women. Others feel that the government should not make any special effort to help women because they should help themselves. Where would you place yourself on this [seven-point] scale, or haven't you thought much about this?" Similar in construction to the equal roles question, this scale runs from one extreme, strong belief that government should help women, to the equally intense belief that women should help themselves. There may, of course, be interpersonal cognitive disagreement among those responding to the question over whether "women helping themselves" signifies *individual* women engaged in lonely self-help or women *collectively* eschewing reliance on government and helping one another instead. Within the bounds of individualistic American culture, the former is more likely to be in the minds of respondents who opine that self-help is better.

In either case, though, the direction of belief cannot influence other attitudes or behaviors unless it also has salience for the individual. There, too, we have an opportunity for analysis. Respondents were also asked whether it is extremely important, very important, somewhat important, or not at all important "that the federal government do what you think is best on this issue of women's economic and social position."

The direction and salience of women's beliefs about government's responsibility to women are collapsed in Table 4.8, and direction and salience are also combined in a composite that shows them both simultaneously. Gender identification/gender ideology strikingly discriminates among belief, salience, and the interaction of the two. Comparing the breakdowns of direction and salience for each category of consciousness, we see immediately that egalitarian women have higher expectations of governmental obligations, but that in each pairing of identified and unidentified women among the privatized, the ambivalent, or the egalitarian, the identified expect more from government than do the individualists. For the identified, the issue is also more salient than it is for women who have the same gender role ideology but who do not identify with other women. For privatized women as a whole, the question is not a very salient one. For identified egalitarians, it is highly salient. And this, theoretically, is as it should be. It is entirely intellectually consistent, if one thinks collectively, casting one's fortunes with the lot of all women, and if one believes in role equality, that one would also think it legitimate to make demands on government to act as women's guarantor.

Women certainly have come to the realization that equality has "gotten harder." Mason and Lu (1988), analyzing data from the General Social Surveys of the years between 1977 and 1985, found a steady profeminist change in the population during the period. In both sexes and across all generations and demographic groups, people were more likely to espouse equality in and out of the home. But women were more feminist than men, men were least feminist on questions of equal responsibility for childrearing, and the authors noted that women were more conscious of the double workload they were facing, since men had not yet changed enough to ease women's burden. But realizing the difficulty of achieving equality, the authors concluded, had not made women less egalitarian. The responses in Table 4.8 suggest that what it may have done, instead, is to make many women increase their demands on the system.

ABORTION, RELIGION, MORALITY, AND GENDER CONSCIOUSNESS

Few issues could become quite the cauldron of competing beliefs and conflicting demands that abortion has become in the United States. Questions of whether women should be free to control their reproductive lives and thus to obtain abortions, or whether this is an act of murder and thus to be prohibited, trigger a bewildering array of political and less obviously political beliefs. We *do* find

TABLE 4.8   PERCENTAGE OF EACH CATEGORY OF IDENTIFICATION/ IDEOLOGY FOR EACH DIRECTION AND DEGREE OF SALIENCE OF BELIEFS ABOUT GOVERNMENT'S RESPONSIBILITY TO WOMEN, 1984

	Ind/P	ID/P	Ind/A	ID/A	Ind/E	ID/E
A. Direction***						
women help selves	64.4	42.2	31.5	23.8	32.0	25.9
neither	17.8	37.8	47.9	41.3	23.0	21.9
govt. help women	17.8	20.0	20.5	34.9	45.1	52.2
B. Salience***						
not important	69.0	53.4	68.6	61.0	49.2	41.0
important	31.0	41.6	31.4	39.0	50.8	59.0
C. Direction × salience***						
help selves, important	17.1	18.4	9.7	8.6	13.6	12.0
neutral and/or not important	70.7	68.4	77.4	68.6	53.6	44.7
govt. help, important	12.2	13.2	12.9	22.9	32.7	43.3

SOURCE: American National Election Study, 1984.
Note: Ind/P = individualist privatized, ID/P = identified privatized; Ind/A = individualist ambivalent; ID/A = identified ambivalent; Ind/E = individualist egalitarian; ID/E = identified egalitarian.
***Differences significant at p < .01.

relatively straightforward positions articulated: the liberal feminist argument for reproductive freedom clearly emerges from a philosophy of individual autonomy and liberty, while some antiabortion arguments appear to proceed directly from orthodox interpretations of Christianity.

But we are in danger of being misled by the simplicity of this picture of Enlightenment rationality pitted against obedience to religious precepts. Pollack Petcheskey (1984) makes a compelling argument for a statist interest in controlling women's reproduction. Nice (1988) paints an alarming picture of political culture in which tolerance of domestic violence against women is associated with incidents of abortion clinic bombings, suggesting that something less noble than a belief in the sanctity of life motivates some antiabortion activities. That something may be a misogyny that I have also uncovered in the history of British and American maternal health care policies (Tolleson Rinehart, 1987), the troubled, almost medieval joining of a sanctified and highly abstracted view of the purity of motherhood to fear and loathing of actual women's sexuality. In the nineteenth century, abortion and even contraception were vilified at least in part because they would allow women to "get away with" adultery. Two such pronouncements, the first from a Dr. G. L. Austin in 1882 (p. 102) and the second from an American Medical Association report in 1871 (quoted in DiBacco, 1992: 13), make the misogyny clear:

This young wife, but lately so innocent and so chaste, who has been polluted by such immorality [the use of contraception], will soon know the ingenious strategem invented by debauchery. Then, if seduction seizes upon her heart, if her virtue fails, she will know that she will be able with impunity to violate the conjugal faith.

She yields to the pleasures—but shrinks from the pains and responsibilities of maternity. . . . Let not the husband of such a wife flatter himself that he possesses her affection. Nor can she in turn ever merit even the respect of a virtuous husband. She sinks into old age like a withered tree, stripped of its foliage; with the stain of blood upon her soul, she dies without the hand of affection to smooth her pillow.

Although it would not be fashionable to express these sentiments in such extreme terms today, there can be little question that they continue to exist. And women's awareness of this view of them might well first be heightened by, and then be a reinforcement of, their gender consciousness.

Complicating any simple view of attitudes toward abortion as the result of misogynist or feminist orientations is women's supposed role as the sustainers of society's moral and religious beliefs. Women have, after all, been celebrated for their roles as the community's moral guardians and the keepers of the flame of religious piety. Indeed, when women have been allowed a role of any sort in the public realm, this has been the one reserved for them, or, as many have argued, the role effectively preventing them from taking any other. But as we have seen (and will see again in the next chapter), although women's "spirituality" or "angelic" purity were advanced as arguments against enfranchising women, feminists on both sides of the Atlantic from the nineteenth century to the present have also seemed to acknowledge women's special moral status, albeit to celebrate the contribution it would make to public life.

Women's assumed position of moral and religious guardianship has led to (frequently unexamined) claims that women would hold more generally conservative political attitudes than would men, claims that have not been supportable for the last two decades, at least in the United States (Sapiro, 1983: 147; Carroll, 1989: 314–315; Tolleson Rinehart and Perkins, 1989). Apart from assumptions about conservative ideology, though, women's attitudes toward abortion may well be influenced by religiosity or moral beliefs because of the potential importance of religiosity and morality to one's conception of what it means to be a woman. Both Judeo-Christian religious beliefs and "traditional" morality powerfully reinforce the view that women's most important roles are those of wife and mother. Abortion, in this view, would undermine both roles. How, then, does gender consciousness "fit" as a cognitive organizing principle for one's attitudes toward abortion, and how does gender consciousness interact with religiosity and morality? Recent attention to religious and moral beliefs in the American National Election Studies makes it possible for us to address these questions.

The findings in Table 4.9 show us that privatization is associated with a pref-

TABLE 4.9   BELIEFS ABOUT ABORTION, BY CONSCIOUSNESS, 1972–1988

	1972***	1976***	1980***	1984***	1988***
% agreeing abortion should never be permitted:					
individualist/privatized	16.2	21.9	27.3	32.3	31.7
identified/privatized	19.9	14.9	23.4	21.3	31.0
individualist/ambivalent	7.2	3.9	15.4	14.4	10.4
identified/ambivalent	8.9	7.9	12.3	15.9	12.2
individualist/egalitarian	9.3	6.1	6.1	10.8	13.2
identified/egalitarian	4.5	8.4	6.6	7.1	7.4
% agreeing abortion should be a matter of personal choice					
individualist/privatized	13.5	10.5	16.9	13.8	12.2
identified privatized	8.6	9.9	21.9	14.8	22.4
individualist/ambivalent	20.1	18.2	25.6	24.4	16.9
identified/ambivalent	21.8	24.4	31.6	27.6	25.0
individualist/egalitarian	29.7	30.5	39.9	35.5	34.1
identified/egalitarian	37.0	38.3	54.0	52.8	51.7

Note: The intervening choices, chosen by remaining respondents, were, in 1972 and 1976, to permit abortion only to save the life of the mother, or for personal reasons; from 1980 to 1988, the intervening responses were to permit abortion in cases of rape or incest or to save the life of the mother, or if a "clear need" is established.
*** Differences among categories of consciousness significant at p < .01.

erence for prohibiting abortion, just as egalitarianism is more likely to correspond to a prochoice position on abortion. But we also see that, by the 1980s, identification with other women begins to soften the prohibitive position, moving almost twice as many identified privatized women to be "prochoice" as is true of their individualist counterparts by 1988. These differences by gender identification are even more notable among ambivalent and egalitarian women. This does not mean that identified privatized women are becoming a prochoice majority: they are not. It does perhaps mean that their identification with, and sympathy for, other women makes them more tolerant of an action (abortion) that other sources of beliefs would direct them to reject. The same phenomenon of identification with other women moves identified egalitarian women toward the strongest prochoice position of all groups by 1980, and they remain the only group to give a majority opinion on the side of freedom of choice through 1988. They may be uniquely strong in their prochoice beliefs because they rely less on traditional religiosity or morality as cognitive structuring principles.

Although it cannot be demonstrated that women's religious beliefs cause them to hold more conservative political attitudes generally, women espouse a more intense religiosity than do men (Tolleson Rinehart and Perkins, 1989). One can interpret women's religiosity on a number of levels: women care for and sustain the church, they are its handmaidens, and as a result of the same socialization

TABLE 4.10   GENDER CONSCIOUSNESS AND RELIGIOSITY, 1980–1988

	1980***	1984***	1988***
% with "high" religious commitment			
individualist/privatized	50.0	57.6	70.4
identified privatized	60.9	55.5	55.0
individualist/ambivalent	51.9	50.0	40.3
identified/ambivalent	54.2	51.4	57.4
individualist/egalitarian	30.7	45.4	39.3
identified/egalitarian	33.7	31.2	33.1

SOURCE: American National Election Studies, 1980, 1984, 1988.

Note: "High" religious commitment reflects those who say *both* that "religion is important" *and* that religion offers a "great deal" of guidance in one's life. Those for whom religion is not important or for whom it offers less than a "great deal" of guidance are not coded "high." See Tolleson Rinehart and Perkins (1989) for more discussion of the use of these indicators.

***Differences in religious commitment among categories of consciousness significant at p < .01.

to other-regardingness and nurturance that makes them the center of family life and the guardians of community morality. So, too, from their socialization, would women adopt more submissive and obedient religious roles. On another level, the medieval search for the *vita apostolica* and a compassionate Christ created wonderful opportunities for women to find new lives in communities of their own devising, such as those of the Beguines in Europe, and to influence piety (Bynum, 1982), just as nineteenth-century evangelism in Britain and the United States potentially empowered women by granting them a moral autonomy and an unmediated relationship to God (Cott, 1978).

Thus has Western religion sometimes worn the benign face of liberation and succor for women. But although the Bible may support "feminist" arguments, and while the Holy Spirit may be the scriptural underpinning for a small and misunderstood band of contemporary feminist evangelicals (Fowler, 1985; Wilcox, 1989), most orthodox religious commentary would be better characterized as antifeminist than as the reverse. And so it must seem to many women, since the data in Table 4.10 show clearly that greater egalitarianism means lower religiosity. The question of gender identification is not so straightforward, since religiosity could—perhaps should—imbue the idea of "sisterhood" with added force. Some research suggests at least indirectly that the context in which one exercises one's religious beliefs (for Protestants, one's denomination, watching televangelists, or adhering to biblical inerrancy are factors of note) may affect one's attitudes toward other women as much or more than one's internal religious beliefs do (Wilcox, 1989; Tolleson Rinehart and Perkins, 1989); certainly, within the fundamentalist Religious Right active in recent American political campaigns, women who embrace feminist precepts may not be "sisters" but rather part of the liberal enemy to be fought; feminists might not feel much less hostile in their turn.

In 1988, after several prior tests, the Board of Overseers of the American

TABLE 4.11   GENDER CONSCIOUSNESS AND MORALITY, 1988

	Agree (%)	Neither (%)	Disagree (%)
A. "The world is always changing and we should adjust our views of moral behavior to those changes."***			
individualist/privatized	38.3	6.2	55.5
identified/privatized	41.6	8.3	50.0
individualist/ambivalent	39.5	14.5	46.0
identified/ambivalent	41.8	6.0	52.2
individualist/egalitarian	49.1	10.5	40.4
identified/egalitarian	44.7	11.5	43.9
B. "We should be more tolerant of people who choose to live according to their own moral standards even if they are very different from our own."***			
individualist/privatized	45.1	18.3	36.6
identified/privatized	46.7	15.0	38.8
individualist/ambivalent	55.9	16.9	27.3
identified/ambivalent	58.9	16.2	25.0
individualist/egalitarian	67.3	13.2	19.5
identified/egalitarian	67.0	13.9	18.1
C. "This country would have many fewer problems if there were more emphasis on traditional family ties."***			
individualist/privatized	91.4	2.5	6.1
identified/privatized	83.4	11.7	5.0
individualist/ambivalent	87.0	10.4	2.6
identified/ambivalent	86.8	8.8	4.4
individualist/egalitarian	82.8	14.6	2.7
identified/egalitarian	78.0	15.2	7.0
D. "The newer lifestyles are contributing to the breakdown of our society."***			
individualist/privatized	91.5	3.7	4.9
identified/privatized	86.4	8.5	5.1
individualist/ambivalent	79.3	15.6	5.2
identified/ambivalent	83.3	12.1	4.5
individualist/egalitarian	73.5	16.9	9.6
identified/egalitarian	69.0	15.2	15.8

SOURCE: American National Election Study, 1988.
***Differences by category of consciousness significant at p < .01.

TABLE 4.12　THE SCALE OF MORAL TRADITIONALISM, 1988

% who are ...	Traditional	Neither	Tolerant
Individualist/privatized	67.5	28.8	3.8
Identified/privatized	67.8	22.0	10.2
Individualist/ambivalent	64.5	26.3	9.2
Identified/ambivalent	56.1	36.4	7.6
Individualist/egalitarian	50.6	31.7	17.8
Identified/egalitarian	49.1	26.3	24.7

SOURCE: American National Election Study, 1988.

Note: Figures are from a simple additive scale of the four items, collapsed so that a "traditional" response (either strongly agree or disagree, or agree or disagree, depending on question wording) is coded -1, "neither" is coded 0, and a "tolerant" response (either strongly agree or disagree, or agree or disagree, depending on question wording) is coded 1. Range of scale is -4 to $+4$. Mean scores: individualist/privatized $= -1.86$; identified/privatized $= -1.63$; individualist/ambivalent $= -1.39$; identified/ambivalent $= -1.41$; individualist/egalitarian $= -0.89$; identified/egalitarian $= -0.75$; scores differ in analysis of variance at $p < .01$. See Appendix for further discussion and analysis. Differences among categories of consciousness are significant at $p < .01$.

National Election Study included new questions meant to elucidate American morality. Ongoing research leads to the conclusion that, for some purposes of measuring morality, the four items represent two different dimensions of tolerance and "family values" (see the Appendix for further discussion). But for our purpose of examining the relationship between moral beliefs and gender consciousness, the two dimensions are intimately connected: one's readiness to accept change and diversity on the one hand and to resist developing an ideology based on the "traditional family" on the other should both resonate with one's willingness to be a part of the "group" of *all* women and to challenge the status quo in and on behalf of that group. The results in Tables 4.11 and 4.12 show individualist privatized women to be the least tolerant, while the most tolerant women are the identified egalitarians. In between those two poles lie the rest of our respondents. In truth, tolerance is not the favored position for any group— "traditional family ties" and fear of "newer lifestyles" compete robustly against fabled American respect for individual freedom in our popular culture. Here, as elsewhere, tolerance may be more honored in the breach than in the observance. Nonetheless, gender role identification seems mildly associated with increased tolerance, even among privatized women.

　　In order to test the interactive influences of gender consciousness, religiosity, and morality on attitudes toward abortion, I broke gender consciousness into its separate components of identification and role ideology (Table 4.13). These joined the scales of religiosity and morality as independent variables that might explain abortion attitudes. All four variables have a significant influence; religiosity's effect is the greatest, followed in strength by egalitarianism, morality, and identification. We can also see that the two components of consciousness, religiosity, and morality all have an *independent* effect, since none is especially strongly correlated with another. Higher religiosity drives respondents toward a

TABLE 4.13 ATTITUDES TOWARD ABORTION REGRESSED ON GENDER IDENTIFICATION, GENDER ROLE IDEOLOGY, RELIGIOSITY, AND MORAL TRADITIONALISM, 1988

	Beta	r^0	MorTrad	ID	Egal
Religiosity	−.276	—	−.303	−.067	−.175
Moral traditionalism	.135	—	—	.055	.175
Identification	.102	—	—	—	.134
Egalitarianism	.172	—	—	—	—
R^2	.192				

SOURCE: American National Election Study, 1988.
Note: First entries are standardized regression coefficients, second set of entries are zero-order correlations of independent variables to one another. All regression coefficients are significant at p < .01, and all Bs are at least 2 (Std. Error B). All variables are coded in the direction of the quality: ranges are 0 to 4 for religiosity, −4 to 4 for moral traditionalism, and 0 to 1 for identification and egalitarianism.

greater desire to prohibit abortion, while more moral tolerance, identification with women, and egalitarianism all support a more prochoice position. Finally, and perhaps most important, we see that gender consciousness, religion, and traditional morality can exert strong and potentially opposing forces on women when questions such as that of abortion stimulate so many of the "meanings" of being a woman.

Thus far in this chapter we have engaged the inner woman, examining how her gender consciousness influences other broad orientations about women and their political roles. Now, as we did in the last chapter, we turn to the "outer" woman and ask whether women are more or less likely to develop gender consciousness in a variety of the contexts of life.

IDENTIFICATION, GENDER ROLE BELIEFS, AND DAY-TO-DAY LIFE

Demographic Influences

Journalists, analysts, and feminists themselves have talked much of the overwhelmingly white, middle-class appearance of the Women's Movement, despite the fact that black women have played crucially important roles as activists and elected officials (see, for example, Hartmann, 1989). No doubt white middle-class women had more freedom from economic pressures or from racism to consider and embrace *feminism*, but gender consciousness, even of the traditional form—the generalized, heightened sensitivity to the political meaning of being a woman—is something that feminist movements, although they draw attention to it, do not completely contain. No more than a minority of women have ever identified themselves as feminists; feminism carries any number of different ideological meanings that, however well or imperfectly understood, all demand an unusual amount of self-assertion and commitment, and "feminist" thus is not lightly worn even by those who most fervently embrace it. For others, the label will not fit at all: traditional women may see feminism as a rejection of their most cherished roles; women of color may see it forcing them into a choice that they do not want to make between itself and the imperatives of their race. What women's movements can and do accomplish, however, is to legitimize gender consciousness. Even if feminism itself seems illegitimate to many, it prods and questions the culture, making room for women to think about themselves. Its impact is often indirect but nonetheless clear (Carroll, 1989); even quite antifeminist women feel empowered to take greater action in times of feminist activity (Hartmann, 1989; Klatch, 1987). The irritant of feminism stimulates gender consciousness, always present among some women, within many others. We have already seen very few differences in the propensity to identify with other women by race. We should expect to see decreasing differences by class as well.

Respondents' subjective assessments of their social class become less and less able to differentiate women in different categories of consciousness as time goes by. As we see in Table 4.14, the 1970s begin with identified egalitarian women claiming the highest social status, but the differences weaken by 1980 and become insignificant by 1984. Before the mid-1980s, privatized women were quite a bit more likely to come from the working class, and this finding comports well with our general understanding of the social conservatism of the American working class and its preservation of traditional distinctions among gender roles. Wendy Luttrell's (1988: 151) detailed participant-observation of working class white and black women's efforts to improve the quality of secondary education in their Philadelphia neighborhood is evocative of the thinking of identified but privatized women. One woman, who was asked in 1979 what she thought of the Women's Movement, said: "I just knew you were going to ask me about that eventually. And I'm just not the right person to talk to. I don't believe in abortion under any circumstances. I don't like what I see in the news from women libbers and I don't think that women should be in the army or in the Presidency." She had worked with energy and acumen on the school campaign, had gotten to know black women, had seen their common concerns, and her new experiences changed many of her attitudes about race. She sees the resonance between the personal and the political, although she might not describe it that way. She has the attributes of the privatized identified: for her, the Women's Movement is middle class, not for her class, and it seems to her to oppose what she believes is right. But she became effective and politically empowered, working in and on the behalf of the women in her community, on an issue that mattered to them very much. She does not like feminism or identify with feminists, and yet her

TABLE 4.14   DEMOGRAPHIC POSITION ACROSS CATEGORIES OF
IDENTIFICATION/ROLE IDEOLOGY, 1972–1988

	1972	1976	1980	1984	1988
A. social class:					
% saying middle or higher					
individualist/privatized	53.5***	51.0***	46.0***	59.1	42.1
identified/privatized	41.6	52.4	42.4	59.7	43.6
individualist/ambivalent	57.9	57.6	48.0	56.8	43.8
identified/ambivalent	57.3	57.1	51.8	59.6	54.7
individualist/egalitarian	55.1	57.6	47.9	52.2	49.8
identified/egalitarian	67.8	65.4	58.5	63.0	49.6
B. Mean family income					
(thousands of dollars)					
individualist/privatized	6.9***	8.7***	11.7***	12.9***	13.8***
identified/privatized	7.1	9.0	11.3	13.5	14.0
individualist/ambivalent	8.0	10.5	13.4	14.2	16.0
identified/ambivalent	8.6	11.2	12.6	13.9	16.4
individualist/egalitarian	7.9	11.2	13.6	17.6	16.0
identified/egalitarian	9.1	11.4	14.5	18.6	20.4
C. Mean, respondent's own					
income (thousands of dollars)					
individualist/privatized	——[a]	2.9***	5.0***	6.2***	8.8***
identified/privatized	——	3.1	4.8	6.6	9.3
individualist/ambivalent	——	4.2	5.3	9.5	10.3
identified/ambivalent	——	4.3	7.2	8.8	9.2
individualist/egalitarian	——	4.6	6.3	10.0	10.4
identified/egalitarian	——	5.4	7.2	11.3	11.8

SOURCE: American National Election Studies, 1972, 1976, 1980, 1984, 1988.
[a]Data not available in 1972.
**Differences significant at p < .05.
***Differences significant at p < .01.

awakening political effectiveness was precisely what feminists have striven for a century and a half to make possible.

Income might be a more straightforward indicator than one's subjective description in a nation that seems so relentlessly middle class. And income remains a sharp delineator, particularly when we are speaking of an individual woman's own income. It seems perfectly logical that privatized women would have lower personal incomes than their egalitarian counterparts, given that fewer of them work outside the home. Their family incomes would be concomitantly lower without their economic contributions, all other things being equal, although no doubt there are individual cases of privatized women whose husbands earn more than the combination of an egalitarian woman's income and that of her spouse. This is certainly true of the comparative affluence of many women New Right activists (Klatch, 1987; Andersen, 1988b). But, as we have seen, it has also been true that privatized women are more likely to call themselves working class.

There is another possibility. A woman with little to no income of her own is economically dependent, usually on a man if not on the welfare state. As we will see below, when that dependence occurs because a woman stays at home to care for her family, it appears to be part of a schema that makes her role an ideological position as well. By the same token, a wage-earning woman is equally ideologically consistent when she is egalitarian and sees her economic fortunes interdependent with those of other women. In the multivariate analysis at the end of the chapter, we see that subjective social class becomes an insignificant discriminator, but a woman's own income retains some association with identification/role ideology in two of the years, even or perhaps especially because women's earnings have continued to lag behind men's.

How Does One's Position in the Life Cycle Matter?

The age and generation of women at each point in the intersection of gender identification and gender role are found in Table 4.15, and here we see the period effects of ebbs and flows in challenges to women's privatization. Privatized women are, on the average, older than their egalitarian sisters, with women who are ambivalent in their beliefs falling in between. The egalitarian identifiers are the youngest of all, having been in the attitudinally malleable condition of adolescence and young adulthood when the third wave of the Women's Movement broke on American shores.

But mean age alone is only a partial clue to the influence of period effects. In the second and third parts of Table 4.15 we see the proportion of the "second wave," or suffrage generation, and the "baby boom" making their presence felt at each point of the role/identification continuum. Some intergenerational differences are certainly evident, but groups within each generation behave in contrast to simple expectations about them. Allowing for increasing mortality in the second wave generation, the entry into adulthood of the "trailing edge" of the baby boom, and the baby boom's simply enormous size, two things deserve note. First, older women showed a considerable propensity both to identify with other women and to express egalitarian views from the beginning—and indeed, well into middle age as they were by 1972, their seasoned maturity would be grist to the mill of political cognition should they choose to frame such experiences in such terms. In 1972, even the oldest of the baby boomers were too young to have reached mature politicization; nor had they yet had much time to play adult gender roles.

Second, as time has passed, the baby boom has not experienced the period effects of the 1970s and 1980s uniformly, but what one can say about these women is that they share a tendency to identify with other women and to make up their minds in favor of egalitarianism. Relatively few baby boomers profess

TABLE 4.15   LIFESPACE: AGE AND GENERATION, 1972–1988

	1972	1976	1980	1984	1988
A. Mean age in each category					
individualist/privatized	48.7***	50.4***	48.9***	52.7***	52.2***
identified/privatized	48.3	50.8	45.5	47.1	51.8
individualist/ambivalent	44.8	45.3	45.3	49.8	52.4
identified/ambivalent	45.7	46.7	49.9	46.6	50.3
individualist/egalitarian	42.5	45.3	45.0	44.0	45.8
identified/egalitarian	40.5	38.5	40.1	37.8	40.0
B. % in each category born in or before 1919					
individualist/privatized	44.0***	40.9***	29.5***	30.3***	23.2***
identified/privatized	40.8	43.4	31.3	20.0	28.3
individualist/ambivalent	34.3	31.5	24.1	28.9	27.3
identified/ambivalent	37.9	38.5	35.6	21.6	16.2
individualist/egalitarian	30.8	29.0	23.5	15.6	13.0
identified/egalitarian	27.8	16.7	15.4	6.6	5.3
C. % in each category born from 1946 to 1964					
individualist/privatized	16.0***	25.2***	28.2**	25.8***	28.0***
identified/privatized	14.5	17.5	35.9	40.0	33.3
individualist/ambivalent	18.2	30.6	39.2	28.9	35.1
identified/ambivalent	12.6	30.0	28.8	40.5	27.9
individualist/egalitarian	24.9	22.8	39.2	38.3	43.0
identified/egalitarian	27.3	43.4	47.1	58.5	56.8

SOURCE: American National Election Studies, 1972, 1976, 1980, 1984, 1988.
**Differences significant at $p < .05$.
***Differences significant at $p < .01$.

doubt about gender ideology, although there may be considerable intragenerational argument about the ideologically "correct" position. The cohort's relative decisiveness exists despite the fact that this is the generation most terribly caught between the Scylla of changing political and economic opportunities for women and the Charybdis of still vigorous desires for a rewarding family life. It is baby boomers toward whom newspaper and magazine articles have aimed advice about "mommy tracking," stopping the effort to be superwoman, the "new traditionalism," and the like. The changes in societal attitudes toward gender have hit this generation in very real and urgent ways, yet it has responded not with uncertainty but with considerable attitudinal assertiveness.

Marital status presents the most immediate, tangible, and consequential context in which gender role practice and gender role belief must coexist. Marriage is the modal state for adult Americans—a large majority of people are married at some point in their lives. But that does not imply a state of perfect stability. Census data for the year 1986 offer us a contemporary snapshot: among all married women, almost 20 percent had been married more than once. About 12 percent of both adult white and black women were widows; 8.2 percent of white and 10.8 percent of black women were divorced. A fifth of white women and just over a third of black women had never married (Rix, 1988: 354–356). Some white women and rather more black women will never enter into marriage with a man, for reasons of vocation, choice, sexual preference, or circumstance. For others, divorce or widowhood will end their marriages.

The possible combinations of gender identification/gender ideology and marital status range from the committed egalitarian identifier in a marriage of long standing to the privatized identifier who has never married. Table 4.16 (which should be read by summing each marital status across each identification/role category in each year) shows, in fact, that all the possibilities are represented, but that our commonsense expectations are also correct. Egalitarian identifiers are more likely never to have been married or to be divorced or separated, and widows are disproportionately likely to be privatized individualists from 1976 on. But most women in all categories are married; under the assumption that marriage will continue to be the modal status for most women, women will have to find a place for their gender consciousness amid their lives with men.

The Socialization Environment

A conceptual bridge between broader socioeconomic patterns such as income or marital status and the more tangible environments of political socialization is the context of homemaking. By definition, of course, housewives have married, and some of those who have never worked outside the home will spend some part of their lives as "displaced homemakers" if divorce or widowhood ends their marriage and, with it, their principal source of economic support. While housewives are not breadwinners, their contributions to their families have been called as much or more valuable than economic ones by both conservatives and feminists. Feminists who have attempted to place dollar figures on housewives' work, in order to emphasize the value of these noneconomic contributions, have inadvertently provoked the wrath of some New Right women, who reject the assignment of dollar figures to what they view as selfless acts of love and devotion (see Andersen, 1988b).

Some women leave the paid labor force temporarily, especially to tend the needs of young children, and some enter the workplace at least partly as a result of changes in attitudes and orientations. The behavior of the maternal generation of the Youth-Parent Socialization Panel Study is, as always, an excellent way to illustrate these patterns. From 1965 to 1982, about 30 percent of the mothers were never employed outside the home, and about 20 percent never *left* the paid labor force. The remaining half of the sample, though, engaged in considerable movement back and forth. Of the half with a varied employment history, 50

TABLE 4.16   LIFESPACE: MARITAL STATUS, 1972–1988

	1972***	1976***	1980***	1984***	1988***
% in each category who are . . .					
A. . . . married					
individualist/privatized	60.0	56.5	59.0	60.0	53.7
identified/privatized	62.3	61.5	57.8	54.1	48.3
individualist/ambivalent	67.6	69.4	59.5	52.8	53.2
identified/ambivalent	68.9	61.1	49.2	50.3	57.4
individualist/egalitarian	59.2	57.0	64.7	53.9	53.7
identified/egalitarian	63.0	55.4	50.3	54.0	50.8
B. . . . widowed					
individualist/privatized	22.2	27.3	24.4	24.6	25.6
identified/privatized	24.5	23.0	17.2	19.3	23.3
individualist/ambivalent	19.7	18.7	15.2	18.0	24.7
identified/ambivalent	18.4	20.7	30.5	18.4	17.6
individualist/egalitarian	16.3	16.9	13.1	15.6	13.3
identified/egalitarian	10.7	10.5	11.8	8.3	7.7
C. . . . divorced or separated					
individualist/privatized	10.7	9.8	11.5	7.7	13.4
identified/privatized	6.0	7.4	12.5	14.7	16.7
individualist/ambivalent	7.7	10.2	12.7	15.7	18.2
identified/ambivalent	4.9	13.0	8.5	16.3	22.1
individualist/egalitarian	11.1	16.9	12.4	14.2	19.3
identified/egalitarian	8.5	16.6	17.6	17.0	21.5
D. . . . never married					
individualist/privatized	7.1	6.3	5.1	7.7	7.3
identified/privatized	7.3	8.1	12.5	11.9	11.7
individualist/ambivalent	4.9	1.7	12.7	13.5	3.9
identified/ambivalent	7.8	5.2	11.9	15.0	2.9
individualist/egalitarian	13.5	9.1	9.8	16.3	13.5
identified/egalitarian	17.8	17.5	20.3	20.8	19.9

SOURCE: American National Election Studies, 1972, 1976, 1980, 1984, 1988.
***Differences significant at p < .01.

percent were employed in one of the three years (1965, 1973, or 1982) when Jennings and his colleagues interviewed them, but not in either of the other two years. The remaining 50 percent either began work in 1973 and were still working in 1982, or were working from 1965 on, with either a brief break at some point or retirement by 1982 (figures are from my own analysis of data made available by M. Kent Jennings). Among all the women studied, while only a fifth had a continuous labor force history, 70 percent had *some* labor force participation from 1965 to 1982. Many of these women may have worked outside the home because it was economically necessary for them to do so, and not because they were pursuing exciting or glamorous careers. Just over 40 percent of the mothers in the panel study were unmarried at some point from 1965 to

1982, and less than half of that group remarried. Their own financial security, as well as that of their children, would surely be a significant determinant of their labor force activity.

But whatever their families' economic circumstances, just under a third of the women remained at home. For some, that must have meant economic sacrifice, even if many of them would only have been able to earn low wages and even if one breadwinner's real income went further than it does today. And that sacrifice must have been less important than their own (or their husbands') gender role ideology—that women belong in the home. That, however, is precisely the point. In this case as in few others, ideology and lifespace would need to be congruent if severe and daily cognitive dissonance is not to exist.

This congruence can be seen in Table 4.17, where housewives' versus all women's gender identifications/gender ideologies are shown. Housewives are much more likely to be privatized and individualistic and far less likely to be egalitarian. The trend strengthens as time passes. We cannot know whether one's presence in the home creates the need for a gender ideological justification or whether gender ideology has dictated women's choice of sphere; although some have argued that a "marriage gap" dividing married from single people is more important than the gender gap, careful examination of marital status actually leaves us with more questions than answers about the conservatizing effects of being a homemaker (Plutzer and McBurnett, 1991).

Although housewives seem considerably more likely to be privatized individualists, it is also true that fewer and fewer women are housewives. Fully 46 percent of all women were housewives in 1972; that proportion had declined to less than a quarter of all women by the late 1980s. This does not mean that most women have moved from the home to the boardroom: more women have *jobs* (with limited opportunities for advancement and authority, with low pay, usually in the form of an hourly wage) than *careers* (with salaried rank and a clear path for advancement), and the apparent success of affluent dual-career couples may depend on their ability to pay for the domestic services they do not perform themselves. In other words, the "dual career couple can prosper professionally in part because there are other couples or individuals who do not" (Hertz, 1986: 5–6.) In between homemakers and women who are halves of affluent dual-career couples are the many women who have "double shifts," who work outside the home but find themselves responsible for most of the work inside the home as well. Women's ability to identify with one another across such different contexts surely takes conscious effort.

If homemaking or employment outside the home can say something about the correlation of women's immediate, daily contexts with their gender ideologies, other measures of the socialization environment are also revealing. Table 4.18 presents some of those measures. One significant early socialization process is children's use of their parents as models of adult role-filling. The American

TABLE 4.17 PERCENTAGE DIFFERENCES IN HOUSEWIVES' AND ALL WOMEN'S DISTRIBUTIONS ACROSS GENDER CONSCIOUSNESS CATEGORIES, 1972–1988

	1972	1976	1980	1984	1988
% housewives—% all:					
individualist/privatized	+4.5	+6.3	+7.9	+8.0	+6.2
identified/privatized	+4.8	+5.8	+2.7	+4.9	+3.2
individualist/ambivalent	+1.2	+4.4	+0.6	+4.5	−0.7
identified/ambivalent	−1.6	−0.5	−1.8	+2.0	+5.5
individualist/egalitarian	−4.3	−2.4	−0.2	−4.9	−1.1
identified/egalitarian	−4.7 .	−13.7	−9.1	−14.5	−13.1

SOURCE: American National Election Studies, 1972, 1976, 1980, 1984, 1988.
Note: A positive number indicates that housewives are more likely than are all women to fall into a given category; a negative number indicates, conversely, that housewives are less likely to fall into a given category. Ns of housewives are 548 in 1972 (46% of all women), 441 in 1976 (36.3% of the total), 195 in 1980 (26.4% of the total), 211 in 1984 (21.5% of the total), and 231 in 1988 (24.7% of the total).

National Election Studies ask almost nothing about respondents' early experiences, but they do contain questions about mothers' employment outside the home. In 1972, only about a third of all women had had employed mothers during their childhoods, and this relatively low number did not differentiate daughters' later adoption of identification and gender ideology. But as time passes, we see that more women recall having had employed mothers and that women with employed mothers are more likely to be identified or egalitarian— even the privatized but *identified* women are more likely to have had mothers in the labor force than their individualistic and privatized counterparts—but the memory of a mother working outside the home while one was growing up is strongest among women who are *both* identified and egalitarian.

Numerous voices in Western culture have loudly insisted that a mother at home is the single most important influence on a growing child's "healthy" development; what was loud became a hysterical shout in the two pop-Freudian decades after World War II. That equation can be inverted to suggest that a mother *not* "at home" would be powerfully influential, too. But in what way? My own panel study of college and community women in the early 1980s showed that women who had grown up in homes where mom worked for pay saw their mothers as models of strength and independence (Tolleson Rinehart, 1985). The participants in my study who had homemaking mothers were more likely to have used their fathers as models for adult political and economic life, in most cases because they had not wished to make the choices their mothers had made. Others have reported similar findings (Mason and Lu, 1988; Thornton and Freedman, 1979; Thornton, Alwin, and Camburn, 1983); something of the sort surely transpires in the figures presented here.

The effects of education are much simpler to decipher. The most egalitarian women are the most educated; the difference in postsecondary education be-

TABLE 4.18   PAST AND PRESENT SOCIALIZATION ENVIRONMENTS, 1972–1988

	1972	1976	1980	1984	1988
A. % with wage-earning mothers					
individualist/privatized	32.6	32.6***	39.0	33.3***	15.9***
identified/privatized	31.1	25.5	43.8	40.0	30.0
individualist/ambivalent	36.2	34.9	43.0	44.4	39.0
identified/ambivalent	33.3	35.6	34.5	46.9	27.9
individualist/egalitarian	37.8	38.4	46.4	53.9	43.7
identified/egalitarian	36.8	49.9	49.7	55.1	58.6
B. Mean years of education					
individualist/privatized	10.5***	10.5***	10.7***	11.0***	11.5***
identified/privatized	10.4	10.8	11.4	11.9	11.5
individualist/ambivalent	11.2	11.4	11.9	11.7	11.9
identified/ambivalent	12.0	12.0	12.1	12.0	12.3
individualist/egalitarian	11.6	11.9	12.5	12.5	12.5
identified/egalitarian	12.7	13.0	13.0	13.4	13.1
C. % with more than high school education					
individualist/privatized	13.3***	14.1***	14.1***	17.0***	23.2***
identified/privatized	15.8	15.4	18.8	24.5	31.6
individualist/ambivalent	16.8	17.5	25.4	27.8	27.6
identified/ambivalent	28.2	26.3	34.0	30.5	39.7
individualist/egalitarian	28.8	34.5	37.3	39.0	40.0
identified/egalitarian	45.1	47.1	48.5	56.0	54.0
D. % with more than bachelor's degree					
individualist/privatized	0.9***	1.9***	2.6***	3.1***	6.1***
identified/privatized	0.0	0.7	7.8	2.7	5.0
individualist/ambivalent	0.7	0.9	1.3	2.2	2.6
identified/ambivalent	1.0	3.0	5.1	1.4	10.3
individualist/egalitarian	2.1	4.1	5.2	7.8	7.4
identified/egalitarian	5.2	9.3	12.1	13.1	9.5
E. Mean job segregation (nonhousewives)					
individualist/privatized	42.4	64.0***	66.2	70.5**	61.4
identified/privatized	42.9	66.8	62.0	67.5	69.1
individualist/ambivalent	44.5	66.9	65.9	63.5	62.2
identified/ambivalent	36.1	62.2	60.6	62.2	69.0
individualist/egalitarian	39.7	57.5	62.4	61.7	62.8
identified/egalitarian	38.6	57.5	61.5	60.2	64.9

TABLE 4.18 *(continued)*

	1972	1976	1980	1984	1988
F. Mean job segregation (college grads only)					
individualist/privatized	75.9***	82.1***	70.3	83.1***	77.1
identified/privatized	80.1	86.6	74.8	76.2	72.9
individualist/ambivalent	73.4	92.5	82.6	76.5	70.9
identified/ambivalent	61.5	75.6	68.6	79.1	75.5
individualist/egalitarian	63.5	72.2	67.1	64.2	66.7
identified/egalitarian	62.2	67.3	68.5	64.3	62.4

SOURCE: American National Election Studies, 1972, 1976, 1980, 1984, 1988.
Descriptions of the calculation of job segregation from census figures and education-job segregation interactions from census figures can be found in the Appendix.
**Differences significant at $p < .05$.
***Differences significant at $p < .01$.

tween the egalitarian and the privatized is particularly striking. Again, though, we see a pattern emerge by the 1980s: identified privatized women are better educated than the privatized individualists. I have already said that I think the significance here lies not in formal schooling itself, but in the ethos it provides. The more time a woman spends in school, especially in a college or university, the more commentary about women, views about their socioeconomic and political status, and prescriptions for change she will hear, and perhaps comment on herself. And if Newcomb's Bennington College studies tell us anything, those cues are likely to be absorbed and used for decades to come (Newcomb, Koenig, Flacks, and Warwick, 1967).

The Bennington alumnae who were so profoundly influenced by their college experience in the 1930s were exposed to what was an essentially liberal political climate, and at least in regard to gender ideology, that climate would have long-term residual effects. Our respondents, too, would be much more likely to find egalitarian messages than the reverse at college. We have come increasingly to recognize and document the fact that the ivory tower harbors considerable sexism, up to and including the sexual harassment and assault of women students. But contact with such practices would, if anything, drive a student further toward egalitarianism and, in many of the same ways, toward identification with other women. What I am saying, in short, is that women with a very conservative gender ideology would find comparatively little *overt* reinforcement for their views on most campuses in the last two decades. *Covert* cues are another matter: the student newspaper on one campus with which I am familiar accepts large, graphic advertisements for wet T-shirt contests for women in local bars but frequently editorializes about the harm feminism does to "traditional values." Such behavior notwithstanding, college women even on conservative southern campuses virtually take equality today as a given and as their unquestioned right (Tolleson Rinehart, 1988).

Sociobiologists and other extreme conservatives such as George Gilder echo Rousseau in acknowledging only one justification for women's higher education: an educated woman is better able to be a wifely companion and competent mother. Oddly enough, John Stuart Mill ([1869] 1970) made a similar argument at the height of the Victorian era as a justification for *removing* the sources of women's subjection. Although Gilder and Mill use a similar justification, they do so to very different ends. And polls on most college campuses today would reveal more sympathy for Mill's feminism than for the other view. Higher education, then, is associated with stronger gender identification and an egalitarian gender ideology, partly because of the reinforcing context and partly because higher education and greater economic independence interact with each other. But this finding should not obscure the *range* of educational levels of women in each category, nor should education be seen as some sort of sine qua non to the formation of either gender identification, or prescriptions about gender roles. While college education is increasingly available to women, it is not available to nor desired by all, and it is not by any means the only place where gender consciousness can grow.

The workplace, like the home and the campus, is another immediate environment of great importance. We spend large portions of our days at work, and it can be the context of intense political learning, attitude reinforcement, and behavior, from the union shop at the factory to the behavioral norms of managers and executives (Finifter, 1974; Sigel and Hoskin, 1977). Until recently, with some exceptions, women were not a large presence in either the union shop or the boardroom. Women in managerial positions continue to hit "glass ceilings," women in skilled labor continue to face hostility or ambivalence, and over the years, although unprecedented numbers of women have entered the labor force, gendered segregation into "pink collar" jobs is on the increase.

But the same hypotheses about segregated versus "nontraditional" occupations that were so useful in chapter three are useful once again. This time, we see that the privatized and individualistic are somewhat more likely to be in segregated occupations, but since housewives are excluded from this analysis, the distinctions do not appear to be as large. When job segregation—this time including housewives—interacts with education, it is clear that among women with at least some college, identified egalitarianism is associated with having a less segregated occupation in three of the five years.

SEEING THE PICTURE IN MORE DETAIL

The foregoing discussion has presented patterns emerging from a comparison of women in the different categories of consciousness by features of their socioeconomic status, position in the life cycle, and scenes of their daily lives and earlier environments. While they show us what we might think of as end results—privatized women are more likely to be housewives; identified egalitarians are the best educated of all women—they cannot tell us everything we would like to know about the processes women employed and were engaged by as they came to these orientations. An emphasis on *individual* change in women's beliefs over time, an emphasis that always should be kept in mind, is also less well served by cross-sectional survey data.

Panel studies such as the Youth-Parent Socialization Panel Study, or long, indepth, open-ended interviews, help to reveal these processes at work in individual minds, as the different illustrations above have shown. But we can also see and understand the *collection* of individual circumstances that produces society-wide trends. This can be done, as I did for gender identification alone in the last chapter, by regressing identification/ideology on all the demographic, lifespace, and socialization measures in each year from 1972 to 1988. In Table 4.19, the distribution of cases across categories is not even, and so the regression coefficients presented here should be treated as indications of relationships, rather than population parameters.

In 1972, neither identification nor gender role ideology was particularly affected by a woman's context—only education and the propensity toward "group thinking" separate the privatized from the egalitarian at this early point of the feminist renascence. This most likely means that women were not yet connecting their gender role ideologies in a conscious way to the myriad other cognitive schemas with which they navigated the seas of information in their worlds. Jane O'Reilly's "Click! The Housewife's Moment of Truth" had only recently been written, for the first issue of *Ms. Magazine* (O'Reilly, 1980). A few years yet were to pass before it seemed that every woman in the country was talking, defending her particular position, arguing, laughing, raging (and it did seem as if every woman was doing just exactly that as the popular culture of the 1970s waxed).

But not too many years had to pass! By 1976, the lines of intrasex differences were being drawn. Suddenly, everything seems to matter: education, collective thinking, the interaction of education and job segregation, income, age, one's mother's employment status. As I did in chapter three, I solved two sets of regression equations, one for all women and one for white women alone. Any differences in the two solutions might signify patterns peculiar to the experience of women of color, admittedly in a rather weak and diluted way, but it is all that can be done when their numbers in the sample are too small to permit a separate analysis. In 1972, 1980, 1984, and 1988, the results for all women are identical to the results for white women alone. But in 1976, when so much consciousness was apparently being raised, and in relation to so many facets of women's lives, we appear to have our only indication of race differences in the relationships

TABLE 4.19   FACTORS SIGNIFICANTLY ASSOCIATED WITH WOMEN'S POSITION IN THE CATEGORIES OF GENDER CONSCIOUSNESS, 1972–1988

Characteristic	1972	1976	1980	1984	1988
Years of education	.163	.127	.179		
Close to other groups	.059	.122	.174	.217	
Education × job segregation		.097		.152	−.100
Had wage-earning mother		.084			.182
R's income		.076		.110	
Age × being in baby boom		.566			
Job segregation		−.196	−.111	−.178	
Age		−.210		−.277	
Being in baby boom		−.576			
Being born in or before 1919			−1.169		
Age × being born in or before 1919			1.282		
Marital status		.067			
Constant	−.258	.627	−.218	2.180	−.377
R²	.104	.210	.183	.208	.125
Adjusted R²	.093	.200	.157	.193	.105

SOURCE: American National Election Studies, 1972, 1976, 1980, 1984, 1988.
Entries are standardized regression coefficients.
Note: "Significance" refers not only to the fact that coefficients are significant as determined by t-tests at $p < .05$, but also that B > 2 (Std. Error B).

measured here. For white women alone, the interaction of job segregation and education, respondents' age, and respondents' own income, becomes insignificant. This suggests that their significance in the equation for all women is contributed largely by black and other women of color.

By the 1980s, the very vivid, restless picture of associations between life circumstances and patterns of gender identification and gender role ideology has settled down. A propensity for collective thinking continues to be important, as is education in 1980 and the interaction between education and job segregation in 1984. A woman's own income is significantly associated with her position in the identification/roles categories in 1984, and through the first half of the 1980s, there is an association between a woman's having a *less* gender-segregated job and being both egalitarian and identified; in 1988, the interaction of job segregation and education has this effect.

In 1980, as the cohort of women born in or before 1919 begins to suffer the consequences of mortality, the difference between that increasingly small group of women and women born later is enormous. *Within* the cohort, though, the older the woman, the more likely that she will place herself among the egalitarian identified. With other considerations held constant, this is the residual effect of such women's exposure to the heady change in women's status during the first four decades of the twentieth century. By 1984, that striking picture has been obscured by the simple force of the inverse relationship between age and identified egalitarianism: the effect of baby boom women's attitudes is massive. By 1988, only the interaction of a less gender-segregated job and education, and the influence of a mother who was employed outside the home, distinguish between categories of consciousness. I take the failure of other demographic or sociali- zation contexts to discriminate among women by 1988 as a powerful indication of just how potentially universal gender consciousness had become, despite or perhaps because of a decade of backlashes against women and women's issues. My interpretation is strengthened by the fact that, throughout the 1980s, there are no differences in the results for all women and for white women alone, suggesting by implication that white women and women of color were respond- ing to features of their environment in similar ways. Despite the fundamental differences among women that race and racism have meant, women are capable of reaching to one another across the divide.

In any case, even with a confirmation of expectations that different life posi- tions or different points in the life cycle would stimulate cognition, as women correlated their inner and outer worlds—what they believed with what they lived each day—socioeconomic status, work, education, or age are not rigidly deter- ministic of women's beliefs. As much as anything else, the multivariate analyses tell us that the intersection of gender identification and gender role ideology is a highly cognitive, individual, and selective process.

Clearly, in the mid-1970s, women were using their contexts as cues, as bases for testing and holding different combinations of beliefs. It also seems obvious that this process was not proceeding at the same pace for all women. Differences in occupation or education, for example, uncover differences in the rate at which women came to conclusions about whether they identified with women as a group and in which spheres they felt women most properly belonged. By the 1980s, these decisions were less driven by any particular social or economic categorization, and I have argued that the logical interpretation of that "negative finding" is that thinking about women's roles and fortunes has become the com- mon property of women, just as the somewhat uncertain, uneasy use of the term "women's libber" in the 1970s has largely been replaced by people's confident use of "feminist" and the "Women's Movement," whether to praise or vilify.

But we should also recall Sigel's (1988) findings of women's genuine role ambivalence. Women are asking questions: How do I reconcile what I believe with what others expect of me and with what I expect of myself? How do I bring my environment into confluence with my beliefs? These questions represent per- haps larger problems for women now than they did even a decade ago. The 1970s were years of a building desire for role change among American women, but we can read the popular and scholarly literature of the very recent past with a bemused regard for its innocence: women could and should take on more of the public roles heretofore reserved for men; men could and should gain for themselves some of the benefits of the intimate, nurturant roles women were expected to perform. Equality and a better world were just around the corner, we thought.

Since then, the New Right has seized on "traditional values" and a "profamily" agenda as effective means to electoral success, in the process giving some women a consolatory reinforcement for their nonfeminist beliefs, something they might surely have felt they lacked during the feminist salad days of the late 1970s. But New Right successes have also seemed to mean backsliding for many feminist aspirations, at the same time that organized feminist political groups such as NOW have failed to develop alternatives to what seem to be losing strategies. "Average" women, then, have known a kind of puzzled exhaustion. If equality is just around the corner, where *is* that corner it is just around, and what does "equality" mean anyway?

So, while the modal category of consciousness is egalitarian/identified by 1988, and while a minority of women still embrace privatized role orientations, almost a quarter of the sample is ambivalent. Most of them identify with other women, but all of them are unable to choose between woman's place in the home and woman's place in the world. They may be the visionary few who see the ineluctable reverberation between public and private. They are more likely to be the ones most caught in the ongoing conflict over the meaning of gender roles. They and the egalitarian women all appear to wish that men were considering these questions more vigorously as well. Women show few signs of abandoning their heightened consciousness but are understandably struggling to use that consciousness in a world that is not always responsive.

For all women, the convinced and the uncertain, the largest test of their consciousness is its politicization. This is what moves identification, and even the strongest role beliefs, into another realm. We have already seen the first indication of consciousness in the relationship among identification, gender role ideology, and the direction and salience of beliefs about women's political roles and government's obligation to women. Thus it is quite naturally toward a deeper understanding of the association of consciousness with political involvement that we now turn.

Chapter 5

GENDER CONSCIOUSNESS AND POLITICAL ENGAGEMENT

> My professor in my course on the Executive just uses "he" all the time. I mean, I
> know, obviously, that presidents have been "hes," but my professor uses it for
> everything. And I don't like it. It makes me feel uncomfortable. It makes it hard
> for me not to see everybody in politics as a man.
> —Undergraduate political science major (1989)

For the young woman who made this remark, her professor's "standard" usage
of the masculine pronoun is neither neutral nor inclusive. Nor, doubtless, did it
seem so to the generations of women who had been excluded from participation
in formal political institutions. For them, politics was literally as well as figu-
ratively male. Our task in this chapter is a consideration of women's political
engagement within and outside a male paradigm, women's participation as an
end in itself and as a means to other ends. Some women who have been excluded
have accepted their relegation to the nonpolitical; even as the twentieth century
draws to a close, some women continue to eschew the political as something
that belongs among their constellations of roles.

Most Western cultures have expended untold intellectual energy on maintaining distinctions between public and private. Definitions of property as private or
public, to take one example, have been at the center of the West's great competing ideologies. Among the most pervasive of the conceptions of public and private, however, have been those that align them with gender, in any of numerable
public man/private woman formulations. Many women, even when the barriers
were most formidable, have subverted them and have made political statements

in unorthodox ways. There have always been women who have attempted to raise their voices in the language of orthodox political paradigms, as we have seen. But others, extraordinary "ordinary" women, have put the traditional characteristics of femininity to startling uses. Fiction, poetry, religious tenets, even quilting have been the outlets for women's expression of their political selves when no other outlets were available to them. These were certainly expressions of what we might now call gender consciousness.

Now, seventy years after the Anglo-American inclusion of women as citizens with voting rights and more recent, moderate growth in the numbers of women occupying political office, those unorthodox outlets may have been supplanted by conventional modes of participation (although the renascence of feminism in the 1960s itself contributed to contemporary acceptance of peaceful protest *as* a conventional participatory act). Yet the habits and patterns of earlier role assumptions may also remain. This leads us directly to the question of whether women, as political actors, are or should be different from men.

Is there some uniquely female or feminine way to be political? We have raised the "difference question" earlier and will discuss it again in the next chapter as we explore policy preferences. But the difference question has a bearing on political participation as well. Have women been less likely to participate in politics because nature or nurture has made them somehow less political? John Stuart Mill answered no to the question of nature more than a century ago (Mill, [1869] 1970). If it is a question of nurture, will not changes in gender role socialization bring concomitant increases in women's participation? Recent history furnishes evidence that such change is occurring. Or have women participated less because the *forms* of participation have somehow been less congenial to women? In that case, does the form of women's participation escape the notice of those who are not looking for it? Quilting, after all, would not automatically be recognized as political behavior by those who define political behavior in terms of voting or campaigning or lobbying.

These questions have been preeminent concerns for those political philosophers who are or might now be called feminists—just as a major concern of those without such sympathies, obviously, has been to ensure that women remain distinctly nonpolitical. Perhaps such antifeminists would have been no better pleased to acknowledge the political activities of "traditional" women than they have been to accommodate feminist arguments. Unless we are observant, can we see an overtly political act in the making of a quilt composed of "T for Temperance" and "Drunkard's Path" patterns, or a quilt embracing abolition or the suffrage (Ferrero et al., 1987)?

We have already thought about the varying influence of kinds of gender consciousness, from high gender identification joined to privatized gender role beliefs to the equally highly identified egalitarian women, on political behavior. Women who fall in the former category have been less recognized as political activists, at least until the singular emergence of New Religious Right women as a political force in the 1970s and 1980s (Brady and Tedin, 1976; Luker, 1984; Hughes and Peek, 1986; Klatch, 1987). They, like women before them, are impelled into the political arena because they perceive the polis to be failing in its responsibility to them and to their values, although unlike those earlier women, their *right* to political participation has been made possible by a legacy of feminism that may, in fact, be one of the things they are protesting against. But they, too, are perpetuating the long tradition of women who try to assert their point of view when they believe that the community has gone astray. And their efforts are made as much in behalf of normative beliefs about women's rights and duties as are the feminist clarion calls to which they are so antithetical. They, like feminists, are driven by a group identification and a desire to present the group's point of view. And if, as Dennis (1987) argues, group consciousness alone is not sufficient to stimulate participation unless "group-based politics" can also be seen as legitimate, not narrowly self-interested and not already unduly advantaged, then the "group" of women could perhaps make the most legitimate and broadest claim to act as a group—even if women of different beliefs will make such a claim for different reasons and to different ends. In this chapter, we shall see both these forms of gender consciousness expressed in a deeper engagement with politics than is true of women who have neither a strong gender identification nor a strong gender role ideology.

But we are not faced with a mere juxtaposition of mobilized Total Women against feminist Viragos. If there is an overwhelming normative agreement to establish woman as citizen among those thinkers throughout history who might be called feminists were they all gathered in some grand conference today (and few even among antifeminists would now deny women the basic privileges of citizenship), that same conference would be noted for its robust disagreement between those who think there is no inherent distinction between the essential political nature of the sexes and those who believe there is. On the one side, from Plato's sexual equality in the Republic's guardian class to Mary Wollstonecraft, Harriet Taylor, and John Stuart Mill, to current liberal feminist thinkers, the belief that women and men are inherently equally capable to be political actors is usually accompanied by an orientation that sees participation at least partly as an end in itself. On the other, from the Victorian prototypes of the "maternal thinkers" to many radical feminist theorists, women's politicization is thought to be not only inherently different in form but also a different means to different political ends.

Such a debate is weighty for a number of reasons. One of the reasons has methodological consequences for the present work. If women's political involvement is inherently different from that of men, then the picture of participation that we draw from survey research grounded in the conventional "male" paradigm of participation will be partial at best, and for research executed within that paradigm the picture will remain sketchy. If the sexes do not inherently differ, then advocates of "political woman" must still explain differences in the level or amount of women's and men's participation. And the differences must be explored without either making woman out to be a passive, helpless victim of oppression or holding man up as some participatory paragon.

The most cogent of both "difference" and liberal feminist explanations are usually made by taking into account the force of gender role socialization, structural factors, and life cycle or situational considerations, although of course each orientation views them quite differently. I have already employed these explanations in measuring women's gender identification and gender role ideology. Now, however, the argument is put to a serious test, for politicization itself—the transition from simple identification to consciousness—must be shown somehow if it is to be useful to us as more than thoughtful speculation. It cannot be measured directly in extant data bases, and I have suggested that it probably could not be directly measured in any case. Consciousness is dynamic, not a "thing." It is best seen as the relationship between other qualities or as the process that joins them. So, in this chapter, we look for it in the relationship among identification, role ideology, and political engagement, defined here as actual participation in politics combined with the internal psychological resources and involvement that would make such participation seem to be both possible and worthwhile.

It is well to remember that both acts of participation and the psychological resources underlying them exist in a gendered world. Socialization, structure, and situation reinforce one another in an intensely interactive cycle. Gender consciousness offers women one opportunity to break the usual cycle. Before we turn to contemporary political engagement and gender consciousness, however, we need to look on the cycle as it has presented itself through time, at least in the Anglo-American case. We shall be on the alert for the "unconventional" political expressions of women against whom the conventional ways were barred. The simple and not-so-simple consequences of women's privatization are now better understood, although the "chicken and egg" nature of privatization's perpetuation, as the culture reproduces itself within families, has not yet been fully explored (see Jennings, 1983). And we have not exhausted the lode of explanations for the varying meanings of privatization in Western culture.

Thus we seem required to take another look at the history of Western culture, especially with regard to some of the ways it has defined public and private. "Public" and "private" have almost always been gendered, and women have almost always been relegated to a private sphere that has not contained within it norms of political—public—activity. This could be said even of Marx and Engels, who, even when they were denouncing the bourgeois decadence of treating wives as "property" or discussing women's role in the reproduction of labor, were speaking to and for men rather than women (see relevant passages on the family in, for instance, Tucker, 1978; and see Hartsock, 1983).

But a stark division of people into public man and private woman fails to do justice to the extraordinary intricacies of meaning beneath it. "Man: public::woman:private" has not been a simple formula. To take just one example, one of the meanings feminists scholarship has found beneath the proscription that "woman's place is in the home" is the disconcerting fact that one was merely, and pejoratively, a woman, and not a *lady,* if one did *not* stay in the home throughout much of American history. Among more obvious divisions, this subtle use of language also effectively divided women by race and class (for the black feminist perspective on the tragic racial divisions between women, see Collins, 1989, and especially Collins, 1990). Yet another view shows us that despite the clarity with which we have begun to see the implications of gender for women, we have hardly begun to ask how gender and definitions of masculinity have created public *man.* Could it be that norms of gender may have pushed man as relentlessly into the public domain as it has forced woman into the shadow of the private? "Manhood," too, is put to society's uses: how else could society convince young males to go out and risk their lives in its armies but to enshrine such acts as pivotal fulfillments of male gender roles (Gilmore, 1990)? Perhaps thinking about male "gender consciousness" will be another consequence of questioning women's roles, a questioning to which we return now.

SOME HISTORICAL MEANINGS OF PRIVATIZATION TO WOMEN'S POLITICAL ROLES

Popular analyses of women's status may claim blithely that equality between men and women has never been so widespread, and there would certainly be a good deal of evidence supporting such claims. But as we now know, constructions of gender roles have varied through time and according to circumstance. The division of male and female into public and private has been a given, but the precise boundaries have shifted, especially when societies have faced epochal periods of change. In America's recent pioneer past, for example, rigidly drawn gender roles gave way to dire necessity, and men and women were required to relinquish many nicely delineated notions of masculinity and femininity if they were to survive in a hostile environment—ladies and gentlemen cannot play delicate drawing room games of courtship where there are no drawing rooms. Crisis is almost always met with an at least temporary alteration of "traditional" gender roles (Lipman-Blumen, 1984). Rosie the Riveter became an affectionately embraced symbol of "femininity" in World War II. And surely this surprising cultural flexibility helps to explain why women in the Western states and territories were the first to exercise the suffrage and why the first female member of Congress, Jeannette Rankin, was elected by the people of Montana in 1916, four years before women were finally enfranchised nationwide.

I would not wish to claim that historical epochs are neatly comparable; indeed, the future emerges from the past in sometimes puzzling ways. I would also wish to avoid the "sin of anachronism" (Gottlieb, 1985) here, just as I tried not to commit it while discussing Christine de Pizan in chapter three. Nor would I want to tell a story only of the rare elite women in each era who exercised political power, even though, unfortunately, it is more often the women of the elite than of the masses of past periods about whom a detailed historical record exists. But there are enduring themes and responses here, and sexual ideologies have set paradigms for whole societies. So, as we have often done thus far, we shall look back before we look forward. It is important to illuminate the understanding of women's privatization in earlier eras in order to see just what, in those earlier eras, our culture may be inchoately responding to now. This gives us a foundation on which to construct a view of the tumultuous present. In particular, we can see how far "public woman" has had to come and how some form of gender consciousness has been a resource on her journey.

From the Renaissance to Mary Wollstonecraft

In the medieval *corpus mysticum*, each individual was surrounded by an ethos of mutual dependence, born into a divinely ordained and unchanging place in the community. These precise, ascribed roles for men and women seem to have offered women who were born into particular positions, especially at the upper reaches of their community hierarchies, remarkable scope for their talents. During at least some part of the middle ages, that scope was truly broad, especially for women religious who, like their male counterparts, were almost alone in their access to literacy and accumulated knowledge. Such rare opportunity is exemplified in the legendary life of St. Hilda of Whitby, abbess of a large community of men and women and the person who ordered and supervised the first writing of the English language, or in the now legendary lives of Hildegard of Bingen and Heloise.

By the end of the middle ages, though, the blossoming of women's religious orders had been blighted by war, conquest, and the church's newly consolidated power. Powerful, the church was no longer grateful for women's energies. "Reformed," it was now suspicious of and hostile to women's perceived carnality (Schulenburg, 1989). This suspicion and hostility was to be frequently vented on the Beguines, the informal, independent gatherings of religious women who had become established on the Continent in the twelfth and thirteenth centuries (Labarge, 1986).

The dawning of the Renaissance was to introduce even more momentous change. The stable, certain world of the medieval *corpus mysticum* was to be smashed by the rise of the urban market society over feudal agriculture, by the Protestant Reformation, and by a burst of progress in science and the arts. Early in the Renaissance, the new humanism seemed to promise everything: the ancients were brought into the light after long, dark years in monastery libraries, and with the rediscovery of classic Greek and Roman texts came a new appreciation of classical approaches not only to arts and sciences, but to politics as well. European middle and upper classes were engagingly enamored of learning, and republicanism was fervently embraced.

Renaissance women, no less than men, were caught up in this effervescent, often charming recreation of the individual and society. At least some twentieth-century scholars were smitten by it: Jerrold (1928: 88) said that "absolute equality of the sexes . . . was never called into question," and Von Martin (1944: 72) concluded that "the cultural role of woman increased in proportion to the increasingly courtly character of society." This *apparent* equality—and it was not apparent but real in many senses of educational and aesthetic standards—obscures, however, the deeply paradoxical regard in which Renaissance man held Renaissance woman. Medieval suspicion of woman's carnal nature had persisted into the new era, as did notions of courtly love, although both of these sexual ideologies had been reclad in seemingly more elegant garments. Woman was, for all her education and her arts, still most bound by her wifely role—perhaps more so in the new economic climate of shifting property ownership than she had been in the middle ages.

Conceptions of the roles of Renaissance woman actually anticipated our modern understanding of public and private by creating three paradoxical positions for woman: virgin or wife, lover or wife, and independent actor or wife. For all the deliriously erotic celebrations of her, man's poetic exaltation of woman was not at all unmixed with revilement of her supposedly inimical carnality. It was just such a disturbing mixture of sentiments to which Christine de Pizan was making an answer in her *Book of the City of Ladies;* I used her words as an epigraph for chapter three because they illustrate a form (if only a form) of gender consciousness in the Renaissance. And while women might have been prepared by education and cultural expectation to take up a number of roles, they were free to take them only by default. The historian Ruth Kelso (1956: 2) explained it thus:

> In the renaissance, so far as the highborn woman shared the work of men, as administrator of estates and kingdoms, leader in war, and so forth, she was ruled by the same standards as men. What was not granted to her was the common right to share. Circumstances alone gave her that power—the death or absence of her husband, the inheritance of a title through lack of a male heir, or, as in nunneries,

the lack of competition from men. Theory went only so far as to make some occasional slight suggestion that high birth placed her above the lot of ordinary women by making her a prince.

Women of the middle and upper classes were educated to run homes, businesses, even princely states while their men were away for reasons of trade or war. But this does not mean that Renaissance men saw them as their equals or their part-ners. Machiavelli, that master of enigmatical modern political thought, wrote this *Canzone* for an interim in his play *Clizia* (transl. Gilbert, 1965):

> He who once angers a woman,
> rightly or wrongly, is a fool if he believes
> to find in her, through prayers or lament, any
>   mercy.
> When she enters upon this mortal life,
> along with her soul she brings
> pride, anger, and disregard of pardon.
> Deceit and cruelty escort her
> and give to her such aid
> that in every undertaking she gains her wish,
> and if anger harsh and wicked
> moves her, or jealousy, she labors and watches,
>   and her strength mortal strength surpasses.

This abiding suspicion of women is a consequence of the paradigm of auton-omy and manhood that came to rule Renaissance political thought (Pitkin, 1984). If the humanism of the early Renaissance was touchingly optimistic, by Machiavelli's time independent city-states were beset by economic crises, cease-less wars and threats of war. For Pitkin, Machiavelli's thought is made coherent via the understanding that autonomy—a dramatic dismissal of medieval inter-dependence in favor of independence, of self-reliance in all things, but espe-cially in politics and war—is in dialectical tension with gender. The Renaissance meaning of "manhood" was threefold, reflecting the era's appreciation of ancient meanings: man is not God, and man is not beast, but also man is not woman. For man to be womanly in any way was to forfeit his manhood and, at the same time, his autonomy. Certainly, Machiavelli's accounts of the astonishing female prince Caterina Sforza in the *Prince* and the *Discources* shows mingled scorn, fear, awe, and respect. She had, after all, bested him in a diplomatic negotiation. But beyond even this apprehension of manhood/autonomy as the key to the po-litical thought of Niccolò Machiavelli, it also signifies the modern Western be-ginning of a consciously gendered division of the world, and the two sexes, into public and private. (The Eastern, Confucian division, though far older, seems to have served similar purposes of ordering the state, especially in its application as "neo-Confucianism" in, for example, medieval Korea.)

This tempted but fearful and suspicious stance of men toward women was to continue, marking the seventeenth century in numerous ways. The English Civil War and the puzzling status of widows provide two perhaps unlikely examples of the uninterrupted influence of the modern public/private conception first introduced in the Renaissance. The position of English widows who had inherited the freehold of their husbands' property reveals the conundrum nicely: only when a woman could not be characterized as maiden or wife could she slip free of patriarchy. Local authorities often found themselves having to go to court or seek explicit legislation to keep propertied widows from exercising political power, since English common law had not accounted for the possibility of female property holders. Women's activities were seen as dangerous, and perhaps with good reason—from 1648 to 1651, *The Petition of Women* and the behavior of women Levellers were two large thorns in Cromwell's side (Fraser, 1984). With the Restoration and the reopening of English theaters, Aphra Behn carried women's anger to the stage, as we see in those words of hers with which I began this book.

Despite Aphra's rage and despite the hapless efforts toward educating women carried on from the Renaissance by women like Mary Astell (Kinnaird, 1983), women's status at the close of the seventeenth century was probably less than what it had been when Queen Elizabeth, that greatest of female princes, died. And by the eighteenth century, fear of women's sexuality had given way to a selfish manipulation of it. Novels like Daniel Defoe's *Moll Flanders*, published in 1722, and Henry Fielding's *Tom Jones*, published in 1749, certainly provide evidence that the potential power of women when they were seen as strongly carnal—almost as sexual predators—was diluted by a new depiction of them, no longer only as predators but also, particularly, as sexual prey. Woman was now "created to be the toy of man, his rattle, and it must jingle in his ears whenever, dismissing reason, he chooses to be amused" (Wollstonecraft, [1792] 1975: 118). Mary Wollstonecraft, a gifted autodidact in Enlightenment rationalist philosophy, could not but believe that women too, if enabled by education, would worship at the Shrine of Reason—that they were men's toys only because a misguided culture had made them the slaves of passion.

The most significant individual target of Wollstonecraft's arguments in the *Vindication of the Rights of Woman* was, of course, Jean-Jacques Rousseau. Despite the sweep of his communitarian political thought, his view of women and their roles in society—or, to put it better, his sharp proscription on any roles for them at all outside the home—leaves women so privatized that there is not even room for the rare woman prince allowed for, by circumstances, in Renaissance thought. His educational plan in *Emile,* for Sophie's transformation into "natural woman," startles us now because we would not call it an education at all. She was quite purposefully to be reared as a virtual illiterate, learning some domestic skills but many erotic ones, so as to retain Emile's protection. Her purpose was to lure him sexually and, through carefully contrived wiles, to prolong his sexual interest in her as far as she could. She would receive, in exchange, a home for herself and their children. But because no man would accept a cuckoo in his nest, her contact with the world beyond the house must be drastically restricted so that Emile could be certain that their children were, indeed, his. Women, for Rousseau, were "responsible" for the corruption in society because they inflamed men's lust; in this, the most respectable housewife did not differ from the Parisian actress. All women made themselves available as objects of desire, whether in a walk to the market or in displaying themselves on the stage. This dire threat to the virtue of the male republican citizen could be obviated simply by placing women in a sexual quarantine and denying them the intellectual development that might empower them to resist entrapment in a domestic dungeon.

Rousseau's words do not require torturing, or even twisting, into such a representation. This perspective on women fairly leaps from the page, not only in *Emile*, but in Rousseau's *Julie* and *Letter to M. d'Alembert* as well. His view of women is also not simply an eighteenth-century version of the straightforward belief that woman's place is in the home, for Rousseau's educational plan for women must go to extraordinarily contrived lengths to trick woman (that really seems the word for it) into thinking that the home sets the boundaries on her place. For Rousseau, as Pitkin argues was also true for Machiavelli, it is not merely that women could not have appropriate public roles: it is that women were a *threat* to the public (see Rousseau, 1979, 1960, 1968; Okin, 1979).

Nor did Mary Wollstonecraft see things very differently than we would. She might have cheered from her grave when, sixty years later, John Stuart Mill made his acerbic pronouncement on the absurdity of forbidding women from doing what by their "nature" they could not in any case do. To Rousseau's argument that women must be passive and submissive to the mastery of men, while men must endeavor to please women in order to obtain "her consent that he should be strongest," she exclaims, "What nonsense!"—this is only giving "a little mock dignity to lust" ([1792] 1975: 129).

But as her argument builds, it becomes an increasingly sophisticated rationalist theory of the absence of civic virtue when the socialization of one of the sexes has been so deranged: "If any class of mankind be so created that it must necessarily be educated with rules not strictly deducible from truth, virtue is an affair of convention. How could Rousseau dare to assert, after giving this advice, that in the grand end of existence the object of both sexes should be the same?" ([1792] 1975: 138). This is an error double-dyed: woman's understanding is sacrificed to the altar of man's sensuality when even Rousseau acknowledges that man's desire will soon wane.

The sacrifice, moreover, is not only futile in the case of one couple; it is the death knell as well of the virtuous republic. The brainless, dizzily sensual creatures who are Rousseau's ideal women could never be rational citizens themselves, of course, but no more could they be teachers and exemplars for their children, the citizens-to-be. Wollstonecraft did not, unlike many of the Victorian thinkers to follow her, believe that there were meaningful differences in men's and women's capacities or ends if they were not differently educated. But she was the first modern thinker to emphasize the harm done by public/private polarizations not only to individual women who, she argued, should in simple justice be vested with rights, but to the health of a republican polis as well.

The "Angel in the House": Victorian Passionlessness and Women's Purity

Mary Wollstonecraft was immediately attacked on publication of the *Vindication;* her work, her whole life were to become anathema after her death five years later. In large part, this horrified reaction to her greatest work *was* a reaction to her life. Her passionate defense of women's virtue and her demand for women's rights as citizen were overshadowed in the public mind by condemnatory portraits of her own vices. She had borne a daughter, Fanny, out of wedlock and had lived with the philosopher William Godwin after being abandoned by her former lover. She married Godwin only just before the birth of their daughter Mary. Mary Wollstonecraft, who died apparently of puerperal fever after that birth, had lived a genuinely unconventional life, certainly by the emerging middle class's standards.

But if a belief first in woman as lusty sexual predator and then in woman as enticing sexual prey had so colored the seventeenth and eighteenth centuries, whence came the horrified reaction to Mary Wollstonecraft? It emerged from Evangelicalism, which began to percolate through Anglo-American culture almost contemporaneously with Wollstonecraft's own writings and which, in another three decades, had become (among other things) the paradigmatic cultural ideology that Nancy Cott (1978) calls "passionlessness." By the mid-nineteenth century, its strains were the top notes in the Victorian refrain. The ideology of passionlessness no doubt had its effects on Mary's two daughters: Fanny committed suicide at the age of twenty-two. Mary Godwin Shelley, on being urged to teach her small son Percy to think for himself, responded in anguish, "Oh God, teach him to think like other people" (Tomalin: 1974: 255–257).

Cott tells us that passionlessness represented the translation of the earlier definition of woman as *particularly* sexual into "the view that women (although still primarily identified by their female gender) were *less* carnal and lustful than men" (1978: 220–221). From the 1790s to the 1830s, the ideology of passionlessness was tied to, and rose with, Evangelicalism for three reasons. First, the novels of Defoe and others depicted promiscuity and aristocratic excess as a threat to middle-class morals and made woman's chastity the archetype of human morality. Second, etiquette manuals such as Fordyce's *Sermons to Young Women* joined the two strains by advocating a modest, demure (albeit distastefully coy) demeanor. Third, and most important, women were such an enormous majority of Protestant congregations by the mid-nineteenth century that "Christian" and "female" values began to be used interchangeably. Women were the armies of Christian soldiers in the Evangelical revival.

At first, this growing ideology seemed potentially liberating for women. In it, woman was for *God's* purpose, not man's; she was an independent moral agent, and her morality was salutary for society even though—or perhaps because—it was still privatized. Many women joined Wollstonecraft in her outrage at woman's degrading reduction to the status of a sexual toy. But while Wollstonecraft offered Reason as the anodyne, the Evangelicals offered religion and morality. Women could rid themselves of coy sexual stereotypes, remove themselves to some degree from men's power, and assert, through their embracing of female/ Christian values, a measure of self-preservation and constructive self-control. Today, we would call this a profound assertion of the political self, almost a political movement.

Male institutions derived benefits from passionlessness as well: religion, as it had done in the early middle ages, could welcome women and thereby gain their energy and loyalty, during a time when men's religious commitment had been declining. Passionlessness also offered male institutions a way to eclipse women's putative power of sexuality over men. The "tacit condition" for women's empowerment in this regard, of course, was the "suppression of female sexuality" (Cott, 1978: 227)—passionlessness. But suppression of this alleged carnality, in fear of which men constructed modern notions of public and private in the first place, meant that "private" became even more privatized, partly because women who internalized passionlessness could become their own and other women's jailers. Quickly, the potentially empowering moral agency of passionlessness became the travesty of the "Woman's Mission" school, the "cult of true womanhood," and the "angel in the house"—a travesty, moreover, that would not only unbearably confine middle- and upper-class women's lives, but would make poor women's lives impossibly more burdensome by imposing on them a standard of "true womanhood" that barest economic necessity made unreachable.

Mary Wollstonecraft's was the first voice of dissent, her voice, indeed, being raised just as the Evangelicals were beginning to raise voices of their own. There were other protests in the liberal rationalist strain, although the effectiveness of what we would call feminist novels, like Harriet Martineau's *Deerbrook* or Mrs. Gaskell's *Mary Barton,* were diminished, as with Mary's *Vindication,* by popular rejections of their authors' lives or beliefs; Martineau's atheism and Mrs. Gaskell's nonconformism certainly did not resonate with the popular tenets of Evangelicalism. In the United States, women subverted the cult of domesticity ingeniously, by putting the requirement that women be ceaselessly engaged in "fine sewing" to unintended uses. This was the ethos surrounding Quaker and other abolitionist women who began using quilts as political statements, and quilts were to figure as prominent symbols in the nineteenth-century temperance and suffrage movements (Clark, 1988; Cozart, 1988; Herr, 1988; Ferrero et al., 1987).

The dissent that burned through Anglo-American culture, however, came quite surprisingly, and certainly without the author's conscious *political* intent, from the wild moors of the West Riding of Yorkshire. Charlotte Bronte's *Jane Eyre* electrified readers with passages that spoke directly to the ideology of passionlessness:

> Nobody knows how many rebellions besides political rebellions ferment in the masses of life which people earth. Women are supposed to be very calm generally: *but women feel just as men feel;* they need exercise for their faculties, and a field for their efforts as much as their brothers do; they suffer from too rigid a restraint, too absolute a stagnation, precisely as men would suffer; and it is narrow-minded in their more privileged fellow-creatures to say that they ought to confine themselves to making puddings and knitting stockings, to playing on the piano and embroidering bags. It is thoughtless to condemn them, or laugh at them, if they seek to do more or learn more than custom has pronounced necessary for their sex. (Brontë, [1847] 1966: 141; emphasis added)

Charlotte Brontë received immediate praise for *Jane Eyre,* but just as quickly came the vilifications. In her brave unworldliness, she battled back. Her next novel, *Shirley,* renewed her appeal: "The cleverest and acutest men are often under an illusion about women: they do not read them in a true light; they misapprehend them, both for good and evil; their good woman is a queer thing, half doll, half angel, their bad woman almost always a fiend. . . . If I spoke all I think on this point, if I gave my real opinion of some first-rate female characters in first-rate works, where should I be? Dead under some cairn of avenging stones in half an hour." "Or a cairn of angry newspaper reviews at least," adds Brontë's biographer (Fraser, 1988: 339). But Charlotte, like Mary Wollstonecraft, remained utterly dedicated to her Truth: even if Mary's was the Truth of Reason, and Charlotte's was the Truth of the "natural heart," neither could bear to see women so painfully and artificially confined. Nancy Cott calls passionlessness a double-edged sword: woman's sexuality could not have called forth such sweeping repression had the salacious image of it not lingered as a shadow on the Victorian mind.

Just as woman had become a slave to sensuality in the eighteenth century, the ideology of passionlessness made her, in the Victorian era, a slave to bleak duty. Just as her putative sensuality became the justification for disallowing her reason, passionless moral purity became the justification for denying her the use of her judgment in the real world. Women, John Stuart Mill ([1869] 1970: 213) said, "are declared to be better than men; an empty compliment which must provoke a bitter smile from every woman of spirit, since there is no other situation in life in which it is the established order, and considered quite natural and suitable, that the better should obey the worse." Still, passionlessness, although it deepened woman's privatization (by making her, symbolically at least, even less capable of entering passionate politics) and threw further obstacles in her path to a place in the public arena, could, when it rose above the caricature of the "Woman's Mission," robe women in a seductive moral power. As his comment above suggests, John Stuart Mill and even Elizabeth Cady Stanton did seriously believe in women's implicit moral superiority—but they used it as a reason for including her in, not excluding her from, the polis. It is no coincidence that the first mass woman suffrage movements also arose in the Victorian era.

Freud reminds us, though, that the duality of men's portrait of woman—as pure and yet evil or, as Charlotte Bronte said, as half doll, half angel, and yet fiend—persisted into the twentieth century, just as we still struggle to mesh eighteenth-century belief in Reason with Victorian morality and sentiment. If Stanton and Mill believed that woman's moral superiority was salutary to political society, Freud thought that woman's utter *inability* to achieve moral maturity was one of civilization's greatest threats. "Women," he said,

> soon come into opposition to civilization and display their retarding and restraining influence—those very women who, in the beginning, laid the foundations of civilization by the claims of love. Women represent the interests of the family and of sexual life. The work of civilization has become increasingly the business of men, it confronts them with ever more difficult tasks and compels them to carry out instinctual sublimations of which women are little capable. Since a man does not have unlimited qualities of psychical energy at his disposal, he has to accomplish his tasks by making an expedient distribution of his libido. What he employs for cultural aims he to a great extent withdraws from women and sexual life. His constant association with men, and his dependence on his relations with them, even estrange him from his duties as a husband and father. Thus the woman finds herself forced into the background by the claims of civilization and she adopts a hostile attitude towards it. (Freud, [1930] 1961: 50)

If we compare these words to Eleanor Roosevelt's belief that government's "increasing cognizance of humanitarian questions" was the result of women's new political influence (see chapter two, above), the collision of views could not be more evident. Women might understandably have difficulty recognizing themselves in Freud's portrait.

But it is men's portraits of women against which gender conscious women have always objected. Whether it is Christine de Pizan protesting against Renaissance man's revilement of her; Aphra Behn or Mary Wollstonecraft angrily rejecting the role of thoughtless sexual plaything; Elizabeth Cady Stanton, Charlotte Brontë, and Sojourner Truth claiming independent personhood; or Eleanor Roosevelt believing that women's participation would make a better world, gender consciousness has always been present, and it has always been political.

Seeing the Patterns

Three things now seem clear. First, as each epoch echoes and reacts to what has gone before, so we, in the late twentieth century, are continuing to weave a tapestry. The most recent patterns in it were set for us by the Victorians, but Enlightenment rationalism has left its mark as well, especially in the United States. Although individual political actors or theorists seem seldom to be addressing the past, the Victorian refrains of women's moral purity can nonetheless be heard beneath contemporary discussions of the "difference" question, just as Enlightenment contradictions are echoed in our uncertainties about gender roles and political equality. Passionlessness has partly given way to renewed celebrations of women's sexuality, but woman's putative moral superiority and her equal right to a political voice are still the claims of a new generation of feminists, just as they underlaid the motivations of Eleanor Roosevelt and the women of the New Deal. And privatization and its profound influence on women's political behavior continue to be the background.

Our second lesson is that the relationship of privatization to women's politicization has been anything but a simple one. We see that, far from "natural," Western women's privatization has emerged from very complex ideologies about women, sexuality, and the state, and it has been enforced only at a cost to society of considerable intellectual and emotional energy. This is not to say that no woman would choose a private role for herself without societal coercion. Nor can it be reduced to slogans about the domination of one group, women, by another, men, for within the public man/private woman formula, the meaning of manhood has conferred not only privileges and powers but anxious constraints, and some women have always been able to participate in men's public privileges. It is to say, however, that public/private constructions, although they seem to be clear frameworks for viewing gender in society, are in reality teeming with ambiguities, both for those who accept existence within the frameworks and for those who try to take a critical stance from outside.

Some of these ambiguities are poignantly illustrated in the results of a 1989 *New York Times* poll on attitudes toward women's roles (Belkin, 1989). A majority of married women said that they thought that men did their "fair share" of the work at home, even though men themselves felt that they *didn't* do a fair share. A similar majority of women agreed that "men are willing to let women get ahead, but only if women do all the work at home." A large majority of white women thought that men's attitudes toward them had improved, but they also asserted that men still considered themselves to be "superior." Men agreed that attitudes toward women had improved, but also thought that "most men they know" still considered themselves superior to women. Black women were less sanguine, and perhaps more realistic: 43 percent of them thought men's attitudes had improved, but fully a quarter of the sample thought attitudes had worsened (the recent escalations of violence against women portrayed in popular literature, music, and comedy, and still more in terms of actual crimes, offer chilling evidence for that view). Both young and older women, both black and white women, strongly endorsed the statement "The United States continues to need a strong women's movement to push for changes that benefit women," and by bare majorities, so did their male counterparts. It seems, as Sigel found in her New Jersey study, that most women are aware of ambivalence and discrimination, but many are wearily resigned to it and are coming to the conclusion that the only sympathy women are likely to get is from other women (Sigel, 1988)— just as Christine de Pizan thought six hundred years ago.

This deeply ambiguous, portentous construction of the public and the private is transmitted from one generation to another through socialization, and it is abetted by structural arrangements such as education, childrearing, and socioeconomic resources. Little girls continue to receive verbal and symbolic messages that politics is mostly male. They grow into women for whom major childrearing responsibilities and economic insecurity are real constraints on the time and energy that might be given to politics. Change is slow; only in the 1980s have American women finally achieved numbers proportional to their share of the population in colleges and universities or in the voting booth. A representative share of other forms of political power remains a very distant goal.

But change *has* occurred, and therein resides the third conclusion to be drawn. No matter what the shape of the privatization, and no matter what the historical epoch, there have been gender conscious women (and some uniquely thoughtful and sympathetic men) to raise their voices against the portrayal of woman as "other," as too sexually threatening, or too much a sexual toy, as too morally puerile or too passionless, to merit a public role. Those voices have sometimes implicitly, but more often explicitly, joined their rejection of otherness to their claims on the polis. Even women who have been deeply conscious of their gender in a "traditional" sense have demanded the right to bring that standpoint to the public arena, for they *do* have standpoints, and where else but in the public domain can they make themselves heard? All gender conscious women, regardless of a given time or ideology, have understood that the world sees them not only, or not even at all, as an individual, but as one of a gendered type: "woman." Now, particularly when legal barriers to women's participation have fallen, consciousness is a political mobilization resource that counteracts the depoliticizing influences of privatization. Gender conscious women, even those women for whom consciousness is of the "traditional role" variety, should be more deeply politically engaged than are women who lack this resource. As we see in the pages to follow, that is very often the case.

GENDER CONSCIOUSNESS, INTERNAL POLITICAL RESOURCES, AND POLITICAL BEHAVIOR

Americans are becoming notorious for being apolitical, a disengagement from politics variously ascribed by pundits to apathy, disgust, disinterest, indolence, or frustration. The American system of formal election procedures is considered one of the most daunting among the Western democracies, entailing cumbersome voter registration requirements and perhaps too frequent elections: the voter who does succeed in becoming registered may find herself called to the polls numerous times in a single twelve-month period, for primaries, and possibly runoffs, as well as different elections for local, state, and national offices. Because of the growing influence of electronic media in campaigns, she may well find state and national campaigns to be slickly packaged, "negative" television events rather than informative exchanges; and because of the much reduced level of attention paid to most local races, she may find information about them even more difficult to obtain.

Because the American political culture has often been one of shunning politics, and because political parties have been seriously weakened since World War II, in a structure that impeded "party government" in any case, our voter is not likely to feel intimately connected to politics through various local party organizations or clubs—her party "membership," if she has one, is more symbolic than substantive. She may belong to one or more interest groups, and a particular event—the condition of public schools, a proposal to build a hazardous waste dump or a prison near her home—may rouse her to considerable action.

But because she has grown up in a society that tells her that "politics" is a nasty business (and indeed she may see enough evidence for that in the conduct of recent campaigns), because good political information easily come by is a scarce commodity, and because her own life is full of other demands on her time and energy, our voter may do little more than vote. And if she does vote, she is one of a bare majority of eligible voters who actually go to the polls in presidential elections, and she would be a member of a minority of people turning out to vote in most state and local elections.

Looming over all this is gender: in addition to the many forces driving Americans away from political participation, our voter must have overcome the subtle and not-so-subtle messages that politics is not only a nasty business, but men's business as well. Our voter's psychological battle in this regard has been made easier in the last two decades, but logistics may have made things even more difficult for her, as ideals of equality have outstripped practical divisions of labor inside and outside the home. As these factors converge, then, we should not be astonished to see that relatively low numbers of Americans are politically engaged and that women's political engagement may be lower than that of men. Amid such general disengagement, can gender consciousness have influence?

I have spoken not merely of political participation but of political *engagement* to indicate the spectrum of politicization, from internal feelings of confidence and interest, the connection to the political system and the commitment to acquire political information, to the performance of actual participatory acts. The American National Election Studies permit us to build a scale including these qualities and behaviors. Psychological resources are measured by internal political efficacy—the belief that voting is *not* the only way that an individual can influence politics (except in 1984 and 1988 when this variable was not available) and that government is *not* "too complicated" for an individual to understand— and political interest, measured here by those who claimed to be "very interested" in the election campaigns. Political *information* is measured by those who read "a good many" or "several" magazine articles about the campaign. (Magazine article consumption was chosen over newspaper reading because there was much less variability in newspaper reading, with the vast majority claiming to have followed the campaigns in the papers.)

Partisanship, "folded" to measure identification with either major party as opposed to independence from or refusal to identify with a party, was included as a measure of integration into the mainstream political system. The object here is not which party one identifies with, but *whether* one is willing to call oneself a Democrat or Republican. Weak though the parties may be, they still provide ideological cues and a sense of membership in the political community, and they are still the conduits to most political offices. (Partly for these reasons, the minuscule number of members of other parties in each year were included with independents and nonpartisans.)

Actual political behavior included claiming to have voted for president in the year of the survey, attempting to influence others' votes, displaying campaign insignia such as buttons or bumper stickers, attending political meetings or rallies, and working in a campaign.

These items, coded such that holding each orientation or committing each act earned a score of 1 while its absence was scored zero, were combined to form a simple additive scale of political engagement. The scale is straightforward and coherent (in each year, all items loaded highly on a single factor in a factor analysis, although partisanship scaled somewhat more weakly than the others; Cronbach's alpha coefficient of scalability is shown in Table 5.1a). It is also exceedingly generous: one would not have to exert oneself much either intellectually or physically in order to score rather well; we even err on the side of generosity by accepting people's claims that they voted for president at face value, although we know that some who claimed to have done so did not in fact. Yet, as we see in Table 5.1a, in any given year, around 10 percent of the population is utterly politically disengaged, and about 20 percent can reach a score of no more than 1 on a scale of 9 or 10, and even these modest levels have declined since the 1970s. Less than 1 percent of the population in any given year is completely politically engaged, at least in the orthodox terms of this scale. Unconventional domains of political life—protests, demonstrations, and the like—are not accounted for in the scale, but could we include them, the overall rates of activity probably would not change much. The omission of less obvious forms of political action, akin to the nineteenth-century quilting of abolitionists, temperance women, or suffragettes, is more regrettable. On the other hand, since full engagement with the political system is now possible for women, a straightforward measure of that engagement is necessary to any discussion of women's influence on politics.

The second part of the table (5.1b) shows the mean scores of all in the samples, of all men, of all women, and finally, of women at different levels of gender consciousness and its components, gender identification and gender ideology. Immediately, we see that women are significantly less likely than men to report their involvement in various aspects of politics. Whether this is a matter of relative over- and understatement of activities on the parts of men and women cannot be ascertained, but if men did feel compelled to overstate their political engagement, while women were inclined to practice false political modesty, this too would signify the power of gender to shape our presentation of ourselves to the world.

When we look at the emergence of gender consciousness in political engagement, though, we see that women differ considerably among themselves. A virtually linear relationship between the categories of consciousness and political engagement would exist were it not for the hypothesized exception of identified but privatized women, who are uniformly more politically engaged than their equally privatized but individualist sisters and who, in 1984, are more engaged

TABLE 5.1a PERCENTAGE FREQUENCY DISTRIBUTIONS OF THE POLITICAL ENGAGEMENT SCALE, ALL RESPONDENTS, 1972–1988

Scale Score	1972	1976	1980	1984	1988
0	8.1	12.6	8.6	10.7	15.0
1	19.4	20.3	21.4	23.2	22.9
2	24.4	19.5	21.3	22.9	25.3
3	19.2	15.1	18.0	18.0	16.9
4	12.8	12.9	14.3	11.6	9.8
5	7.5	9.1	8.4	7.7	5.6
6	3.9	5.7	4.3	3.2	3.0
7	3.1	2.5	2.2	1.9	1.0
8	1.1	1.7	0.8	0.4	0.2
9	0.5	0.5	0.6	0.4	0.2
10	0.0	0.1	0.1	—	—
Chronbach's alpha	.676	.720	.624	.647	.616

SOURCE: American National Election Studies, 1972, 1976, 1980, 1984, 1988.

TABLE 5.1b MEAN SCORES ON POLITICAL ENGAGEMENT SCALE, 1972–1988

	1972	1976	1980	1984	1988
A. All respondents	3.01	3.09	2.71	2.48	2.21
B. By sex					
men	3.24*	3.37*	2.89*	2.66*	2.39
women	2.84	2.90	2.56	2.32	2.07
C. By consciousness					
Ind/P	2.32*	2.60*	2.53*	2.09*	2.55
ID/P	2.46	2.74	2.59	2.55	2.23
Ind/A	2.75	2.77	2.57	2.11	2.06
ID/A	3.06	3.14	2.54	2.30	2.40
Ind/E	3.02	3.07	2.94	2.57	2.20
ID/E	3.47	3.27	3.16	2.93	2.39
D. By components					
individualist	2.72*	2.83*	2.74[.06]	2.32	2.20
identified	3.10	3.14	2.99	2.73	1.98
privatized	2.57*	2.80	2.55*	2.29*	2.32*
egalitarian	3.24	3.21	3.09	2.84	1.99

SOURCE: American National Election Studies, 1972, 1976, 1980, 1984, 1988.
Note: Ind/P = individualist privatized; ID/P = identified privatized; Ind/A = individualist ambivalent; ID/A = identified ambivalent; Ind/E = individualist egalitarian; ID/E = identified egalitarian.
*Indicates that differences from analysis of variance are significant at p < .01. Less but still significant differences are reported in the superscript.

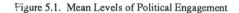

Figure 5.1. Mean Levels of Political Engagement

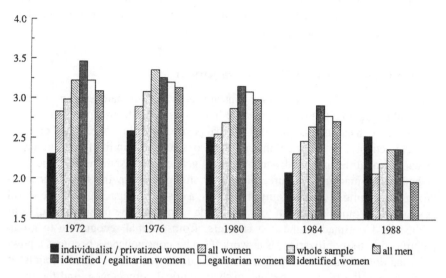

SOURCE: American National Election Studies, 1972 - 1978

even than individualists who are ambivalent in their gender role ideologies. Even identified privatized women are not as engaged as egalitarian women are, and this is appropriate given the beliefs of each group about gender roles. But gender identification, even in the group of women who believe that their place is in the home, seems to spur them to greater involvement with politics. Of fifteen possible pairings of identified and individualist women who have similar role ideologies (privatized, ambivalent, or egalitarian), gender identified women are the more politically engaged half in thirteen pairs (the exceptions occur in 1980, when women with ambivalent roles are indistinguishable by gender identification, and in 1988, when privatized individualists are more mobilized than any other group).

This is shown most obviously when we simply compare the mean engagement scores of identified and individualist women: gender identification provides a significant boost to political engagement. As we would expect, the spur to engagement is even more evident when we compare egalitarian and privatized women. The two components, reinforcing each other, mean that privatized individualist women are the least, and identified egalitarian women are the most, politically engaged. The stark effect gender consciousness has on women's political engagement is brought home in Figure 5.1. The rates of engagement for either identified or egalitarian women exceed those of all women and of men, with the rate for women who are both identified and egalitarian reaching the greatest heights, and the rate for privatized individualists falling far below sample norms—except in 1988 when, amid general political disengagement, the privatized individualists are the most engaged of all. In the analysis of separate scale components below, we shall see that this group of women was unusually mobilized by the 1988 campaign.

Particular Aspects of Political Engagement

Why should differences in gender consciousness discriminate among women's political engagement? From all that we have considered to this point, it is clear that gender consciousness provides internal psychological resources and external spurs to action. The historical instances of consciousness in the foregoing pages reveal two qualities in abundance: a using of gender, a translation of the meaning of being a woman into a source of interior strength; following this inner revolution of meaning, a looking outward occurs, a desire of engaging with the world emerges, a "women's point of view" is made manifest. The progression of consciousness I outlined in the first chapters, from internal recognition to group identification to mobilization, is at work. Gender consciousness becomes a powerful antidote to gendered political socialization and structural constraints; it gives women the means to believe in their political competence, and the motivation to act.

Those two benisons of consciousness, psychological robustness and action, make themselves evident in the separate indicators of which the political engagement scale is composed. Given the general disengagement of Americans with politics, disappointingly few people do more than vote (or claim to do so) or express an identification with one of the two major political parties. But despite this general lack of involvement, gender consciousness affects women's engagement in two broad ways, as we see in Tables 5.2 and 5.3.

First, gender role ideology has an almost across-the-board influence: the egalitarian are nearly always more engaged than the ambivalent, who are in turn more involved with politics than the privatized. Second, gender identification has its own enhancing effect apart from the sweeping and expected influence of gender role ideology. And among the indicators for which these different effects are significant, we see the internal psychological strength and the readiness to act that we would expect gender consciousness to provide. Internal political efficacy and political interest, and the motivation to acquire political information, to try to influence others, to vote, and even to attend political meetings are all affected by gender consciousness. The exception to this pattern in the five election years is 1988, when political engagement is at its lowest ebb. In that year, even differences between men and women are insignificant, and as I have said, the privatized individualists are the most mobilized of all groups. While they are not especially more efficacious or active than other women, they are more interested and try more to influence others than the hypothesis would allow

TABLE 5.2   GENDER CONSCIOUSNESS AND PSYCHOLOGICAL RESOURCES, 1972–1988

	1972	1976	1980	1984	1988
% who are . . .					
A. Highly efficacious[a]					
Ind/P	7.1*	6.6*	2.6*	18.2*	17.1
ID/P	8.6	10.4	9.4	20.9	18.3
Ind/A	14.0	7.7	8.9	21.1	11.7
ID/A	12.6	14.8	1.7	15.5	20.6
Ind/E	13.5	13.7	14.4	25.5	16.7
ID/E	20.7	15.8	12.7	33.1	15.1
B. Very interested					
Ind/P	22.7*	34.3	21.8*	19.7	37.8
ID/P	25.0	26.5	21.7	29.4	25.0
Ind/A	23.1	31.3	21.8	22.2	20.8
ID/A	29.1	37.8	30.5	26.4	32.4
Ind/E	29.1	40.9	30.3	27.5	28.5
ID/E	38.4	36.2	30.5	28.9	23.6
C. Used magazines[b]					
Ind/P	6.2$^{.05}$	23.0*	14.1$^{.05}$	9.1*	9.8
ID/P	5.3	21.4	17.2	15.5	5.0
Ind/A	7.0	30.6	11.4	11.1	2.6
ID/A	14.6	26.7	16.9	11.5	5.9
Ind/E	6.9	29.0	19.6	17.0	7.8
ID/E	11.8	36.3	26.8	25.4	11.1
D. Were partisan[c]					
Ind/P	65.3	57.5	69.2	57.6	78.0
ID/P	71.7	56.0	75.0	73.6	78.3
Ind/A	65.0	57.0	70.9	65.6	70.1
ID/A	68.9	40.4	67.8	63.5	67.6
Ind/E	71.3	47.2	60.1	65.2	59.6
ID/E	62.7	50.7	66.0	69.2	67.4

SOURCE: American National Election Studies, 1972, 1976, 1980, 1984, 1988.
Note: Ind/P = individualist privatized; ID/P = identified privatized; Ind/A = individualist ambivalent; ID/A = identified ambivalent; Ind/E = individualist egalitarian; ID/E = identified egalitarian.
*Differences by analysis of variance greater than p < .01. Less but still significant differences are reported in the superscript.
[a]Proportion *disagreeing* that "voting is the only way" *and* "government is too complicated," except in 1984 and 1988, when "voting only way" was unavailable.
[b]Proportion who read at least "several" campaign articles in magazines.
[c]"Folded" to include only strong and weak identifiers with the major parties.

for or indeed than was true of their counterparts in earlier years. (The point of Smith [1989] about the "muddle" of media attention and interest in the campaign in the questions about following the campaign in newspapers or magazines is well taken, but here I am trying to establish not ideological sophistication but engagement. "Magazines" were chosen instead of newspapers because the two are highly multicollinear, with even more people saying they followed the campaign in newspapers than in magazines. In an already quite mild measurement of engagement, I chose to use the somewhat more rigorous item of the pair.) We can speculate that, in 1988, the long-term trend of disengagement was abetted by the unsavory, bitter conduct of the presidential campaign. While this seems to have further dampened most people's sense of political involvement, it mobilized the privatized individualists. Perhaps, in some less than straightforward fashion, they were expressing a sub rosa "group consciousness" of their own, rejecting the legitimacy of other groups'—including the "group" of women's—current high political profile.

Feelings of internal political efficacy and political interest, and the desire to acquire political information—which may be at least partly a consequence of the former qualities—are the casualties of gendered political socialization, as numerous socialization studies have documented. If politics is presented as a man's world, or engagement with it puts women at risk of being called "unfeminine," then women who are nonetheless engaged in and with a political system that does not seem to want to be engaged with *them* must erect a psychological fortress against the assaults of such socialization, at least until such time as the assaults cease. We see these processes at work from 1972 to 1984 in the tables: men, overall, are still more likely than women to evince efficacy, interest, and the pursuit of information about politics. What is even more clear, though, is the boost that gender role ideology and gender identification provides for women. In every case of significant differences among women but one, that of 1988, the egalitarian are more involved than their privatized sisters. And if we compare identified to individualist women in each category of role ideology in those same significant cases, we find that identified women are more involved than the individualists more than 60 percent of the time. Obviously, women who are both identified and egalitarian are best armed with motivations for their political involvement, but especially in the case of efficacy, a sense of gender identification helps obviate the effects of a privatized role ideology. The anomaly of 1988 is probably just that.

Attempting to influence the votes of others and attending political meetings are even bolder acts: they not only require internal psychological fortitude but the hardiness to risk confrontation with others—something that has long been portrayed as "unfeminine"—as well as a commitment of time and energy. Rapoport (1981) found that among adolescents in the early 1970s, girls were likely to express fewer political attitudes than boys, but girls' attitudes were more coherently structured. Evidence of psychological hardiness emerges from the finding that girls who *did* have more political attitudes were more likely to try to persuade others. Boys' attempts to influence others were not obviously associated with the number of attitudes they held themselves. I would argue that this is a classic result of gender role socialization. While boys are encouraged toward leadership of and influence over others, girls are taught to respond, rather than initiate, in their interactions with people. Women even learn that a tentative

TABLE 5.3   GENDER CONSCIOUSNESS AND PARTICIPATORY ACTS, 1972–1988

	1972	1976	1980	1984	1988
% who . . .					
A. Voted for president					
Ind/P	52.9*	59.4.05	55.1	68.2*	69.5
ID/P	65.1	70.2	64.1	73.6	71.1
Ind/A	69.2	60.0	57.0	60.0	64.9
ID/A	76.7	72.2	67.8	66.9	73.5
Ind/E	68.9	65.8	68.6	70.9	64.4
ID/E	76.4	71.0	59.5	75.6	71.9
B. Influenced others					
Ind/P	24.9.05	32.1	34.6	27.3*	24.4
ID/P	22.4	29.1	34.4	26.4	18.3
Ind/A	29.4	25.5	24.1	21.1	18.2
ID/A	26.2	35.9	28.8	26.4	24.1
Ind/E	29.1	40.2	32.0	34.8	27.9
ID/E	36.9	35.1	38.9	37.3	28.9
C. Used button/sticker					
Ind/P	9.3	5.7	5.1	6.1	12.2
ID/P	9.2	4.9	3.1	8.2	5.0
Ind/A	9.8	8.1	3.8	6.7	6.5
ID/A	14.6	10.7	1.7	10.1	2.9
Ind/E	18.3	7.5	7.2	7.8	9.3
ID/E	20.3	10.2	9.5	9.4	9.8
D. Attended meeting/rally					
Ind/P	4.4.05	5.0.05	5.1	1.5*	1.2
ID/P	5.3	3.9	4.7	4.5	1.7
Ind/A	7.7	5.1	5.1	0.0	9.1
ID/A	7.8	12.6	1.7	6.8	4.4
Ind/E	9.7	5.7	9.2	5.7	5.9
ID/E	12.9	8.4	9.5	10.3	7.4
E. Worked in campaign					
Ind/P	4.9.05	2.5	2.6	1.5	4.9
ID/P	2.0	3.2	3.1	2.7	0.0
Ind/A	3.5	4.3	3.8	3.3	2.6
ID/A	5.8	10.0	0.0	2.7	4.4
Ind/E	6.9	5.2	3.9	2.8	3.7
ID/E	9.2	4.5	5.9	4.0	3.7

SOURCE: American National Election Studies, 1972, 1976, 1980, 1984, 1988.

Note: Ind/P = individualist privatized; ID/P = identified privatized; Ind/A = individualist ambivalent; ID/A = identified ambivalent; Ind/E = individualist egalitarian; ID/E = identified egalitarian.

*Differences from contingency tables significant at p < .01. Less but still significant differences reported in superscript.

verbal style elicits more response from men than does an assertive style (a nuance complicated by the fact that *women* prefer other women to be direct; see Carli, 1990). But strong feelings about something can impel women out of a passive role, as we may be seeing, contrary to our expectations, among the 1988 privatized individualists. Gender conscious women, in contrast, appear to be unusually discouraged by politics.

In this study, too, men are significantly more likely than women to say that they have tried to influence the vote choices of others, although they are not generally more likely to attend political meetings—perhaps because, as we have seen, women have always gathered together for the community's good. Identified egalitarian women are rather more likely than other women to try to influence people's votes, but identification has its own separate effect on attending political meetings and on voting. Too few women or men work in political campaigns for significant differences to emerge in this behavior by itself.

In many of these cases as Table 5.4 shows, we see that where there are systematic, significant differences *between* men and women, there are often (but not always) differences *among* women as well. Theoretical considerations would have led us to expect this, and the initial analyses gave us our first hint of it. When socialization and structural factors depress women's overall levels of politicization, we would expect to see gender consciousness differentiating women from one another. When the overall level rises, a new norm is being established, and we would expect most people to adjust their behavior accordingly. Observe such norm-setting taking place in reported voting behavior: in 1972, 72.3 percent of men said they voted for president, significantly more than the 66.8 percent of women who said they did. Gender consciousness markedly distinguished among women at that time. In the subsequent decade, as women's actual and reported turnout rates began to surpass men's (Kenski, 1988), voting became less susceptible to distinctions by gender socialization, with the result, by the late 1980s, of a "new" norm that women, even privatized women, vote.

An exception to the general pattern is partisanship, the case where women are consistently more likely than men to seem politically engaged. Women have been strikingly more likely to claim attachment to a party (or, conversely, to eschew independence) since 1972. Except in 1976, two-thirds or more of women are partisans. Even in 1976, when only a bare majority of women identified with a political party, only 41.9 percent of men did. Claiming partisanship is even easier than voting, it has cognitive utility for people while making few explicit demands on them, and partisanship has been a prevalent norm of the political culture. Claiming partisanship and claiming to vote are the only aspects of political participation in which large numbers of the sample—male or female—are likely to be engaged. But because so many women are partisan, gender consciousness does not notably differentiate them. Why women have such a propensity to partisanship is quite another question; the answer may lie in nu-

TABLE 5.4 CORRELATIONS OF SEX, IDENTIFICATION, AND ROLE IDEOLOGY WITH COMPONENTS OF THE POLITICAL ENGAGEMENT SCALE, 1972–1988

	1972	1976	1980	1984	1988
A. Efficacy					
by sex	.121*	.126*	.123*	.135*	.154*
by identification	.068*	.111*	.026	.049	−.043
by egalitarianism	.149*	.124*	.168*	.142*	−.058
B. Interest					
by sex	.122*	.088	.064*	.089*	.070*
by identification	.078*	−.018	.030	.045	−.057
by egalitarianism	.101*	.055	.062	.036	−.057
C. Magazine use					
by sex	.043	.112*	.078*	.142*	.078*
by identification	.068	.042	.097*	.086	.029
by egalitarianism	.031	.102*	.117*	.142*	.036
D. Partianship					
by sex	−.071*	−.092*	−.080*	−.068*	−.089*
by identification	−.014	−.033	.025	.048	.011
by egalitarianism	−.003	−.032	−.069	.025	−.088*
E. Presidential vote					
by sex	.060*	.078*	.043*	−.005	.049
by identification	.103*	.094*	−.010	.066	−.102
by egalitarianism	.096*	.040	.021	.078*	−.139*
F. Influencing others					
by sex	.098*	.129*	.071*	.051*	.100
by identification	.032	.003	.065	.041	−.024
by egalitarianism	.081*	.060	.065	.119*	−.013
G. Attending meetings/rallies					
by sex	.029	−.023	.018	.045	.056
by identification	.040	.055	.012	.101*	−.020
by egalitarianism	.095*	.020	.094*	.103*	.023
H. Using button/sticker					
by sex	−.002	−.022	.011	.037	.016
by identification	.036	.039	.029	.037	−.052
by egalitarianism	.128*	.040	.096*	.013	.005
I. Working in campaign					
by sex	−.035	−.002	−.025	.056*	.001
by identification	.021	.027	.028	.021	.030
by egalitarianism	.085*	−.004	.066	.029	−.011

SOURCE: American National Election Studies, 1972, 1976, 1980, 1984, 1988.
Note: Entries are Pearson's product-moment correlations; those followed by * are significant at $p <$ .01. Independent variables are dummied; for sex, male = 1; for identification, identified = 1; for egalitarianism, egalitarian = 1.

merous studies of party elites that show women's partisanship to be an extension of their "community housekeeping" roles (see, for example, Fowlkes, Perkins, and Tolleson Rinehart [1979]; Sapiro and Farah [1980]; Jennings and Farah [1981]).

A different exception is the case of attendance at political meetings and rallies. Unlike the relative ease with which we can claim partisanship, this is "hard": the time and effort required to attend such events would only be invested by the truly politically engaged. And unlike the usual trend of our findings, this is a case where differences between men and women are minuscule, but women's behavior is nonetheless affected by their role ideology in 1972, 1980, and 1984 and, in 1984, their gender identification. We can speculate that the motivating force of egalitarianism and the group orientation of identification sends women into political gatherings, to cheer or to protest.

In the case of political efficacy, where men seem to maintain a daunting advantage, egalitarian role ideologies genuinely benefit women, as identification also did in the 1970s. Both gender ideology and gender identification succored women's political interest in 1972, but as men's advantage over women begins to shrink in the 1980s, the effect of gender consciousness on women's interest is correspondingly muted. We have already noted a similar pattern for voting. By 1984, egalitarianism remains influential, as it does among women's attempts to influence others. Identification, however, has become less powerful a discriminator, except in the act of voting in 1988, when the privatized individualists make their unusual degree of mobilization felt.

One vital point must be made here. "Men" are not the group against which women should be measured, and men's participation does not set an ideal standard of participation to be held up for women. Early studies of women's participation, bent on filling the gaps in our knowledge, were sometimes interpreted this way. My inclusion of men in the tables, however, should not be construed in this fashion. It is true, for example, that women seem to be less politically efficacious than men, and most of us today would call that a shame. We know why this could occur, and we also understand how gender consciousness could remedy it. But we should not assume that women's goal is to become *as* efficacious as men; rather, we should ask whether women are becoming *more* efficacious. As we answer that question, men's levels of efficacy are sources of comparison for us, not some sort of sine qua non of political confidence.

We can also see that the entire picture of the relationship of gender consciousness and women's political engagement is by no means clear. It is complicated by the fact that identification and egalitarianism complement each other, while identification and privatization may be in conflict. As we recall from historical examples, identification and privatization are likely to combine as a source of mobilization into the public arena only when privatized women see a threat to *their* conception of all women's ability to fulfill their traditional roles, and under those circumstances, they may be mobilized into conflict with other women (Koonz, 1976). They may also experience some tension between their traditional values and their success as political actors, as several of the women studied by Klatch (1987) recognized. But overall, notwithstanding some surprises in 1988, we see what we would expect to see: if women require special resources to overcome the lack of welcome they may find as they try to become political, gender consciousness can provide them. Gender identification and gender role ideology furnish these means by providing an intrinsic belief system: I can and should participate; and a sense of extrinsic support: I do this with and for others like me.

The Shape of One's World and the Articulation of One's Political Self

In the first part of this chapter, we could indulge in the luxury of setting the scene. From history, political philosophy, and fiction, we could draw out the richness, or bleakness, of *place*, of the location of women's lives. This color and texture combined to reveal the patterns of women's private and public lives. Quantitative research rarely affords such luxury, but it too conveys meaning through studies of structural or socialization explanations of women's politicization. Too often, structure and socialization have been pitted as opposing sources of meaning. This is unfortunate when, in reality, they ceaselessly interact with each other. "Structure," including obvious demographic factors like race or economic class, but also including more subtle contexts like the absorbing responsibilities of parenthood or employment, influences the nature and number of cues on which we draw in adolescent and adult socialization to politics. Political socialization is a process of selective perception that, although it is shaped by environment, can also stimulate an individual to reinterpret her environment, perhaps in the process shaping it as much or more than it has shaped her. To put it another way, how could any woman ever have participated in politics if the structural barriers against her had been invincible? The Anglo-American suffrage movement breached the single most formidable barrier to women's formal membership in the political community, but every woman who then passed through the breach by going to the polls widened it until, seven decades later, not a pebble of the barrier—of *formal* participation, at least—remains. Thus women who, against all the odds, somehow developed extraordinarily vital political selves, managed to change the structure for succeeding women, who in turn have contributed to further change.

Although the meaningfulness, or effectiveness, of voting can be seriously questioned, the suffrage is the foundation stone on which all other formal political participation rests. As Randall (1987: 51) puts it, "The suffragettes, however mistakenly, perceived the vote not simply as a symbol of political emancipation but as a means to effective political participation. In Britain and the United States they endured severe privations to gain it. Women still do not everywhere possess the same formal voting rights as men," and women's historic underrepresentation as participants has been almost breathtakingly cross-cultural. It seems clear that this is a result of the chicken-and-egg/socialization-structure dilemma found in system after system (Christy, 1985; Jennings, 1983).

On the brighter side, gaps between the sexes' participation have shrunk dramatically in the last quarter century. In two generations, American women have gone from virtually total disenfranchisement to holding 14 percent of all elective offices in the United States. Fourteen percent, though, could also be seen as quite a low number. Women continue to face frustrating obstacles in their quest for political leadership and, as we have seen, are far from being fully politically engaged even at less lofty levels. Here, despite some real shifts in gendered political socialization, we detect still significant structural ramparts, especially when they reinforce traditional gendered divisions of labor. Most of the attention to these interactions of structure and socialization has been paid to employment, childrearing, and education.

Andersen (1975) showed that, from 1952 to 1972, women working outside the home participated more than homemakers and more than most men. Gurin (1986: 170) has elucidated the meaning of that distinction: "The political arena," she says, "is alien in many ways to the demands, values, and relationships that prevail in the private sphere. In this way, the adult experience of the truly cloistered homemaker [who is neither employed nor involved in community or volunteer activities] reinforces the values and expectations of childhood socialization that politics is a man's world." She concluded that employed women were more politically conscious and electorally active because they possessed more resources for political life—but she also found that "nontraditional" homemakers, those involved in professional, civic, community, or political associations, resembled employed women more than they did their cloistered sisters.

The presence of young children in the home and the concomitant childrearing responsibilities that continue to fall disproportionately on women have also been posited as limiting factors on women's participation. Although women are the bearers and transmitters of the political culture, playing vital roles in the political socialization of their children (Jennings and Niemi, 1968; Niemi, 1974), the daily demands of motherhood can squeeze politics out of a busy life (Stanley, 1985; Sapiro, 1983). On the other hand, some studies have not found that childrearing depresses political participation (Welch, 1977), and others have found that motherhood and its attendant concerns, such as education, health, or child welfare, can stimulate political activity (Jennings, 1979; Luttrell, 1988; Lynn and Flora, 1977).

Duverger (1955) called education the single most important factor affecting women's political participation, and if it is not the most important, its importance can hardly be overestimated (Jennings and Niemi, 1981; Sapiro, 1983). "Education" as a measurable concept also represents a vital interaction of socialization and structural considerations. Higher education, in particular, almost functions as a surrogate for socioeconomic status, since college education is so strongly associated with higher income in the United States. Education is also a powerful socialization context; more years in school not only means more opportunities to acquire knowledge about politics, but more implicit and explicit encouragement of participation. Its influence on political attitudes can be astonishingly durable: even decades after one has departed the campus, the attitudes one formed there persist (Newcomb et al., 1967).

Education is especially critical for women in times or places of limited political opportunities, as Duverger's postwar comparative analysis showed. And efforts to broaden the scope of educational opportunities for women seem to occur simultaneously with efforts to improve women's political status, no doubt because women see that one is very difficult to achieve without the other. One has but to think of the Anglo-American suffrage and "university degrees for women" movements in the second wave of feminism or the drive to integrate sex-segregated universities early in feminism's third wave.

Until very recently, women were markedly underrepresented among the college-educated, but the total population of American college and university students now includes a proportionate or even overrepresentative number of women, as we saw in Table 3.7. This means that education is no longer the rare resource of the few and that differences solely attributable to education among women, as well as between women and men, should eventually diminish. Education's influence on politicization will not concomitantly decline, however; rather, it is simply a context to which more and more women (and men) will be exposed. The campus is not a perfect haven for women. There is sexism and even sexual violence in the academy. With few exceptions, much generational replacement will be required before women are as likely to be the professors as they now are to be the students. But more years in school are still a real political luxury, a genuine wealth of stimuli, information, and opportunities. This is potentially true for everyone, but for women, especially, there are few environments so overtly supportive of women's individual development, and this extends to the development of gender consciousness, as we see in Table 5.5

The relationship of education to political engagement is consistently very strong for women, as it is for the whole sample. When the effects of education are held constant, men remain more politically engaged than are women, affirming an intuitive suspicion that lingering educational differences alone do not fully explain differences between the sexes in so thoroughly a gendered a culture. But the relationship between education and the components of gender consciousness is strong enough that when educational differences among women are held constant, the bivariate associations among gender identification, gender role ideol-

TABLE 5.5   CORRELATIONS OF SEX, GENDER IDENTIFICATION, AND GENDER ROLE IDEOLOGY WITH POLITICAL ENGAGEMENT, 1972–1988

	1972	1976	1980	1984	1988
A. Education × political engagement					
all	.379*	.378*	.345*	.337*	.333*
women only	.374*	.366*	.313*	.363*	.347*
B. Identification × education	.121*	.181*	.148*	.170*	.089*
C. Egalitarianism × education	.213*	.272*	.246*	.273*	.122*
D. Sex × political engagement (controlled for	.106*	.115*	.089*	.099*	.094*
education)	.091*	.097*	.080	.092*	.075*
E. Identification × engagement (controlled for	.100*	.074*	.069*	.109*	− .069*
education)	.059	.009	.024	.052	− .107*
F. Egalitarianism × engagement (controlled for	.176*	.103*	.145*	.159*	− .089*
education)	.106*	.004	.075	.067	− .141*

SOURCE: American National Election Studies, 1972, 1976, 1980, 1984, 1988.
Note: Entries are Pearson's product-moment correlations. Entries followed by * are significant at p < .01.

ogy, and political engagement are weakened. This is true in an unusual converse way even in 1988, when controls on education actually strengthen the difference between those mobilized privatized individualists and other women. (This odd relationship in 1988 aside, very similar patterns occur in a separate analysis of nonwhite women, but the tiny Ns of cases mean that they rarely achieve statistical significance.) We should not conclude from this that gender consciousness is a mere artifact of education, however. A more appropriate conclusion would locate higher education as one of the best and most widely available contexts in which the seeds of gender consciousness can germinate. In this way, gender consciousness is like the kind of political awareness that the environment of higher education fosters generally, as it has always been thought to do for men.

Homemaking versus work outside the home, and the constraints of parenthood, are the two structural factors most frequently thought to depress women's politicization. If we add employment and children to education as covariates in an analysis of the variance in political engagement, these relationships are elaborated (Table 5.6). Of the structural and socialization factors, education is overwhelmingly important; the presence of small children is significant in 1976, 1984, and 1988; and employment has influence only in 1972. In other words,

TABLE 5.6   GENDER CONSCIOUSNESS, SOCIALIZATION, AND STRUCTURAL FACTORS, 1972–1988

	1972	1976	1980	1984	1988
Effects of covariates					
employment	3.767*	.014	.068	.006	2.106
children at home	.419	19.811**	1.751	19.696**	4.167*
education	199.974**	208.401**	68.133**	152.993**	50.374**
Main effects					
gender conscious-					
ness	4.844**	.375	.823	2.507*	2.579*
Effects of covariates					
employment	3.755*	.014	.069	.006	1.265
children at home	.418	19.829**	1.754	19.676**	3.780
education	199.323**	208.584**	68.281**	152.841**	61.492**
Main effects					
identification	4.680**	.003	.215	2.487	1.955
egalitarianism	12.708**	.135	1.329	6.202**	4.081*

SOURCE: American National Election Studies, 1972, 1976, 1980, 1984, 1988.
Note: Entries are F values from analysis of variance. Entries followed by * are significant at $p < .05$; those followed by ** are significant at $p < .01$. Two-way interactions between identification and egalitarianism are insignificant in all years.

both structure and socialization are important, and education is probably the clearest way to see the interaction between the two.

But these leading indicators of structure and socialization are hardly the sole direct determinants of women's political engagement. As I had hypothesized, they are vital contexts within which politicization develops. Gender consciousness is the form of much of women's politicization, and it can be seen apart from structural and socialization considerations. In the table, engagement is strongly reflected in our measure of consciousness in 1972 and 1984 (but not in the intervening years); it is not as strong but still significant in 1988. If we know the degree and direction of a woman's consciousness, then, we can say that we know something about her level of political engagement. We can also see that both the components of consciousness, egalitarian role ideology and gender identification, reveal themselves. This imperfect tool of survey research is also saying what women, throughout history, have said more clearly and in their own words.

POLITICAL WOMAN

Sporting analogies, even more than the analogies of war, litter contemporary political discourse. From describing campaigns as "horse races" to calling a clever policy initiative an "end run," what politics and athletics have in common, aside from obvious commonalities like competition, conflict, "teamwork" and strategy, is a more subtle, clubby atmosphere of masculinity. Women who have wished to be athletes or fans have quickly found that it is hard to enter the club. The athlete has until quite recently found few facilities or means of support, and the spectator finds herself overlooked or greeted with an astonished stare. Neither is thought to be as good at doing or at appreciating what is done as are men. Except for the admiring role of cheerleader, the other roles women might take have only recently been granted a space. With hundreds of thousands of small American girls now playing soccer, basketball and other sports, women's athletic prospects have improved markedly. This is good not only for talented women athletes, but for all women who can improve their physical well-being, athletic star or not. Privatization was not only psychologically but literally physically confining. But the improvement did not come about without the struggle of hardy, often lonely pioneer sportswomen.

So it has been with politics. Political involvement has been treated as a uniquely male preserve, throughout history and in almost all the world's cultures. That is no longer so in most of the West. Although decades more will have to pass before women achieve something like parity in officeholding, the foundation of mass activity on which the parity will rest is already being constructed, and gender consciousness has supplied the mortar.

There is much to be said for the simple liberal argument that women's participation is a worthy goal in itself. Recently, liberalism's unfashionableness has meant that too little attention has been paid to the justice and benefit of equal political participation. These liberal goals have been abandoned by many before they have been fulfilled. At the mass, and certainly at the elite, levels, women do not yet occupy the secure place that pure arguments of democratic representation would grant them. But to what ends will women's political activity be put? We are beckoned once again to the question of how and why women's ideological dispositions and policy preferences may differ from men's. This is the next chapter's task.

Chapter 6 ———————————————————————————————

GENDER CONSCIOUSNESS AND
POLICY PREFERENCES

> There was a side of Sloan, [Priss] had decided, that she mistrusted, a side that
> could be summed up by saying that he was a Republican. Up to now this had not
> mattered: most men she knew were Republicans—it was almost part of being a
> man. But she did not like the thought of a Republican controlling the destiny of a
> helpless baby.
>
> Mary McCarthy, *The Group* ([1954] 1980: 258)

What do women want? This question, no matter its importance to men who
purport to be puzzled by the women they can't live with and can't live without,
has only recently been asked with seriousness about women's political beliefs.
Before that, except when forced to consider demands for women's political representation, political elites and scholars assumed that it doesn't much matter
what women want: women were either too uninterested in the business of the
polis or too ignorant about it to merit a concern for their opinions. In either case,
even if women voted and otherwise undertook civic responsibilities, they would
only reflect the preferences of the men in their lives, voicing the opinions of
fathers and husbands (see Campbell, Converse, Miller, and Stokes, 1960; and
Converse, 1964, to which we shall return). The scholarly mind thought it safe
to draw interpretations about women's political behavior that, if used to explain
men's behavior, would be called ecological fallacies. Butler and Stokes (1969),
for example, "explained" British women's partisanship by saying that women
more frequently attended church, and religiosity makes one more conservative;
ergo, women were more conservative. No actual analysis of women's beliefs and

behavior is necessary in the face of such elegant logic (for a penetrating early critique of political science's curious relaxation of scholarly rigor when it came to women, see Bourque and Grossholtz, 1974). But even in Mary McCarthy's trenchant novel, written in the 1950s about the same 1930s milieu that engendered Eleanor Roosevelt's feminism, some women voiced quite different assumptions about women's political roles. Though the somewhat befuddled Priss is often drawn with sly humor in *The Group,* McCarthy does not belittle her sincere political engagement. And Priss's sentiments, in this fictionalized account of the 1930s, foreshadowed the genuine "gender gap" in American politics of the 1980s and 1990s.

The point here is not to quarrel with findings of British women's greater preference for the Conservative than the Labour party in the Britain of the 1950s and 1960s, nor with other, similar findings. As Mary Wollstonecraft said of Rousseau, "But peace to his ashes! I war not with the man, but" with unscrutinized assumptions about women. The resulting legacy of ignorance obscured the true dimensions of women's historical political engagement, as we have already seen. It left scholars unprepared for the reemergence of feminism and for the mass political changes that the new Women's Movement would stimulate. When the gender gap appeared on the electoral horizon in 1980, the heritage of scholarly neglect of women impaired our ability to understand—even to see—what might be one of the most important developments in mass electoral behavior in postwar America. After a decade of gender gaps in state and national campaigns and more than a decade of research on women and gender, one can still be surprised by the extent of the marginalization not just of women but of research about them. The research is there now, but it is not yet "mainstream." Voting-behavior scholars and journalists do not consult gender politics research for explanations of the gender gap, because "that's about women, and I'm doing a voting behavior study,"—and as a consequence, they are all too ready to leap to the wrong conclusion about what issues "caused" the gender gap (for a clear demonstration of such errors, see Mansbridge, 1985). Exasperated gender politics scholars can only sigh.

Nor do the difficulties end here. Among gender politics scholars, the "difference question" is unresolved. Are women, indeed, fundamentally different from men, more nurturant, less bellicose, more protective of the well-being of the commonwealth, more concerned for the environment? How large is the difference, and if it is not natural (something we cannot ascertain with perfect certitude), is the conventional gender role socialization that produces it so uniform and pervasive that it can overwhelm the many differences among women? Why should it be more obvious now, after a quarter century of liberal egalitarian attempts to remove many of the differences between women and men, than it was in that decade of epic privatization, the 1950s? Does the dismantling of barriers to women's participation free them to voice preferences they have previously suppressed? Or is "maternal thinking" merely our fin de siècle fashion?

The historical record directs us to answer this last question with a qualified no. Gender role socialization is unquestionably profound and is strikingly similar from culture to culture. In these pages I have used the illuminating work of women's historians, feminist philosophers, and even fiction and literary criticism to show that something like contemporary gender consciousness can be found, at least in the European and American traditions, for centuries. Gender consciousness, once it is awakened, transcends many of the otherwise large racial, economic, and class differences that characterize women in a polyglot society. But it must be awakened; it is not awake in some women, and is not awake in the same way in others. Sisterhood is indubitably powerful, but feminists can be as unkind to other women as nonfeminist women can be, and ideological beliefs are not universally shared among all "feminists," as diverse as that group is, let alone all women. If we use only a few of the rare women who have led their states as examples, we see that a Prime Minister Gro Hartland Bruntland of Norway may be applauded as a model of the new political woman, but the phenomena of Prime Ministers Margaret Thatcher of Britain and Edith Cresson of France are more difficult to explain, and Presidents Violeta Chamorro of Nicaragua and Cory Aquino of the Phillipines are more reflective of the old pattern of the widow succeeding to her husband's ambitions rather than to her own.

Surely the answer to women's privatization in the 1950s *is* the Women's Movement of the 1960s. The stultifying cultural impositions women endured, particularly following the relaxation of gendered strictures in the 1930s and 1940s, finally produced a reaction, at first among women with the resources to enable them to raise a challenge. Levine (1987: 133) shows how a similar reaction helped to characterize British Victorian feminism: "The very notion of justice, they felt, had been perverted [by outrages like the Ripper murders and marital violence]; a recourse to moral superiority was an obvious and logical position, more especially given the role ordained them by [Victorian] ideology. Feminists took hold of the position to which they were limited by Victorian ideology and inverted its precepts, turning the duties of moral guardianship into a crusade." American feminism in the last two decades also has seemed like a crusade. In turn, the contemporary antifeminist backlash can be taken as a measure of just how large feminism's challenge to vested interests has become (Chafetz and Dworkin, 1987).

But while these cycles of debate over women's roles may explain women's politicization directed toward explicit questions of women's political rights, it does not yet answer questions about women's political attitudes generally and the degree of their departure from the generality of political attitudes held by man. As Conover (1988b) pointed out, relatively little attention has been paid to gender gaps in public opinion, compared to gaps in turnout or candidate preference, and "the research that has been done has concentrated on documenting the existence of this gap rather than on explaining it" (p. 986). Conover concluded that the gender gap in political values could not be attributed to women's sex but could be attributed to women's *identity*—in this case, as feminists. Taking the broader perspective once again, we can argue that feminism is itself a particularly politicized manifestation of gender consciousness. Just as we have seen that gender consciousness motivates political engagement, we can show that it also structures numerous general political beliefs.

This is a less than easy task because, particularly in the American case, it is difficult to demonstrate that *any* organized cognitive structure shapes citizens' beliefs. Very few Americans are avid participants in politics, as we know, and underlying this disinclination to participate are correspondingly low levels of political interest, knowledge, and sophistication. Despite an enormous cottage industry bent on explaining American political "ideology," few can agree even on what it is, whether it exists, and if so, how it is to be identified.

Once again, though, scholars fall prey to a curious lapse in rigor when it comes to examining the beliefs of the female portion of the public. The debate continues to rage over whether American ideological "sophistication" exists, and who, if it does, is sophisticated. But all controversy seems to subside in the general agreement that, whatever it is, and no matter how few men seem to possess it, women have less of it—if, indeed, questions of differences between the sexes are addressed at all.

We thus have two opportunities. The first is the opportunity to assess women's policy preferences in a variety of domains, not merely by using sex as the independent variable, as has already been done (see, for example, Frankovic, 1982; Baxter and Lansing, 1983; Poole and Zeigler, 1985; Shapiro and Majahan, 1986), but by exploring how consciousness of gender shapes political views. Our question is not simply whether gender consciousness and feminist orientations are associated: that question has already been explored. While it is certainly important to them, the role of gender consciousness in shaping women's beliefs about their political roles is primarily foundational, or motivational. By undergirding women's belief in their right, or responsibility, to participate, gender consciousness accomplishes its first task. Its next, according to our theoretical perspective, is the direction of that participation to certain ends. In other words, we would ask not only whether gender consciousness stimulates political engagement, as we have already seen that it does, or whether it stimulates a correspondence between attitudes and behavior, as we shall see that it does when we observe that there is a stronger correlation between the political engagement and policy preferences of gender conscious women than is true for women without such consciousness. Conceptually speaking, though, something lies in between the motivation to participate and the political attitudes in behalf of which participation is supposed to take place. The medial, connecting concept is the organization or structure of the attitudes themselves. Students of political behavior have assumed, and political philosophers have hoped, that attitudes are not randomly held, that our beliefs are meaningfully bound to one another and not just chaotically bundled into our heads.

I am suggesting, in short, that gender consciousness directs and constrains policy preferences. In that assertion lies our second opportunity, that of assessing gender consciousness as such an organizing device. In particular, we can make a simple test of the competitiveness of gender consciousness's components against the most studied source of supposed attitudinal constraint, the liberal/conservative ideological spectrum. Before we proceed to the test, however, we need to enter the thickets of ideological sophistication and the levels of conceptualization about politics.

IDEOLOGY: SOPHISTICATION, NAIVETÉ, OR INDIFFERENCE?

A century and a half ago, Alexis de Tocqueville presciently limned American democracy for a curious European audience. But while his analysis of the young society retains an ability to predict aspects or outcomes of our mass behavior even to this day, a satisfyingly complete explanation of the inner political life of those individuals who constitute the mass remains a maddeningly elusive quarry. We know some things: we know that, because politics is not, except in times of perceived "crisis," seen by most people to be relevant to their day-to-day lives, politics is not something many Americans care passionately about, unless they are passionately disgusted with the whole business. What is not relevant is not interesting and is not worth the investment of time, energy, money, and thought that informed participation would require. We know that civic education is shallow and that political socialization is superficial for most citizens most of the time.

Recently, this state of affairs has been manifested in decreased levels of voter turnout and in the apparent weight of candidate affect and short-term economic forces in the decisions of those who do vote. "Negative" campaigning has (perhaps justifiably) increased cynicism and hastened the demise of citizen efficacy, concomitantly weakening the citizenry's willingness to be the watchful overseers demanding accountability from an open system. Disinterest and a lack of vigilance maintain the space in which mountebanks and opportunists maneuver, perpetuating a belief that "politics" is a pejorative, something to be avoided. Who, struggling to find, say, affordable but excellent childcare, can be persuaded that sacrificing all her free time and money to political efforts on behalf of children is the way to find it? If she could be persuaded, and perceptions of group and self-interests do sometimes effect such transformations, what could she, alone, reasonably hope to achieve? Put this way, meaningful political participation does sound formidable. But let us simplify the proposition: let us assume not that our hardworking mother will become an activist, but merely that, when she votes, policies about childcare are high priorities in her decision-making. Would they have been so before her children were born? Will they be so after her children are grown? How are those policies connected to her other beliefs about other issues? *Are* they connected in some discernible way?

Scholars continue to wrestle with the problem of ideological constraint for good reason. Theories of democratic representation all require some kind of agreement on ends between the governed and the governing, even if the agreement is passive. The legitimacy of the state founders otherwise. The most participatory of democratic theories assumes that these linkages of beliefs and values are not only a matter of necessity to the structure of the political system, but of great developmental benefit to the individual citizen as well. Forming considered opinions about politics and acting on them are central activities in the growth of the whole person for thinkers as widely different in time and outlook as John Stuart Mill and Benjamin Barber. All this implies, as do general theories of human cognition, that attitudes are connected to one another, that an individual opinion does not exist in isolation from others. But how are we to measure the connections?

The three great bodies of theory about attitudinal connections have devolved on perceptions of self-interest (latterly most discussed in terms of economic self-interest), group identification, and ideology. Until recently, gender as a theoretical and analytical concept has received little welcome from these schools of thought. Public choice models of economic self-interest have not considered whether one's gender role orientation may contribute to different constructions of economic self-interest, and as I discussed at length in chapter three, the idea of women as a "group" with group consciousness was raised by gender politics scholars, without even now gaining much attention from political psychologists generally.

But the theoretical construct of ideological sophistication and constraint, in its character as the dominant paradigm of political behavior and public opinion, has had the greatest influence on our understanding (or misunderstanding) of gender and political attitudes. Two works, *The American Voter* (Campbell, Converse, Miller, and Stokes, 1960) and "The Nature of Belief Systems in Mass Publics" (Converse, 1964), had an extraordinary impact on political science by defining "belief systems" as "configurations of ideas and attitudes in which the elements are bound together by some form of constraint or functional interdependence" (Converse, 1964: 207). Having arrived at this deduction, Campbell, Converse, and their colleagues proceeded to the assumption that the source of constraint for belief systems was ideology, specifically a unidimensional, linear progression from conservative to liberal, as the concepts were employed in mid-century American politics.

Relying on data from the 1956 National Election Study, the *American Voter* scholars used their concept of ideological constraint to limn political behavior in ways that would profoundly influence subsequent generations of political scientists. They found very little of the constraint for which they searched, and even less of its concomitant, ideological sophistication, the term they gave to the ability to use and understand abstract ideological concepts. Because they chose to distinguish ideological sophistication from "group benefits" or "nature of the times" explanations for policy preferences, and deemed the latter two to be less constrained or sophisticated, they inadvertently or otherwise helped to doom progress in group consciousness research for some time. And their empirical analysis was primitive compared to the elegance of their reasoning. But no matter how deductive and on how thin an empirical thread their argument hung, it irresistibly affected a discipline and initiated decades' worth of argument about whether the American populace was more sophisticated than they had claimed, or was getting more sophisticated (Nie and Andersen, 1974), or was even more politically naive than Converse and Campbell had thought (Smith, 1989). Bennett (1977: 472) mournfully predicted that the endless and growing debates about ideological sophistication would cause the field to crumble under its own conceptual weight.

Smith (1989), after an astonishingly thorough investigation, makes it almost impossible to argue that American voters were or are more "sophisticated" than Converse and Campbell had first thought, and in fact Smith concludes with Bennett (1977) that we would do better to stop arguing about how much and instead argue about what ideological sophistication is. Others (Kinder, 1983; Conover and Feldman, 1981, 1984) have turned in other directions—to group consciousness and cognitive schemata—with considerable benefit. And so shall we have to as well, since one thing the *American Voter* scholars did to which almost nobody objected (for an exception, see Jennings and Farah, 1980) was to blithely assume that no matter how ideologically unsophisticated men were, women were ideological dodos. Converse put it this way in "Mass Belief Systems" (p. 233):

> Now there is one type of relationship in which there is overwhelming evidence for vigorous opinion-leading [of the more sophisticated by the less sophisticated] where politics is concerned in our society. It is the relationship within the family: The wife is very likely to follow her husband's opinions, however imperfectly she may have absorbed their justifications at a more complex level. We can do a fair job of splitting this relationship into its leader-follower components simply by subdividing our total sample by sex . . . our expectation that the presence or absence

of intervening belief systems is of reduced importance among sets of people who are predominantly opinion followers is well borne out by the relatively flat and disordered progression of bars [representing descending categories of sophistication] among women.

Of course, Converse could not do a "fair job" at all. Tests of the opinion leadership and followership of individual husband-wife pairs cannot be accomplished by dividing the sample into aggregate groups of men and women—this is a classic ecological fallacy, not to mention a whopping attribution of the flow of opinion causation, from husband to wife, for which his data simply cannot permit a test.

But I do not wish to argue that women were more sophisticated than men in the 1950s and that researchers just missed it or couldn't hear what women were saying (for such gendered communication breakdowns, see Carli, 1990). And I do not think that a female conspiracy to hide women's political sophistication from men was abroad in the land, even if Campbell and Converse overestimated the significance of the gap between men and women. Two genuine barriers to women's politicization loomed large in the 1950s: first, women had been propagandized *out* of traditional gender roles and *into* the war industry during World War II (and turned out heavily to vote in the 1944 presidential election), but were equally vigorously sent back to traditional roles after the war. Second, in this pop-Freudian wilderness of the 1950s, women's rates of higher education were to plummet to lows that had not been seen since the 1920s and were not to recover until the 1970s. Enforcement of traditional roles and less education both exacerbate apolitical orientations, and women may well have exhibited little ideological sophistication.

Neither did, or do, men: a claim of equality for women in this instance would not be much of a claim. The point is that the search for alternatives to ideological sophistication has provided a broader theoretical underpinning for gender consciousness as a source of constraint. We are freer now to consider what besides our external impositions of ideology might organize political beliefs. Carroll (1989: 315) offers this kind of different consideration: "The logic that seems to underlie these traditional differences in perspective [between men and women] is not a logic based on liberal/conservative ideology, but rather one based on sex differences in objective life circumstances and on the socialization of women and men to different roles . . . women's more marginal and vulnerable position in society may have led them to be more conservative than men in their voting choices and more opposed to social forces that might threaten the social fabric." Reasoning of this sort does more to help us understand women's shift from preferences for the Republican party in the 1950s to the Democratic party in the 1980s, for example (Kenski, 1988). We know now that ideological self-identification is not as bipolar and issue-oriented as it is simply symbolic (Conover and Feldman, 1981). We know that multidimensional cognitive structures, multiple schemas for organizing beliefs may be *more* sophisticated, rather than less (Conover and Feldman, 1984). We know that group identification, enduring values, personality, group identification, the historical context, and their modes of presentation all may affect the way we perceive issues (Kinder, 1983; Smith, 1989). No longer limited by a given paradigm, our thinking about women is liberated.

CONSCIOUSNESS AND POLICY

The gender gap in American politics may be singular—that is to say, unlikely to develop in the same way in Europe or elsewhere—in part because of American political fluidity (see Norris, 1988). The same looseness of political identity and political organization that leads to weak ideological constraint and weak political parties frees women to think of themselves as a "group." Gelb (1989: 2) attributes the relative success of the American Women's Movement to its ability to develop "independent strategies and political agendas of their own choosing," in contrast to the insistence on ideological purity of British feminists and their consequent subsumption in the Labour party. This independent Women's Movement, even when it failed to achieve goals like ratification of the Equal Rights Amendment, and even among women who would not call themselves feminists, helped to create an environment in which increasing numbers of women could mobilize both internal and external political resources from the early 1970s on (Costain, 1988).

Gelb notes that the existence of what she calls American "interest group feminism" means that women in elected office, though not terribly cohesive, could come to identify as "women" often as readily as they identify with the political parties. She and others (see the essays in Dodson, 1991) note that female elected officials are more liberal on the issues that have been thought to characterize the gender gap—consumerism, children, "compassion issues," peace—regardless of party affiliation. Republican congresswomen, for example, significantly differ in their behavior from Republican congressmen. These gender differences do not emerge in the British Parliament. Nor have we seen any British phenomenon that compares to the Congressional Caucus for Women's Issues, formerly the bipartisan Congresswomen's Caucus (Gertzog, 1984), because no large, vibrant movement independent of political parties has existed as a broad base from which female elites can emerge.

While, as Sapiro (1981: 712) notes, the "increased representation of people who 'look like women' will effect powerful symbolic changes in politics," American women's increasing politicization is not a matter of virtual representation alone. Surely most people would applaud the increase of women in elected office as a simple manifestation of justice, but as Gelb forces us to see in the British case, women in Parliament (few as they are) have not yet been distinctive advocates of a particular women's policy perspective. Rather, they have been partisans, as have their male counterparts. And as the title of Sapiro's essay reminds us, interests are not *interesting*, to political scientists or the political system, if they are not the reflection of a distinct point of view. Sapiro warns that she is not discussing women by using the concept of the "interest group" in the usual way, a way that "seems to require an organized group of people inter-acting through conventional political channels in opposition to other organized groups" (p. 703). On the contrary, she argued, women have been denied the means to achieve self-consciousness and identification, the very psychological cornerstones of groups in politics.

Sapiro speculated, a decade ago, that we could argue both that "women" as a group share unique statuses and problems and that "women" have a distinctive view of solutions to political problems. Not *all* women need partake of this group perspective, nor does the "women's" perspective have to be utterly differ-ent from the perspective of other groups. This does mean, however, that "women" becomes a group whose interests can be represented. And this is pre-cisely the work that consciousness does: consciousness, beyond stimulating women's beliefs about their own political roles, also reorganizes orientations toward other issues by motivating women to believe that they have unique per-spectives on public problems and can offer unique solutions. Gender conscious women, in short, are the women who create gender gaps.

The Choice of Policy Preferences for Analysis

The research on the gender gap generally concludes that women in the aggregate are increasingly liberal on the so-called compassion issues, including govern-ment intervention to secure people's welfare, and we have long seen evidence that women are generally more pacific than are men. Thus I have chosen six identical, or nearly identical, measures of policy preferences, a choice restricted by the contents of the survey and by comparability over time, to examine sepa-rately and as a simple additive scale. The case of 1976 offers our only exception, since there is no measure in that year comparable to questions about Vietnam in 1972 or the Soviet Union in the 1980s; in 1976, then, the maximum score on the policy scale is 5, and in all other years it is 6. Because of its long tradition in the literature, ideology, measured according to respondents' self-placement on a seven-point liberal-conservative scale, is the construct I chose to oppose to consciousness as a source of explanation for policy preferences.

Five of the measures (four in 1976) were asked in forced choice form, and one, the most important problem facing the nation, was open-ended. All measures were coded in the direction of a more liberal response, since that is what research on the gender gap has led us to expect. The measures were collapsed into dummies of two categories, 1 (liberal response) and 0 (all other responses) for inclusion into the additive scale, but in separate analysis of the items their full range of responses was preserved. Policy preferences in the realm of domestic and economic policies are represented by two questions: whether the government should guarantee everyone a job and good standard of living or whether people should help themselves; and whether the government should help minorities or whether they should help themselves (seven-point scales). Candidate preference is represented by the presidential vote, coded in the direction of a vote for McGovern in 1972, Carter in 1976 and 1980, Mondale in 1984, and Dukakis in 1988; in each case, although with considerable variation and appeal, the Democrat and his platform was more responsible to "women's preferences" than were Nixon, Ford, Reagan, Bush, or their platforms.

"Women's preference" also became the driving force behind the coding of the open-ended, most important problem questions in each year. Using only my theoretical perspective and accumulated results from other gender gap research, I made an a priori division of the entire code of mentioned issues into 1 for "women's preference" and 0 for all other issues mentioned, and I did not revise the division after reviewing the resulting frequency distributions, other than checking for coding omissions. My reasoning was, I think, simple: if we think we know what women's policy preferences are, or should be, as a result of our research, then we ought to be confident enough to make such an a priori test of the distribution of open-ended responses. In the event, the measure is not a splendid discriminator, for reasons that are discussed below. (The Appendix contains all issue mentions and the directions in which they were coded.)

Opposition to war and more irenic orientations toward international affairs were captured by questions about whether defense spending should be cut or maintained (with dichotomous response choices in 1972 and 1976), or cut, maintained, or increased in the 1980s (to which respondents chose a point on a seven-point scale). In 1972, a question asked respondents whether we should withdraw from Vietnam; and in 1980, 1984, and 1988, respondents were asked whether we should "try harder to cooperate" with the Soviet Union. Each of these questions had seven-point scale response formats. No equivalent question was found in the 1976 survey.

Combined into an additive scale, these six items (five in 1976) touch on most of the dimensions of the gender gap as we have seen it discussed. A preliminary glimpse of the distribution of the scales among the whole samples in each year, and corresponding coefficients of scalability, can be found in Table 6.1a. Using either liberalism or gender consciousness as the criterion for constraint, we nonetheless see that comparatively few Americans take consistent positions across several issues, although we withhold any further judgment at this point.

TABLE 6.1a   PERCENTAGE FREQUENCY DISTRIBUTIONS AND SCALABILITY OF POLICY SCALES, ALL RESPONDENTS, 1972–1988

	1972	1976	1980	1984	1988
Number of policy positions in "women's" direction					
0	28.0	34.0	29.6	22.7	22.9
1	25.0	32.3	34.4	26.9	28.7
2	19.1	20.6	17.5	21.5	23.8
3	15.2	8.9	10.5	13.4	14.2
4	7.2	3.3	5.5	9.5	7.2
5	5.6	1.0	2.1	4.9	2.8
6	0.0	—	0.4	1.0	0.4
Chronbach's alpha	.634	.412	.495	.532	.436

SOURCE: American National Election Studies, 1972, 1976, 1980, 1984, 1988.

As we have assumed, and as Conover has also concluded, simple divisions of the citizenry by sex cannot adequately explain gender gaps (but Shapiro and Majahan [1986] and Klein [1984] both note that, even when distributions of issue positions are roughly equal across the sexes, this does not address possible differences in the salience of issues). Table 6.1b shows that sex alone discriminates among people only in 1984. But gender consciousness shows who, among women, make gender gaps, as we see in both the table and in Figure 6.1. Individualist privatized women are very much less likely to take "women's positions" than are men, and this can be said, to a lesser extent, for the privatized identified women as well as women who are ambivalent individualists. Gender gaps are created most especially by identified egalitarian women. They are joined by egalitarian individualists and, as the 1980s wear on, by identified women regardless of gender role ideology. But the identified egalitarians were on the way to creating the gender gap in the 1970s, and as they became an increasingly large proportion of the population of all women, it is they who would make the difference in public opinion polls and voting booths which would be called the preferences of, simply, women.

We can also see that both of the two components of consciousness, gender identification and gender role ideology, are making a steady contribution. While egalitarianism is somewhat stronger as a discriminator, even our less-than-perfect measure of identification is significant. Additional analysis of the relationship between consciousness and policy preferences (not presented here) showed that controls for race and generation did not alter these patterns. Although the small number of cases of black and other women of color meant that relationships did not always achieve significance (nor can race consciousness itself be ignored as a factor), the patterns for white and nonwhite women were quite similar. The relationships were also quite similar for women of different generations: while we might have expected that gender conscious women in the baby boom generation would show the largest effects, this was seldom the case. Controls for education, introduced following assumptions that the most educated

TABLE 6.1b   MEAN SCORES ON POLICY SCALE FOR WHOLE SAMPLE, ALL MEN, ALL WOMEN, AND FOR CONSCIOUSNESS AND ITS COMPONENTS, 1972–1988

	1972	1976	1980	1984	1988
A. All respondents	1.65	1.31	1.36	1.79	1.64
B. By sex					
men	1.60	1.30	1.31	1.69*	1.59
women	1.68	1.32	1.40	1.90	1.68
C. By consciousness					
Ind/P	1.33*	1.17*	0.88*	1.38*	1.25*
ID/P	1.45	1.32	1.12	1.47	1.83
Ind/A	1.18	1.07	1.06	1.28	1.25
ID/A	1.22	1.16	1.23	1.73	1.59
Ind/E	1.96	1.22	1.36	1.96	1.84
ID/E	2.35	1.69	1.69	2.34	2.12
D. By components					
individualist	1.57.05	1.17*	1.17*	1.63*	1.60.09
identified	1.87	1.52	1.56	2.10	1.73
privatized	1.30*	1.19*	1.07*	1.51*	1.45*
egalitarian	2.16	1.55	1.58	2.25	1.75

SOURCE: American National Election Studies, 1972, 1976, 1980, 1984, 1988.

Note: Ind/P = individualist privatized; ID/P = identified privatized; Ind/A = individualist ambivalent; ID/A = identified ambivalent; Ind/E = individualist egalitarian; ID/E = identified egalitarian.

*$p < .01$ from analysis of variance. Less but still significant differences are reported in the superscripts.

Figure 6.1. Mean Scores on Policy Scale

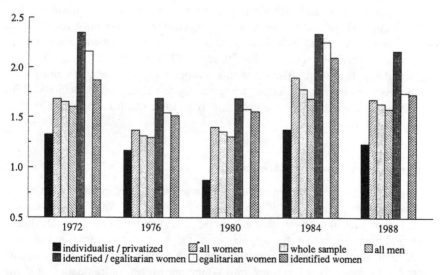

■ individualist / privatized   ▨ all women   ☐ whole sample   ▨ all men
■ identified / egalitarian women   ☐ egalitarian women   ▨ identified women

SOURCE: American National Election Studies, 1972 - 1988

citizens are also the most ideologically constrained, also failed to weaken the relationship between our measure of gender consciousness and the policy scale.

We can look at these relationships in another way, by considering not the mean score on the policy scale, but on how many issues positions are taken (Table 6.1c). Identified egalitarian women are by far the most likely group to take three or more of the "women's preferences" in all years. By 1984, identified women whether privatized or ambivalent were increasingly taking such preferences as well. Surely, whether by virtue of gender role ideology or gender identification—and most certainly via the interaction of the two—increasing numbers of women have come to believe that they have a distinctive perspective on public policy.

Ideology, or self-placement along a liberal-conservative spectrum, is associated with gender consciousness. But as Shapiro and Majahan (1986) noted, female gender role socialization may not comport neatly with externally determined, "pure" notions of liberalism or conservatism, since gender role socialization prompts women toward *both* conserving and compassionate orientations. For example, women may be apparently conservative on questions of drug abuse, pornography, crime, or federal budget deficits, and apparently liberal on questions of government regulation, social welfare, and aid to the helpless, all because gender role socialization directs women toward care and protection of others. This is Gilligan's "different voice," and the reason that Republican congresswomen behave differently than Republican congressmen. Gender consciousness, on the contrary, does not erect artificial barriers between conserving and compassionate orientations. Instead, it serves to organize them into one harmonious schema. This is why we see differences in Table 6.2 between egalitarian individualists and identified egalitarians, just as we see differences between identified and individualist but privatized women. We must recall, from earlier pages, that most Americans attach relatively insubstantial meanings to the terms "liberal" and "conservative," and the 1980s have seen "liberal" become a particularly dirty word. Thus it seems reasonable to assume that gender consciousness is as or more effective an organizing principle than is ideology. With this foundation established, we can turn to a closer examination of individual policy positions.

Differences in Policy Preferences

The idea that the government should guarantee that everyone has a job and a decent standard of living holds a paradoxical place in the American consciousness. It took root in the desperate economic crisis that led to the New Deal, and a job and home seem like the very center of the American Dream. On the other hand, the idea of government guaranteeing such things, as opposed to removing obstacles to them, runs headlong into American rugged individualism and the

TABLE 6.1c   HOW MANY POLICY POSITIONS ARE TAKEN? WOMEN ONLY, 1972–1988

	1972***	1976***	1980**	1984***	1988***
A. % who took none					
Ind/P	30.3	28.9	46.7	20.0	32.9
ID/P	34.5	24.6	28.2	29.5	13.3
Ind/A	40.0	33.2	44.4	33.8	32.5
ID/A	33.0	28.9	28.8	20.7	27.9
Ind/E	20.5	30.3	31.3	20.7	18.1
ID/E	17.7	21.6	20.7	15.3	12.2
B. % who took three or more					
Ind/P	19.1	11.6	11.7	11.1	17.1
ID/P	27.5	13.9	10.3	21.8	28.3
Ind/A	20.0	8.6	15.9	19.0	15.6
ID/A	16.7	11.9	15.4	27.6	22.1
Ind/E	37.6	13.4	19.8	31.0	20.8
ID/E	44.2	24.7	24.1	42.3	37.7

SOURCE: American National Election Studies, 1972, 1976, 1980, 1984, 1988.
Note: Ind/P = individualist privatized; ID/P = identified privatized; Ind/A = individualist ambivalent; ID/A = identified ambivalent; Ind/E = individualist egalitarian; ID/E = identified egalitarian.
***p < .01.
**p < .05.

TABLE 6.2   GENDER CONSCIOUSNESS AND IDEOLOGICAL SELF-IDENTIFICATION, 1972–1988

	1972***	1976***	1980***	1984***	1988***
A. % "liberal"					
Ind/P	10.1	11.9	7.9	22.5	7.6
ID/P	17.8	8.2	3.1	30.6	22.8
Ind/A	16.7	14.5	24.4	21.0	36.0
ID/A	13.5	16.6	12.5	28.4	45.1
Ind/E	33.5	22.5	24.0	34.2	20.4
ID/E	38.9	29.4	35.4	46.9	33.2
B. % "conservative"					
Ind/P	51.7	45.3	65.8	77.5	69.8
ID/P	41.1	56.5	49.0	65.9	57.2
Ind/A	39.4	47.2	46.6	63.1	10.0
ID/A	40.6	31.2	37.5	70.8	15.7
Ind/E	29.1	33.5	41.0	60.7	46.3
ID/E	29.6	25.1	31.1	51.0	30.4

SOURCE: American National Election Studies, 1972, 1976, 1980, 1984, 1988.
Note: Ind/P = individualist privatized; ID/P = identified privatized; Ind/A = individualist ambivalent; ID/A = identified ambivalent; Ind/E = individualist egalitarian; ID/E = identified egalitarian.
***p < .01.

Puritan work ethic, however imperfectly those things are understood and practiced. We wish to see ourselves as self-reliant, perhaps more so than in any political culture. So we are not surprised to find that a plurality, and an outright majority of the privatized individualists in the 1980s, prefers that people should help themselves. Similar inchoate feelings, perhaps tainted by racism among some women, or doubts that further government action would help, make for resistance to the idea that government should help minorities. Once again, pluralities reaching majorities of women, except for the identified egalitarians, said they thought minorities should help themselves through 1980. After that time, there was general movement toward the indecisive middle of the scale. For both questions, though, the more gender conscious a woman is, the more likely she is to seek government guarantees (Table 6.3).

It is difficult to imagine a presidential candidate making flagrant appeals to women, and certainly no major candidate did so in the five elections from 1972 to 1988. Especially since 1980, a recognition of the gender gap has necessitated recognition of women, but this has usually taken the form of placing women in visible positions at nominating conventions or espousing certain issues that women were thought to favor. While the Republican candidates of the period, with the possible exception of Gerald Ford in 1976, eschewed the appearance of support for women's rights, the Democratic candidates took pro-ERA, pro-choice, and pro–women's rights positions, but also—as with the cases of McGovern in 1972 and Carter in 1976 and 1980—angered women by appearing to renege on some of these positions. Dukakis in 1988 is widely thought to have suffered from a clinical, cold image that the conventional wisdom held to be especially offputting to women, but he nonetheless benefited from the "gender gap."

From Table 6.4 we find once again that gender conscious women appear to be responsible for the gender gaps in candidate preference. I must note that the coding of the variable opposes those who claim to have voted for the Democratic candidate to all others: those who claimed to have cast a Republican vote, as well as those who said that they did not vote, and the very small number of women who claimed to have voted for another candidate (usually less than 1 percent of the total except in 1980, when a slightly larger but still very small fraction of the sample cast a vote for Anderson). My purpose here was to search for affirmative statements of policy orientations and candidate evaluation; for this purpose, *not* voting is not "missing data" but is, rather, meaningfully different from voting *for* the Democratic nominee. While this measure does not reveal why a woman did not vote, it shows that she did not vote in the direction that gender gap research would predict. To take 1988 as an example, among all women, 27.6 percent claimed to have voted for Dukakis, 31.0 percent voted for Bush, 0.7 percent said they voted for another candidate, and 39.9 percent said that they did not vote, a slightly lower proportion of nonvoters than was true

TABLE 6.3   THE INFLUENCE OF GENDER CONSCIOUSNESS ON DOMESTIC AND ECONOMIC POLICIES, 1972–1988

	1972	1976	1980	1984	1988
A % who say that govt. should guarantee jobs and standards of living					
Ind/P	33.9	24.4***	17.3**	24.5**	20.7
ID/P	34.5	23.1	25.6	32.6	23.3
Ind/A	26.7	15.2	27.2	26.3	18.2
ID/A	20.6	15.8	18.0	28.0	17.6
Ind/E	36.8	21.8	33.8	40.0	29.6
ID/E	37.2	29.1	37.8	38.8	26.3
B. % who say govt. should help minorities					
Ind/P	21.3***	27.1***	8.3***	25.6***	6.1**
ID/P	29.9	31.7	12.5	19.5	11.7
Ind/A	26.6	20.1	12.1	16.6	9.1
ID/A	22.9	21.4	11.5	18.8	11.8
Ind/E	40.7	36.8	20.6	36.8	15.6
ID/E	50.4	43.5	30.1	39.9	15.6

SOURCE: American National Election Studies, 1972, 1976, 1980, 1984, 1988.
Note: Ind/P = individualist privatized; ID/P = identified privatized; Ind/A = individualist ambivalent; ID/A = identified ambivalent; Ind/E = individualist egalitarian; ID/E = identified egalitarian.
***$p < .01$.
**$p < .05$.

among the men. This means, then, that women's contribution to the "gender gap" in the 1988 election, where male voters sharply preferred Bush and female voters divided almost perfectly between Dukakis and Bush, was actually caused by something less than a third of all women, and as we see in the table, those women were more likely to have been the identified egalitarians. This was also true in 1972 (before women's higher turnout rates and changing policy preferences had led to "gender gaps") and in 1984, the two other years when consciousness distinguishes women's voting behavior.

"Women's preferences" of issues they believe to be the most serious problems facing the nation, as I have already suggested, did not provide as clear a division as I had hoped. The "most important problem facing the nation today," alas, can almost be called a media creation. An open-ended question such as this is intended to free survey respondents of forced choice answers and allow them spontaneously to voice their beliefs about urgent political questions. Unfortunately, given general disengagement among the American citizenry, such beliefs appear to be driven by short-term predilections, especially as they are featured on the media's agendas. We become, as a culture, agitated about what are depicted as crises, some of them quite genuine but others more ephemeral. Our agitation does not subside, from election to election, as much as its focus changes. Given

TABLE 6.4 THE INFLUENCE OF GENDER CONSCIOUSNESS ON PRESIDENTIAL VOTE CHOICE AND "MOST IMPORTANT PROBLEMS," 1972–1988

	1972	1976	1980	1984	1988
A. % claiming to have voted for the Democratic presidential candidate					
Ind/P	30.3***	56.6	32.6***	33.3***	33.3***
ID/P	39.4	58.5	43.9	38.3	22.0
Ind/A	32.3	56.0	35.6	22.2	24.7
ID/A	25.3	49.2	55.0	41.4	41.2
Ind/E	41.7	44.1	44.8	41.0	29.3
ID/E	45.4	52.3	52.2	52.8	38.2
B. % choosing "women's preference" for the most important problem facing the nation[a]					
Ind/P	16.0	38.1	21.8	40.9	32.9***
ID/P	19.1	34.3	20.3	30.9	51.7
Ind/A	22.4	37.9	17.7	41.1	28.6
ID/A	20.4	34.8	16.9	43.9	42.6
Ind/E	22.8	31.3	17.6	29.8	46.7
ID/E	21.4	41.0	19.6	38.0	51.2

SOURCE: American National Election Studies, 1972, 1976, 1980, 1984, 1988.
Note: Ind/P = individualist privatized; ID/P = identified privatized; Ind/A = individualist ambivalent; ID/A = identified ambivalent; Ind/E = individualist egalitarian; ID/E = identified egalitarian.
***p < .01.
[a]See Appendix for coding of "women's preferences" on respondents' choice of the "most important problem" facing the nation in each election year.

the virtually unlimited number of things that could be called "most important" by a diverse populace, it is remarkable testimony to presidential and media power to control the public agenda to see just how tight that focus can be.

In each of the five years, only five to seven issues were mentioned by roughly 50 to 80 percent of women, nor did their choices differ from those of the whole sample. Categories of consciousness, moreover, did not discriminate among preferences until 1988, when identified women of all gender role ideologies became more likely to name a "women's preference" than were their individualist counterparts. In 1972, Vietnam was an enormous preoccupation for the American public, and indeed was probably the most genuine of the "crises" the nation faced in the sixteen-year period. In 1976, the plurality of women were concerned about unemployment and inflation; these pocketbook issues were joined in 1980 by concern about the hostages then held in Iran, and unemployment appeared once again in 1984, this time joined by fear of nuclear war and

Ronald Reagan's favorite issue, government spending. The Reagan agenda was once again reflected in the 1988 Bush campaign, with a plurality of women naming government spending and drug abuse as the most important issues.

Table 6.4 suggests, in fact, that despite a short-term, crisis- and pocketbook-driven approach to what is "most important," a growing proportion of all women stress that issues of human welfare, peace, and the environment should have the highest priority. In 1988, we finally see that significantly more gender conscious women take such positions. Despite what Faludi (1991) has called the antifeminist backlash of the 1980s, it seems that identified women are more confidently raising their voices about the direction government should take.

Woman as amative, as peacemaker, as "beautiful soul" may always have been more a lovely artifice than the reality, and surely the image has been invoked in the past to restrain women's entry into the public realm, as an acceptance of Woman Warrior could not have been (Elshtain, 1987). There is no doubt, however, that women, and feminists, themselves have also invoked this construction of women as less bellicose (recall the discussion in chapter five), and public opinion polls have long documented that women in the mass see this role for themselves (Hero, 1968); we see some evidence of women's rejection of war in Table 6.5. Questions about defense spending, withdrawal from Vietnam, or trying harder to cooperate with the Soviet Union may also be contaminated by questions of just war, patriotism, or individual perceptions of the nature of a given crisis, so the picture of women's pacifism presented here is not unmistakably clear (see Conover and Sapiro, 1992, for experimentation with new measures of these questions, including a measure reflecting concern about the Persian Gulf War). But we do see that identified egalitarian women, occasionally joined by women with other forms of consciousness (identified privatized women often find themselves in this group) appear to want to lead the way to peace.

Liberal ideology or consciousness?

Because the idea of women's conscious recognition of group membership in the group of all women is likely to be regarded as problematic, for all the numerous reasons that we have discussed, many may assume that the connection between consciousness and policy preferences I have presented here is actually an artifact of egalitarianism. That is a legitimate assumption, since the association of the equal roles measure and liberal ideological self-placement has been long established (Fulenwider, 1980). But aside from theoretical speculation about the potentially poor fit between liberal-conservative spectra and women's socialization to both compassionate and conserving orientations, empirical analysis thus far suggests that, indeed, gender identification is making its own distinct contribu-

TABLE 6.5   DEFENSE SPENDING, WAR, AND INTERNATIONAL AFFAIRS, 1972–1988

	1972	1976	1980	1984	1988
A. % preferring to cut defense spending[a]					
Ind/P	28.4**	9.9***	13.8**	23.8**	23.2
ID/P	34.8	16.7	13.3	21.1	35.0
Ind/A	28.4	9.7	6.4	26.3	27.3
ID/A	43.9	16.6	12.3	28.2	22.1
Ind/E	38.9	15.6	8.3	37.5	27.4
ID/E	47.7	29.6	16.7	41.7	35.0
B. % in favor of withdrawing from Vietnam (1972) or trying harder to cooperate with the USSR (1980–1988)[b]					
Ind/P	42.6**		21.7***	22.2***	20.7***
ID/P	35.4		23.1	29.5	28.3
Ind/A	35.5		25.4	20.3	16.9
ID/A	39.3		25.0	34.4	23.5
Ind/E	56.6		43.6	31.9	35.9
ID/E	62.0		47.8	45.4	43.8

SOURCE: American National Election Studies, 1972, 1976, 1980, 1984, 1988.
Note: Ind/P = individualist privatized; ID/P = identified privatized; Ind/A = individualist ambivalent; ID/A = identified ambivalent; Ind/E = individualist egalitarian; ID/E = identified egalitarian.
***p < .01.
**p < .05.
[a]Defense-spending question asked in a dichotomous, favor/oppose format in 1972 and 1976; asked in a seven-point scale format in 1980, 1984, and 1988, of which the three points on the "favor cutting" side of the scale are collapsed and presented here.
[b]Vietnam withdrawal in 1972 and cooperation with the USSR in 1980, 1984, and 1988 asked in seven-point scale format, of which the three points on the "favor withdrawing" or "try harder to cooperate" sides of the scale are collapsed and presented here. No question similar to either the Vietnam or the USSR question was asked in 1976.

tion to consciousness's influence on policy preferences. We can see this more clearly by disaggregating the components of gender consciousness and associating them with individual policy positions.

The first thing that Table 6.6 shows us is the correlation between egalitarianism and liberalism we have already assumed to exist; the relationship is significant if not terribly strong. We also see, though, that gender identification is quite independent of liberalism: while it achieves statistical significance in 1980 and 1988 (perhaps because of the tenor of the presidential campaigns in those years), the coefficients in these years, as in all the others, are substantially smaller than are those representing the relationship between liberalism and egalitarianism.

TABLE 6.6   CORRELATIONS OF THE COMPONENTS OF CONSCIOUSNESS WITH IDEOLOGICAL SELF-PLACEMENT AND POLICY POSITIONS, 1972–1988

	1972	1976	1980	1984	1988
A. Ideology					
identification	.067	.089	.189*	.080	.129*
egalitarianism	.295*	.229*	.247*	.163*	.163*
B. Jobs, standard of living					
identification	.040	.032	.183*	.102*	.029
egalitarianism	.116	−.011	.128	.162*	.110*
C. Aid to minorities					
identification	.159*	.112*	.175*	.111*	.050
egalitarianism	.284*	.143*	.174*	.189*	.107*
D. Choice of Democratic candidate for president					
identification	.043	.096	.171*	.145*	.020
egalitarianism	.158*	.014	.089	.132*	.016
E. "Women's preference" on most important problems					
identification	−.012	.037	.026	.036	.021
egalitarianism	.038	.062	.000	−.028	.041
F. Cuts in defense spending					
identification	.120	.194*	.127	.087	.043
egalitarianism	.140*	.168*	.181*	.162*	.047
G. Vietnam withdrawal					
identification	.029				
egalitarianism	.253*				
H. Cooperation with USSR					
identification			.162*	.089	.051
egalitarianism			.306*	.172*	.148*

SOURCE: American National Election Studies, 1972, 1976, 1980, 1984, 1988.
Note: Entries are Pearson's product-moment correlations; all variables are coded in the direction of the listed quality; identification and egalitarianism are dummies.
An asterisk following the coefficient indicates that $p < .01$.

This is evidence that consciousness can operate independently of ideology as an organizer of political attitudes.

Continuing down the list of policy preferences, we continue to see that both gender identification and gender role ideology exert influence. Generally, in a case where either component has an effect, both components do—albeit each may sometimes operate in different years. We find exceptions in the cases of "women's preferences" on most important problems, where neither component has significant influence, and in defense spending and Vietnam withdrawal, where identification is clearly less influential than is egalitarianism. But overall, given Americans' generally weak ideological constraint, gender consciousness may well rival or replace ideology as an underlying structure for political attitudes.

TABLE 6.7   THE ASSOCIATION OF COMPONENTS OF GENDER CONSCIOUSNESS WITH THE POLICY SCALE, ALONE, AND CONTROLLED FOR IDEOLOGY, 1972–1988

	1972	1976	1980	1984	1988
A. Identification	.106***	.155***	.149***	.143***	.067**
controlled for ideology	.078	.130***	.091	.113***	.025
B. Egalitarianism	.326***	.174***	.206***	.224***	.147***
controlled for ideology	.228***	.081***	.125***	.163***	.098***

SOURCE: American National Election Studies, 1972, 1976, 1980, 1984, 1988.
Three asterisks following a coefficient indicate $p < .01$; two asterisks following a coefficient indicate $p < .05$.
[a]Entries are zero-order Pearson's product-moment correlations of each component of consciousness (dummied) with the policy scale, and first-order correlations of Consciousness components with policy scale controlled for ideological self-placement, coded in the direction of increasing liberalism.

Another and more difficult test is that of controlling for ideology as we measure the association among identification, egalitarianism, and the entire policy scale. The effects of such a control, shown in Table 6.7, cannot diminish the influence of consciousness in eight out of ten instances. In 1972, and again in 1988, holding liberalism constant reduces the effect of gender identification to insignificance. In all other years, and in all years for egalitarianism, removing liberalism from the mental equation yet leaves a demonstrable job for consciousness to do. Most important, gender consciousness is not externally imposed, as "liberal" and "conservative" labels are. Women must, instead, construct their consciousness for themselves. In doing this, women craft something that has meaning and harmony and that can comfortably organize other attitudes.

CONSCIOUSNESS: THE CONNECTION OF BEHAVIOR TO ATTITUDES

If women are to represent themselves, and other women, and a woman's perspective on public policy, they must do more than shape these perspectives for themselves. They must act on them. Group consciousness, as we know, proceeds from a recognition of one's membership in the group, to identification with it, to actions in and on its behalf. I and others have argued in favor of this process as an explanation of women's "group" behavior throughout modern Western culture. I have tried to further the argument by saying that gender consciousness goes beyond feminism and so-called women's issues. I have emphasized that it should be thought of as a process, as difficult as that is to depict in empirical ways; in statistical terms, we might say that consciousness is the "unobserved" connection between political engagement and political attitudes. In theoretical

TABLE 6.8 THE INFLUENCE OF COMPONENTS OF CONSCIOUSNESS ON THE ASSOCIATION OF POLITICAL ENGAGEMENT AND POLICY PREFERENCES, 1972–1988

	1972	1976	1980	1984	1988
Political engagement × policy preferences					
individualist	.104	.124*	.038	.007	.076
	(266)	(470)	(254)	(235)	(464)
gender identified	.264*	.197*	.085	.168*	.213*
	(236)	(745)	(357)	(567)	(704)
privatized	−.001	.164*	−.031	.010	−.015
	(261)	(566)	(214)	(313)	(287)
egalitarian	.251*	.172*	.087	.168*	.216*
	(241)	(648)	(397)	(489)	(881)

SOURCE: American National Election Studies, 1972, 1976, 1980, 1984, 1988.
Note: Entries are zero-order Pearson's product-moment correlations of political engagement scale with policy scale for each category of the components of consciousness. Numbers in parentheses below each coefficient are Ns of cases.
An asterisk following a coefficient indicates $p < .01$.

terms, consciousness represents the living intellectual and affective framework women use in order to make sense of the political world. This process reveals itself in Table 6.8. There we see unmistakably that consciousness knits thought and action.

Women with a sense of gender identification more often act on their political beliefs; for individualists, the connection between political engagement and policy orientations is weak. Despite the potential for privatized women to develop traditional role gender consciousness (some of whom are represented among the identified), egalitarianism provides more fertile ground in which politicization can take root. Political women—women who assume their places in the life of the polis—take confident positions on public questions and believe in their competence to act. Gender consciousness makes political women, women who seek to represent not only themselves but their views of what is good and just for all.

Chapter 7

SOME CONCLUDING THOUGHTS

Lovers of Jane Austen know that the ends of her novels were hurried, almost hasty, as if, once she had tied everything up in a neat package, she could not bear to go on. I know that feeling. I do not want to weary myself or my reader with repetition, and I have tried to draw conclusions throughout this work, and to invite readers to do so, rather than saving them all for the end. I shall close, then, with something more in the nature of a brief epilogue than a reprise. I did not choose an epigraph for this last chapter for much the same reason: I hope that readers will observe the world around us at this moment and find their own resonating comments.

For we are in as great a need for gender consciousness as ever. Scholars—and not just gender politics scholars—need to continue to probe consciousness as a theoretical construct and seek better measures of it. As I write, new measures have been tested in the 1991 American National Election Pilot Study. They are being evaluated now to judge their superiority to the survey questions we have been forced to use thus far. They show promise, and I look forward to watching their behavior in the 1992 survey. But mass survey research alone will never completely capture gender consciousness. I join the chorus of others who plead for a diversity of methods. I hope we will seek other ways of asking women to talk to us, and I hope we will be good listeners when that happens. I hope that gender consciousness scholarship, and indeed all of gender politics, can emerge from its ghetto. I would like to see this book and others like it being read by students of political psychology and political behavior. I dream of the day when

I hear someone say, "Since I'm studying behavior, I must think about gender," rather than, "But that's about women, and I am studying behavior/theory/policy"—the refrain we most often hear today. Consciousness is not only an analytical construct: it is something to be *raised*.

I hope that interdisciplinary efforts will continue; I think that political scientists have not done a good enough job of demonstrating to other scholars just how central politics is to women's fortunes, just as, perhaps, we have failed to communicate this same message—that politics matters—to the citizenry. While we have learned to draw wisdom from other fields of endeavor, we have not sufficiently convinced others that we might be able to contribute to our accumulated wisdom, too.

Far more than to scholarship, though, gender consciousness is important to women. It is spreading rapidly, as the foregoing pages show. It motivates women in their political behavior, and it is a resource from which they can draw the means of organizing their political worlds. Just as important, gender consciousness is a source of fortitude for women in times of backlash against them. We live in an era when some of the successes of feminism—the achievement of some legal and economic guarantees, and the partial reshaping of men's and women's public and private roles—have apparently been great enough to threaten the status quo. As women achieve a larger place in the worlds of politics and work, violence against women is increasing. The popular culture—think of prime-time television or popular music—seems more likely to degrade than to celebrate women.

At the level of the individual, people (especially women) now see how hard change is. The exercise of adult gender roles in the private domain has not changed enough to prevent many women's having to work "double shifts" outside and inside the home. People are struggling: most men have not yet confronted what a change in *women's* gender roles will mean for men's own gender role construction. In the 1970s, people optimistically believed that equality was just and therefore would happen. Two decades later, two decades in which the media have so powerfully influenced our visions of women, women and men see how much harder equality will be.

This challenge has not dampened women's consciousness. On the contrary, gender consciousness is more evident than ever. I saw this impressionistically and empirically as I observed the 1990 gubernatorial election in Texas, between Democrat Ann Richards and Republican Clayton Williams. "Claytie," as Williams was called, tried to evoke the myth of Texas's cowboy past but succeeded only in repelling large numbers of voters, particularly women in both parties, with his repeated sexist and sexually demeaning remarks. As one East Texas man put it, "He's no cowboy. He's just a guy in a big hat running around abusing women." Ann Richards, a liberal running in an increasingly conservative state, was both hampered and benefited by traditional and modern conceptions of gender roles. Believers in traditional roles felt that she was stepping out of her place, and in a very negative campaign, she seemed to such people to be insufficiently "feminine." But holders of more egalitarian beliefs were thrilled by her candidacy, and women with such beliefs were her ardent supporters.

In the end, Richards won a narrow victory. She attracted the votes of a majority of men who traditionally are Democratic voters, and she also got some votes from urban, educated, professional men. But her victory was a victory of women's cohesiveness: white, black, and Hispanic women all supported her strongly. Exit poll results showed that she captured an unheard-of 25 percent of Republican women's votes. Relatively few of Richard's female supporters would call themselves feminists. But most of them were moved by something we *know* to be gender consciousness.

The 1990 Texas race is just one—if perhaps the most vivid—example of the contemporary crucible of gender roles and political roles. Richards's candidacy also illustrates the vulnerability and sense of threat that privatized women can feel. We have seen throughout these pages that the number of women with traditional gender role ideologies is dwindling steadily. For privatized women who also have gender identification, changing roles are less threatening, for they have integrated their traditional roles into the supportive framework of gender consciousness. Here, once again, we can make the otherwise startling argument that women like Phyllis Schafly are gender conscious: they certainly identify more closely with women than they do with men, whom they seem to distrust. But we are more likely to find, among traditional role conscious women, women who have turned their roles into a source of strength and purpose. They are not unlike the Victorian feminists who turned the moralistic roles to which they had been assigned into the justification for a political crusade.

But for women who are both privatized and bereft of a sense of gender identification, the current world must seem cold and alienating. It must seem to have rejected them, at least insofar as questions of women's political roles are concerned. I hope that other women can reach out to them.

Another, larger, more painful division between women is that of race. Mutual suspicion and distrust can be terribly difficult to overcome. And yet some women *do* overcome them, by emphasizing sisterhood. The astonishing victory of Carol Moseley Braun in the 1992 Illinois primary, defeating an incumbent and a wealthy challenger, both white and male, on her way to the Democratic Senate nomination, is a testament to what women can do when they identify with one another across something even as potentially divisive as race. I hope that more and more women can reach across the divide. Gender consciousness is what will enable them to do it.

There are so many battles left to be fought. These battles are formal and institutional—they are the places where the struggle for public policy takes place. But more insidious, because it underlies everything else, including all our constructions of political power, is the psychological battle. Women may disagree among themselves over whether something androgynous should be striven for or whether some distinct constellation of "feminine" virtues should be recast as truly public roles. I believe that we abandoned our consideration of androgyny much too soon. The differences among women, however, pale in comparison to the battle for the hearts and minds of men. As long as anything from beer to hardware is advertised in Western markets by featuring naked or nearly-naked young women, as long as popular music glories in depictions of sexual violence, as long as women's needs remain least and last on our public agendas, gender consciousness will be necessary. One day, when the political world is no longer a gendered place, "gender consciousness" will have taken on new meaning for women, and for men. Perhaps consciousness will then be no more than the awareness of the ways in which *both* gender roles, male and female, enrich the political self. We have started on that road already. When schoolchildren in Texas think about "the governor," they now conjure up a female face. But we have miles and miles and miles to go. Gender consciousness gives women the strength to undertake the journey.

APPENDIX

While most of the variable transformations appearing in chapters three through six are explained in the text, some require additional explanation. This appendix offers readers a review and discussion of the creation and use of the empirical measures.

A. *N*s of cases for the gender consciousness measures:

	N, all women	N, consciousness measure	White women	Women of color
1972	1252	1242	1088	154
1976	1412	1339	1161	178
1980	794	787	682	105
1984	1074	1068	914	154
1988	1168	986	804	182

Black women constitute approximately 86 percent to 93 percent of women of color in the sample.

B. Job segregation, as explained in the text, was created by comparing census codes in the five American National Election Study surveys to occupation figures by sex as reported in *Statistical Abstracts of the United States*. Where exact matches of occupational classification existed (more frequently from 1980 on), exact figures from "Female as Percent of Total" columns were coded. For cases where exact matches could not be made, figures from the appropriate general category or subcategory were coded. Housewives were assigned a score of 100 because of my interest more in whether respondents filled stereotypical roles for women than in the particular job itself, and for this reason the exclusion of housewives seemed an unnecessary loss. But readers will note that job segregation figures for *nonhousewives* in 1972 seem unusually low. This surprising finding is most likely explained by two factors. First, fully 48.2 percent of the 1972 sample were housewives, leaving proportionately fewer women than in other years hypothetically distributed across all other occupational categories. As more and more women entered the workforce after the early 1970s, and as the service economy greatly expanded from 1976 onward, more new "pink collar" ghettos of women's employment developed. Second, the less finely discriminating categories of the early 1970s census codes confound the findings in two ways. "Professional, technical, and kindred workers," for example, are harder to separate from one another than they later would be, so the job segregation figures for women in 1972 may be artificially low. But second, the largest single group of women other than housewives in 1972 are "laborers and operatives," and while the census codes here too are rather lumped together, and the census figures show this category to be male-dominated (with good reason), this probably obscures the picture for particular loci of female-dominated "laborers and operatives," as might be the case with female machinery operators (who are not stitchers or seamstresses) in southern textile factories. Later refinements of census categories helped to remove these problems after 1972.

C. Religiosity and moral traditionalism. As presented in the text, "moral traditionalism" is composed of four items, two of which were asked with responses in one direction (of greater traditionalism), and two of which were asked with responses in the opposite direction (of greater tolerance). This minimizes response-set bias, while Chronbach's alpha may actually underestimate the strength of the scale's reliability under such circumstances. But it must also be noted that the four items actually seem to represent two "subscales," of "family values" and "moral tolerance" (see Stoker, 1987, for a full discussion of item interrelationships and performance).

Although Conover and Feldman (1986) and Stoker (1987) dispute some theoretical and methodological points with each other, and both were working with larger numbers of items from the Pilot Studies of 1985 and 1987, they are in considerable agreement on the question of moment for us: the relationship of moral traditionalism to beliefs about women's roles. They both find that moral traditionalism is distinct from, although related to, religiosity; that it is associated with the New Right political agenda of the 1980s; and that it is strongly associated with evaluations of the Women's Movement, feminists, and abortion.

Following my earlier work on gender and religiosity (Tolleson Rinehart and Perkins, 1989), I have relied on the conceptually more significant psychological measure of religiosity—whether religion is both important *and* offers a great deal of guidance in one's life—rather than on quite problematic measures of fundamentalism or less meaningful measures of denomination or attendance at religious services. And attempting to learn from both Conover and Feldman, and Stoker, I have computed a simple additive scale of the four moral traditionalism items, recoding traditional responses (whether strong or not strong) as −1, "depends" or "neither one way nor the other" responses as 0 (very small numbers of "don't knows" are excluded, following Stoker), and morally "tolerant" responses (whether strong or not strong) as +1. The result is a nine-point scale ranging from −4 (most morally traditional) to +4 (most morally tolerant). The N of cases for the scale is 971 (women only), with 197 missing cases. Scale reliability, with Chronbach's alpha = .477, is moderately strong, and item-to-scale correlations are also moderate, ranging from .224 to .320. Frequencies follow:

Response	Frequency	Valid percentage
−4	156	16.1
−3	49	5.0
−3	218	22.5
−2	104	10.7
0	275	28.3
1	77	7.9
2	69	7.1
3	14	1.4
4	9	0.9

D. The "women's preference" issue choices for the "most important problem" facing the nation were constructed, as described in the text, by making a priori judgments about whether spontaneously mentioned issues would be more likely to be made by women. I created a dummy variable in each year by assigning all such issue codes equal to 1, and all others to 0, *before* examining frequency distributions. Codes for 1972 differ from those for all other years, the latter being virtually identical to one another (but not all issues were mentioned by respondents in any given year). Lists of all issues coded 1, for "women's preference," follow:

Issues in 1972	Issues in 1976, 1980, 1984, 1988
population increase, birth control	population increase, birth control
unemployment and its compensation	unemployment and its compensation
aid to education	aid to education: for
aid to the elderly	aid to the elderly: for
health care	health care: for aid, better quality
mental health care	mental health care
housing, slums, urban renewal	housing policy: for
	urban renewal: for
poverty, the poor	welfare assistance: for
assistance to Negroes and minorities	
general welfare references	general welfare: for
surplus food disposal	food assistance, programs: for
for conservation, antipollution	for conservation, anti-pollution
for beautification programs	

Issues in 1972, cont'd
protection for migrant laborers
protection/expansion, civil rights
narcotics, drug addiction, etc.

Issues in 1976, 1980, 1984, 1988 cont'd
protection for migrant laborers
protection/expansion, civil rights

pro–women's rights
prochoice on abortion
pro–freedom of speech
pro–general human rights
pro–rights of demonstrators (1976)
anti–police brutality
pro–busing of schoolchildren

gun control: for

gun control: for
family problems, welfare
increased government spending: for
anti–"powerful moneyed interests"
regulation of commerce, travel: for

consumer safety: for

consumer safety: for
safety regulation generally: for

Vietnam
better foreign relations

better foreign relations
anti–increased military activity
increased economic development assistance

support for United Nations
prevention of war, wants peace
for disarmament, anti–arms race

support for United Nations
prevention of war, wants peace
for disarmament, anti–arms race
amnesty: for

for honesty, ethics in government
fair election procedures

for honesty, ethics in government
fair election procedures
unifying nation/morale of nation
anti–Watergate conspirators (1976)

BIBLIOGRAPHY

Allport, Floyd H. (1920). "The Influence of the Group upon Association and Thought." *Journal of Experimental Psychology* 3 (1920): 159–182.

Andersen, Kristi. (1975). "Working Women and Political Participation, 1952–1972." *American Journal of Political Science* 19 (August): 439–453.

———. (1988a). "No Longer Petitioners: Women's Political Involvement in the 1920s." Paper presented to the Annual Meeting of the Midwest Political Science Association. Chicago.

———. (1988b). "Sources of Pro-Family Beliefs: A Cognitive Approach." *Political Psychology* 9(2): 229–243.

Atwood, Margaret. (1986). *The Handmaid's Tale.* Boston: Houghton Mifflin.

Austen, Jane. ([1818] 1933). *Persuasion.* Volume 5 of *The Oxford Illustrated Jane Austen.* Edited by R. W. Chapman. London: Oxford University Press.

Austin, G. L., M.D. (1882). *A Doctor's Talk with Maiden, Wife and Mother.* Boston: Lothrop, Lee & Shepard.

Barber, Benjamin R. (1976). *Liberating Feminism.* New York: Dell.

———. (1988). "Spirit's Phoenix and History's Owl or the Incoherence of Dialectics in Hegel's Account of Women." *Political Theory* 16 (February): 5–27.

Baxter, Sandra, and Marjorie Lansing. (1983). *Women and Politics: The Visible Majority.* Ann Arbor: University of Michigan Press.

Beck, Paul Allen, and M. Kent Jennings. (1982). "Pathways to Participation." *American Political Science Review* 76 (March): 94–108.

———. (1988). "Childhood Socialization Environments and Adult Political Involvement." Paper presented to the Annual Meeting of the American Political Science Association. Washington, D.C.

Belkin, Lisa. (1989). "Bars to Equality of Sexes Seen as Eroding, Slowly." *The New York Times.* August 20, p. 1.

Bennett, W. Lance. (1977). "The Growth of Knowledge in Mass Belief Studies: An Epistemological Critique." *American Journal of Political Science* 21 (August): 465–500.

Bentley, Arthur T. (1908). *The Process of Government.* Chicago: University of Chicago Press.

Blair, Diane D. (1988). *"The Handmaid's Tale* and *The Birth Dearth:* Prophecy, Prescription and Public Policy." Paper presented to the Annual Meeting of the Midwest Political Science Association. Chicago.

Blanchard, Paula. (1978). *Margaret Fuller: From Transcendentalism to Revolution.* New York: Delacorte Press.

Blee, Kathleen M. (1991). "Women in the 1920s' Ku Klux Klan Movement." *Feminist Studies* 17 (Spring): 57–77.

Bleier, Ruth. (1984). *Science and Gender.* New York: Pergamon Press.

Bloom, Allan. (1987). *The Closing of the American Mind.* New York: Simon & Schuster.

———. trans. (1979). *Emile,* by J. J. Rousseau. New York: Basic Books.

Boles, Janet K. (1979). *The Politics of the Equal Rights Amendment.* New York: Longman.

Bookman, Ann, and Sandra Morgen, eds. (1988). *Women and the Politics of Empowerment.* Philadelphia: Temple University Press.

Bourque, Susan, and Jean Grossholtz. (1974). "Politics as Unnatural Practise: Political Science Looks at Female Participation." *Politics and Society* 4 (Winter): 255–266.

Bowman, Ann O'M. (1984). "Physical Attractiveness and Electability: Looks and Votes." *Women & Politics* 4 (Winter): 55–65.

Brady, David W., and Kent L. Tedin. (1976). "Ladies in Pink: Religion and Ideology in the Anti-ERA Movement." *Social Science Quarterly* 56 (March): 564–575.

Breckenridge, Sophonisba. (1933). *Women in the Twentieth Century.* New York: McGraw-Hill.

Brontë, Charlotte. ([1847] 1966). *Jane Eyre.* Edited by Q. D. Leavis. London: Penguin.

Butler, David, and Donald Stokes. (1969). *Political Change in Britain.* New York: St. Martin's Press.

Bynum, Caroline Walker. (1982). *Jesus as Mother: Studies in the Spirituality of the High Middle Ages.* Berkeley: University of California Press.

Campbell, Angus, Philip E. Converse, Warren Miller, and Donald E. Stokes. (1960). *The American Voter.* New York: John Wiley & Sons.

Carli, Linda L. (1990). "Gender, Language, and Influence." *Journal of Personality and Social Psychology* 59(5): 941–951.

Carroll, Susan J. (1989). "Gender Politics and the Socializing Impact of the Women's Movement." In Roberta S. Sigel, ed., *Political Learning in Adulthood.* Chicago: University of Chicago Press.

Carroll, Susan J., and Wendy S. Strimling. (1983). *Women's Routes to Elective Office.* New Brunswick, N.J.: Center for the American Woman and Politics.

Chafetz, Janet Saltzman, and Anthony Gary Dworkin. (1987). "In the Face of Threat: Organized Antifeminism in Comparative Perspective." *Gender & Society* 1 (March): 33–60.

Chapman, R. W., ed. (1985). *Jane Austen: Selected Letters.* Oxford: Oxford University Press.

Chodorow, Nancy. (1978). *The Reproduction of Mothering.* Berkeley: University of California Press.

Christy, Carol A. (1985). "American and German Trends in Sex Differences in Political Participation." *Comparative Political Studies* 18(1): 81–103.

Clark, Ricky. (1988). "Mid-Nineteenth-Century Album and Friendship Quilts, 1860–1920." In Jeanette Lasansky et al., eds., *Pieced by Mother: Symposium Papers.* Lewisburg, Pa.: Oral Traditions Project of the Union County Historical Society (University of Pennsylvania Press).

Coles, Robert. (1986). *The Political Life of Children.* Boston: Atlantic Monthly Press.

Collins, Patricia Hill. (1989). "The Social Construction of Black Feminist Thought." *Signs* 14 (Summer): 745–773.

———. (1990). *Black Feminist Thought: Knowledge, Consciousness, and the Politics of Empowerment.* London: HarperCollins.

Conover, Pamela Johnston. (1984). "The Influence of Group Identifications on Political Perceptions and Evaluations." *Journal of Politics* 46 (August): 760–785.

———. (1987). "Gender Identities and Basic Political Orientations." Paper presented to the Annual

Meeting of the American Political Science Association. Chicago.

———. (1988a). "So Who Cares? Sympathy and Politics." Paper presented to the Annual Meeting of the Midwest Political Science Association. Chicago.

———. (1988b). "Feminists and the Gender Gap." *Journal of Politics* 50 (November): 985–1010.

———. (1988c). "The Role of Social Groups in Political Thinking." *British Journal of Political Science* 18(1): 51–76.

Conover, Pamela Johnston, and Stanley Feldman. (1981). "The Origins and Meaning of Liberal/ Conservative Self-Identifications." *American Journal of Political Science* 25 (November): 617– 645.

———. (1984). "How People Organize the Political World: A Schematic Model." *American Journal of Political Science* 28 (February): 95–126.

———. (1986). "Religion, Morality, and Politics: Moral Traditionalism in the 1980s." Paper presented to the Annual Meeting of the American Political Science Association. Washington, D.C.

Conover, Pamela Johnston, and Virginia Sapiro. (1992). "Gender Consciousness and Gender Politics in the 1991 Pilot Study: A Report to the Board of Overseers." Unpublished manuscript.

Converse, Philip E. (1964). "The Nature of Belief Systems in Mass Publics." In David Apter, ed., *Ideology and Discontent*. Glencoe, Ill.: Free Press.

Costain, Anne N. (1988). "Activists, Agitators, and Issues: Mobilizing a Women's Movement in America." Paper presented to the Annual Meeting of the American Political Science Association. Washington, D.C.

Cott, Nancy F. (1978). "Passionless: An Interpretation of Victorian Sexual Ideology." *Signs* 4 (Winter): 219–236.

———. (1987). *The Grounding of Modern Feminism*. New Haven: Yale University Press.

Cozart, Dorothy. (1988). "The Role of Fundraising Quilts, 1850–1930." In Jeanette Lasansky et al., eds., *Pieced by Mother: Symposium Papers*. Lewisburg, Pa.: Oral Traditions Project of the Union County Historical Society (University of Pennsylvania Press).

Daly, Mary. (1984). *Pure Lust: Elemental Feminist Philosophy*. Boston: Beacon Press.

Danelski, David J. (1979). "The Influence of the Chief Justice in the Decision Process." In Walter F. Murphy and Herman C. Pritchett, eds., *Courts, Judges, and Politics*. 3d ed. New York: Random House.

Darcy, R., Susan Welch, and Janet Clark. (1987). *Women, Elections, and Representation*. New York: Longman.

Davies, James C. (1965). "The Family's Role in Political Socialization." *Annals of the American Academy of Political and Social Science* 361 (September): 10–19.

de Beauvoir, Simone. ([1949] 1961). *The Second Sex*. Translated by H. M. Parsley. New York: Bantam Books.

Delli Carpini, Michael X. (1989). "Age and History: Generations and Sociopolitical Change." In Roberta S. Sigel, ed., *Political Learning in Adulthood*. Chicago: University of Chicago Press.

Dennis, Jack. (1987). "Groups and Political Behavior: Legitimation, Deprivation, and Competing Values." *Political Behavior* 9(4): 323–372.

de Pizan, Christine. ([1405] 1982). *The Book of the City of Ladies*. Translated by Earl Jeffrey Richards. New York: Persea Books.

Diamond, Irene. (1977). *Sex Roles in the State House*. New Haven: Yale University Press.

DiBacco, Thomas V. (1992). "Doctors' Role in the Abortion Debate." *Washington Post Health*. January 21, p. 13.

Dodson, Debra L. (1991). *Gender and Policymaking: Studies of Women in Office*. New Brunswick, N.J.: Center for the American Woman and Politics.

Donovan, Josephine. (1985). *Feminist Theory*. New York: Frederic Unger.

Drury, Shadia B. (1987). "Aristotle on the Inferiority of Women." *Women & Politics* 7(4): 51–65.

Duverger, Maurice. (1955). *The Political Role of Women*. New York: UNESCO.

Easton, David, and Jack Dennis. (1969). *Children in the Political System: Origins of Political Legitimacy.* New York: McGraw-Hill.

Eccles, Jacquelynne S. (1987). "Gender Roles and Women's Achievement-Related Assumptions." *Psychology of Women Quarterly* 11 (June): 135–171.

Eisenstein, Hester. (1983). *Contemporary Feminist Thought.* Boston: G. K. Hall.

Eisenstein, Zillah. (1984). *Feminism and Sexual Equality.* New York: Monthly Review Press.

Elshtain, Jean Bethke. (1986). *Meditations on Modern Political Thought.* New York: Praeger.

Elshtain, Jean Bethke. (1987). *Women and War.* NY: Basic Books.

Erikson, Robert S., Norman R. Luttbeg, and Kent L. Tedin. (1980). *American Public Opinion.* 2d ed. New York: John Wiley & Sons.

Faludi, Susan. (1991). *Backlash: The Undeclared War Against American Women.* New York: Crown.

Ferrero, Pat, Elaine Hedges, and Julie Silber. (1987). *Hearts and Hands: The Influence of Women and Quilts on American Society.* San Francisco: Quilt Digest Press.

Finifter, Ada. (1974). "The Friendship Group as a Protective Environment for Political Deviants." *American Political Science Review* 68 (June): 607–625.

Firestone, Shulamith. (1972). *The Dialectic of Sex.* New York: Bantam Books.

Fowler, Robert Booth. (1985). "The Feminist and Anti-Feminist Debate Within Evangelical Protestantism." *Women & Politics* 5 (Summer/Fall): 7–39.

Fowlkes, Diane L., Jerry Perkins, and Sue Tolleson Rinehart. (1979). "Gender Roles and Party Roles." *American Political Science Review* 73(3): 772–780.

Frankovic, Kathleen A. (1982). "Sex and Politics—New Alignments, Old Issues." *PS* 15 (Summer): 439–438.

———. (1985). "The Ferraro Factor: The Women's Movement, the Polls, and the Press." Paper presented to the Annual Meeting of the Midwest Political Science Association. Chicago.

Fraser, Antonia. (1984). *The Weaker Vessel.* New York: Alfred A. Knopf.

Fraser, Rebecca. (1988). *The Brontes: Charlotte Bronte and Her Family.* New York: Crown.

Freud, Sigmund. ([1930] 1961). *Civilization and Its Discontents.* The Standard Edition, translated by James Strachey. New York: W. W. Norton.

Friedan, Betty. (1981). *The Second Stage.* New York: Summit Books.

Fulenwider, Claire Knoche. (1980). *Feminism in American Politics: A Study of Ideological Influence.* New York: Praeger.

Gage, Matilda Joslyn. ([1893] 1972). *Woman, Church and State.* New York: Arno Press.

Garson, G. David. (1978). *Group Theories of Politics.* Beverly Hills, Calif.: Sage Publications.

Gelb, Joyce. (1989). *Feminism and Politics: A Comparative Perspective.* Berkeley: University of California Press.

Gertzog, Irwin N. (1984). *Congressional Women: Their Recruitment, Treatment, and Behavior.* New York: Praeger.

Giddings, Paula. (1984). *When and Where I Enter: The Impact of Black Women on Race and Sex in America.* New York: William Morrow.

Gilbert, Allan. (1965). *Machiavelli: The Chief Works and Others.* Volume 2. Durham, N.C.: Duke University Press.

Gilder, George. (1975). *Sexual Suicide.* New York: Bantam Books.

Gilligan, Carol. (1982). *In a Different Voice.* Cambridge, Mass.: Harvard University Press.

Gilman, Charlotte Perkins. ([1915] 1979). *Herland.* New York: Pantheon Books.

Gilmore, David D. (1990). *Manhood in the Making.* New Haven: Yale University Press.

Golembiewski, Robert T. (1978). *The Small Group in Political Science.* Athens: University of Georgia Press.

Goreau, Angeline. (1980). *Reconstructing Aphra: A Social Biography of Aphra Behn.* New York: Dial Press.

Gornick, Vivian, and Barbara K. Moran, eds. (1971). *Woman in Sexist Society.* New York: New American Library.

Gottlieb, Beatrice. (1985). "The Problem of Feminism in the Fifteenth Century." In Julius Kirshner and Suzanne F. Wemple, eds., *Women in the Medieval World: Essays in Honor of John H. Mundy.* Oxford: Basil Blackwell.

Gurin, Patricia. (1985). "Women's Gender Consciousness." *Public Opinion Quarterly* 49(2): 143–163.

———. (1986). "The Political Implications of Women's Statuses." In F. J. Crosby, ed., *Spouse Parent Worker.* New Haven: Yale University Press.

Gurin, P., A. H. Miller, and G. Gurin. (1980). "Stratum Identification and Consciousness." *Social Psychology Quarterly* 43: 30–47.

Hare, A. Paul. (1973). "Group Decision by Consensus: Reaching Unity in the Society of Friends." *Sociological Inquiry* 43: 75–84.

———. (1976). *Handbook of Small Group Research.* 2d ed. New York: Free Press.

Hartmann, Susan M. (1989). *From Margin to Mainstream: American Women and Politics since 1960.* New York: Alfred A. Knopf.

Hartsock, Nancy C. M. (1983). *Money, Sex, and Power: Toward a Feminist Historical Materialism.* New York: Longman.

Hero, Alfred. (1968). "Public Reaction to Government Policy." In John P. Robinson et al., eds., *Measures of Political Attitudes.* Ann Arbor, Mich.: Survey Research Center, Institute for Social Research.

Herr, Patricia T. (1988). "Quaker Quilts and Their Makers." In Jeanette Lasansky et al., eds., *Pieced by Mother: Symposium Papers.* Lewisburg, Pa.: Oral Tradition Project of the Union County Historical Society (University of Pennsylvania Press).

Herstein, Sheila R. (1985). *Mid-Victorian Feminist: Barbara Leigh Smith Bodichon.* New Haven: Yale University Press.

Hertz, Rosanna. (1986). *More Equal than Others: Women and Men in Dual Career Marriages.* Berkeley: University of California Press.

Hess, Robert D., and Judith V. Torney. (1967). *The Development of Political Attitudes in Children.* Chicago: Aldine.

Hewlett, Sylvia Ann. (1986). *A Lesser Life: The Myth of Women's Liberation in America.* New York: William Morrow.

Hill, David B. (1981). "Political Culture and Female Political Representation." *Journal of Politics* 43 (February): 159–168.

Hirschman, Albert O. (1970). *Exit, Voice, and Loyalty.* Cambridge, Mass.: Harvard University Press.

Homans, George C. (1950). *The Human Group.* New York: Harcourt Brace.

hooks, bell. (1989). *Talking Back.* Boston: South End Press.

Hughes, D. L., and Charles W. Peek. (1986). "Ladies Against Women: Explaining the Participation of Traditional- and Modern-Role Women." *Political Behavior* 8 (2): 158–174.

Hyman, Herbert. (1955). *Survey Design and Analysis.* Glencoe, Ill.: Free Press.

Jaggar, Alison M., and Paula S. Rothenberg. (1984). *Feminist Frameworks.* 2d ed. New York: McGraw-Hill.

Janis, Irving L. (1972). *Victims of Groupthink.* Boston: Houghton Mifflin.

Jaros, Dean. (1973). *Socialization to Politics.* New York: Praeger.

Jennings, M. Kent. (1979). "Another Look at the Life Cycle and Political Participation." *American Journal of Political Science* 23 (November): 755–771.

———. (1983). "Gender Roles and Inequalities in Political Participation." *Western Political Quarterly* 37: 364–385.

Jennings, M. Kent, and Barbara Farah. (1980). "Ideology, Gender and Political Action: A Cross-National Survey." *British Journal of Political Science* 10 (April): 219–240.

———. (1981). "Social Roles and Political Resources: An Over-Time Study of Men and Women in Party Elites." *American Journal of Political Science* 25 (August): 462–482.

Jennings, M. Kent, and Richard G. Niemi. (1968). "The Transmission of Political Values from Parent to Child." *American Political Science Review* 62 (March): 169–184.

————. (1971). "The Division of Political Labor between Mothers and Fathers." *American Political Science Review* 65 (March): 69–82.

————. (1974). *The Political Character of Adolescence*. Princeton: Princeton University Press.

————. (1981). *Generations and Politics*. Princeton: Princeton University Press.

Jennings, M. Kent and Norman Thomas. (1968). "Men and Women in Party Elites: Social Roles and Political Resources." *Midwest Journal of Political Science* 12 (November): 469–492.

Jerrold, Maud. (1928). *Italy in the Renaissance*. Boston: John Luce.

Joseph, Elizabeth. (1991). "My Husband's Nine Wives." *The New York Times*. May 23, p. A15.

Kann, Mark. (1983a). "Legitimation, Consent, and Anti-Feminism." *Women & Politics* 3 (Spring): 1–19.

————. (1983b). "Does Feminist Theory 'Work'?" *Women & Politics* 3 (Winter): 57–65.

Kanter, Rosabeth Moss. (1977). *Men and Women of the Corporation*. New York: Basic Books.

Kaplan, Temma. (1982). "Female Consciousness and Collective Action: The Case of Barcelona, 1910–1918." *Signs* 7(3): 545–566.

Keller, Evelyn Fox. (1985). *Reflections on Science and Gender*. New Haven: Yale University Press.

Kelso, Ruth. (1956). *Doctrine for the Lady of the Renaissance*. Urbana: University of Illinois Press.

Kenski, Henry. (1988). "The Gender Factor in a Changing Electorate." In Carol M. Mueller, ed., *The Politics of the Gender Gap*. Beverly Hills, Calif.: Sage Publications.

Kerber, Linda K., et al. (1986). "On *In a Different Voice:* An Interdisciplinary Forum." *Signs* 11(2): 304–333.

Key, V. O., Jr. (1966). *The Responsible Electorate*. Cambridge, Mass.: Harvard University Press.

Kinder, Donald R. (1983). "Diversity and Complexity in American Public Opinion." In Ada F. Finifter, ed., *Political Science: The State of the Discipline*. Washington, D.C.: American Political Science Association.

Kinnaird, Joan K. (1983). "Mary Astell: Inspired by Ideas." In Dale Spender, ed., *Feminist Theorists*. London: Women's Press.

Kirkham, Margaret. (1983). *Jane Austen: Feminism and Fiction*. Sussex, England: Harvester Press; Totowa, N.J.: Barnes & Noble.

Kirkpatrick, Jeanne. (1974). *Political Woman*. New York: Basic Books.

Klatch, Rebecca E. (1987). *Women of the New Right*. Philadelphia: Temple University Press.

Klein, Ethel. (1984). *Gender Politics*. Cambridge, Mass.: Harvard University Press.

Koonz, Claudia. (1976). "Nazi Women Before 1933: Rebels Against Emancipation." *Social Science Quarterly* 56 (March): 533–563.

Kristof, Nicholas D. (1991). "Stark Data on Women: 100 Million Are Missing." *The New York Times*. November 5, pp. B5, B9.

Labarge, Margaret Wade. (1986). *Women in Medieval Life: A Small Sound of the Trumpet*. London: Hamish Hamilton.

Levine, Phillipa. (1987). *Victorian Feminism, 1850–1900*. London: Hutchinson.

Lipman-Blumen, Jean. (1984). *Gender Roles and Power*. Englewood Cliffs, N.J.: Prentice-Hall.

Lugones, Maria C., and Elizabeth V. Spelman. (1983). "Have We Got a Theory for You! Feminist Theory, Cultural Imperialism, and the Demand for 'The Woman's Voice.'" *Women's Studies International Forum* 6(6): 573–581.

Luker, Kristin. (1984). *Abortion and the Politics of Motherhood*. Berkeley: University of California Press.

Luttrell, Wendy. (1988). "The Edison School Struggle: The Reshaping of Working-Class Education and Women's Consciousness." In Ann Bookman and Sandra Morgen, eds., *Women and the Politics of Empowerment*. Philadelphia: Temple University Press.

Lynn, Naomi, and Cornelia Butler Flora. (1977). "Societal Punishment and Aspects of Female Political Participation: 1972 National Convention Delegates." In Jewel L. Prestage and Marianne Githens, eds., *A Portrait of Marginality.* New York: David McKay.

McCarthy, Mary. ([1954] 1980). *The Group.* New York: Avon Books.

Maccoby, Eleanor. (1974). *The Psychology of Sex Differences.* Stanford: Stanford University Press.

McGlen, Nancy E. (1980). "The Impact of Parenthood on Political Participation." *Western Political Quarterly* 33 (September): 297–313.

Mansbridge, Jane J. (1985). "Myth and Reality: The ERA and the Gender Gap in the 1980 Election." *Public Opinion Quarterly* 49 (Summer): 164–178.

———. (1986). *Why We Lost the ERA.* Chicago: University of Chicago Press.

Markus, Gregory B. (1986). "Stability and Change in Political Attitudes: Observed, Recalled, and 'Explained.'" *Political Behavior* 8(1): 21–44.

Marvick, Dwayne. (1965). "The Political Socialization of the American Negro." *Annals of the American Academy of Political and Social Science* 361 (September): 112–127.

Mason, Karen Oppenheim, and Yu-Hsia Lu. (1988). "Attitudes Toward Women's Familial Roles: Changes in the United States, 1977–1985." *Gender and Society* 2 (March): 39–57.

Merelman, Richard. (1971). *Political Socialization and Educational Climates.* New York: Holt, Rinehart and Winston.

Mezey, Susan Gluck. (1978). "Women and Representation: The Case of Hawaii." *Journal of Politics* 40 (May): 369–385.

Mill, John Stuart. ([1869] 1970). "The Subjection of Women." In *Essays on Sex Equality.* Edited by Alice S. Rossi. Chicago: University of Chicago Press.

Miller, Arthur H., Patricia Gurin, Gerald Gurin, and Oksana Malanchuk. (1981). "Group Consciousness and Political Participation." *American Journal of Political Science* 25 (August): 494–511.

Miller, Arthur H., Anne M. Hildreth, and Grace Simmons. (1986). "The Political Implications of Gender Group Consciousness." Paper presented to the Annual Meeting of the Midwest Political Science Association. Chicago.

Newcomb, Theodore, Kathryn E. Koenig, Richard Flacks, and Donald P. Warwick. (1967). *Persistence and Change: Bennington College and Its Students after Twenty-Five Years.* New York: John Wiley & Sons.

Nice, David C. (1988). "Abortion Clinic Bombings as Political Violence." *American Journal of Political Science* 32 (February): 178–195.

Nie, Norman H., with Kristi Andersen. (1974). "Mass Belief Systems Revisited: Political Change and Attitude Structure." *Journal of Politics* 36 (August): 540–587.

Nie, Norman H., Sidney Verba, and John R. Petrocik. (1976). *The Changing American Voter.* Cambridge, Mass.: Harvard University Press.

Niemi, Richard G. (1974). *How Family Members Perceive Each Other.* New Haven: Yale University Press.

Norris, Pippa. (1988). "The Gender Gap: A Cross-National Trend?" In Carol M. Mueller, ed., *The Politics of the Gender Gap.* Beverly Hills, Calif.: Sage Publications.

Okin, Susan Moller. (1979). *Women in Western Political Thought.* Princeton: Princeton University Press.

O'Reilly, Jane. (1980). *The Girl I Left Behind Me: The Housewife's Moment of Truth and Other Feminist Ravings.* New York: Macmillan.

Petcheskey, Rosalind Pollack. (1984). *Abortion and Women's Choice.* NY: Longman.

Pitkin, Hanna Fenichel. (1984). *Fortune Is a Woman: Gender and Politics in the Thought of Niccolò Machiavelli.* Berkeley: University of California Press.

Plutzer, Eric, and Michael McBurnett. (1991). "Family Life and American Politics: The 'Marriage Gap' Reconsidered." *Public Opinion Quarterly* 53 (Spring): 113–127.

Poole, Keith T., and L. Harmon Zeigler. (1985). *Women, Public Opinion, and Politics*. New York: Longman.

Randall, Vicky. (1987). *Women and Politics: An International Perspective*. 2d ed. Chicago: University of Chicago Press.

Rapoport, Ronald B. (1981). "The Sex Gap in Political Persuading; Where the 'Structuring Principle' Works." *American Journal of Political Science* 25 (February): 32–48.

Rinehart, Steven. (1982). "The Anti-Feminist Impulse." Ph.D. dissertation, Purdue University.

Rix, Sara E., ed. (1988). *The American Woman, 1988–89*. New York: W. W. Norton.

Rossi, Alice S. (1973). *The Feminist Papers: From Adams to de Beauvoir*. New York: Columbia University Press.

———. (1982). *Feminists in Politics*. New York: Academic Press.

Rousseau, Jean-Jacques. (1960). *Politics and the Arts. Letter to M. d'Alembert on the Theater*. Translated by Allan Bloom. Ithaca, N.Y.: Cornell University Press.

———. (1968). *Julie, ou La Nouvelle Heloise*. Translated by Judith H. McDowell. University Park: Pennsylvania State University Press.

———. (1979). *Emile*. Translated by Allan Bloom. New York: Basic Books.

Ruddick, Sara. (1980). "Maternal Thinking." *Feminist Studies* 6 (Summer): 342–367.

Sapiro, Virginia. (1981). "When Are Interests Interesting? The Problem of Political Representation of Women." *American Political Science Review* 75 (September): 701–716.

Sapiro, Virginia. (1982). "If U.S. Senator Baker Were a Woman: An Experimental Study of Candidate Image." *Political Psychology* 3 (Spring/Summer): 61–83.

———. (1983). *The Political Integration of Women*. Urbana: University of Illinois Press.

———. (1986). "The Gender Basis of American Social Policy." *Political Science Quarterly* 101: 221–238.

Sapiro, Virginia, and Barbara G. Farah. (1980). "New Pride and Old Prejudice: Political Ambition and Role Orientation among Female Partisan Elites." *Women & Politics* 1 (Spring): 13–36.

Saxonhouse, Arlene W. (1985). *Women in the History of Political Thought*. New York: Praeger.

———. (1986). "From Tragedy to Hierarchy and Back Again: Women in Greek Political Thought." *American Political Science Review* 80 (June): 403–418.

Schattschneider, E. E. (1975). *The Semi-Sovereign People: A Realist's View of Democracy in America*. Hinsdale, Ill.: Dryden Press.

Schulenburg, Jane Tibbetts. (1989). "Women Monastic Communities, 500–1100: Patterns of Expansion and Decline." *Signs* 14 (Winter): 261–292.

Scott, Anne Firor. (1984). *Making the Invisible Woman Visible*. Urbana: University of Illinois Press.

Sears, David O., Leonie Huddy, and Lynitta G. Schaffer. (1984). "Schemas and Symbolic Politics: The Cases of Racial and Gender Equality." Paper presented to the 19th Annual Carnegie Symposium on Cognition. Carnegie-Mellon University.

Shapiro, Robert Y., and Harpreet Majahan. (1986). "Gender Differences in Policy Preferences: A Summary of Trends from the 1960s to the 1980s." *Public Opinion Quarterly* 50: 42–61.

Shils, Edward A. and Morris Janowitz (1948). "Cohesion and Disintegration in the Wehrmacht in World War II." *Public Opinion Quarterly* 12:280–315.

Shingles, Richard D. (1981). "Black Consciousness and Political Participation: The Missing Link." *American Political Science Review* 75 (March): 76–91.

Sigel, Roberta S. (1988). "Female Perspectives of Gender Relations." Paper presented to the Annual Meeting of the Midwest Political Science Association. Chicago.

Sigel, Roberta S., and Marilyn B. Hoskin. (1977). "Perspectives on Adult Political Socialization— Areas of Research." In Stanley Allen Renshon, ed., *Handbook of Political Socialization Research*. New York: Free Press.

———. (1981). *The Political Involvement of Adolescents*. New Brunswick, N.J.: Rutgers University Press.

Sigel, Roberta S., and John V. Reynolds. (1979–1980). "Generational Differences and the Women's Movement." *Political Science Quarterly* 94: 635–648.

Sigel, Roberta S., and Nancy L. Welchel. (1986a). "Minority Consciousness and Sense of Group Power among Women." Paper presented to the Annual Meeting of the Midwest Political Science Association. Chicago.

———. (1986b). "Assessing the Past and Looking Toward the Future: Perceptions of Change in the Status of Women." Paper presented to the Annual Meeting of the American Political Science Association. Washington, D.C.

Smith, Barbara. (1983). "Introduction." In Barbara Smith, ed., *Homegirls: A Black Feminist Anthology*. New York: Kitchen Table: Women of Color Press.

Smith, Eric R. A. N. (1989). *The Unchanging American Voter*. Berkeley: University of California Press.

Sperling, Susan. (1991). "Baboons with Briefcases: Feminism, Functionalism, and Sociobiology in the Evolution of Primate Gender." *Signs* 17 (Autumn): 1–27.

Spruill, Julia Cherry. ([1938] 1972). *Women's Life and Work in the Southern Colonies*. New York: W. W. Norton.

Staggenborg, Suzanne. (1991). *The Pro-Choice Movement: Organization and Activism in the Abortion Conflict*. New York: Oxford University Press.

Stanley, Jeanie R. (1985). "Life Space and Gender Politics in an East Texas Community." *Women & Politics* 5(4): 27–49.

Stanton, Elizabeth Cady. ([1882] 1915). "The Solitude of Self: Speech Delivered to the Judiciary Committee." *Elizabeth Cady Stanton Papers*. Washington, D.C.: Library of Congress.

Stoker, Laura L. (1987). "Morality and Politics: Conduct and Control. A Report on New Items in the 1987 National Election Pilot Study." Submitted to the ANES Board of Overseers. Unpublished manuscript.

Stratton, Joanna L. (1981). *Pioneer Women*. New York: Simon & Schuster.

Strouse, Jean. (1980). *Alice James: A Biography*. Boston: Houghton Mifflin.

Thornton, Arland, Duane F. Alwin, and Donald Camburn. (1983). "Causes and Consequences of Sex-Role Attitudes and Attitude Change." *American Sociological Review* 48 (April): 211–227.

Thornton, Arland, and Deborah Freedman. (1979). "Change in the Sex Role Attitudes of Women, 1962–1977: Evidence from a Panel Study." *American Sociological Review* 44 (October): 831–842.

Tolleson Rinehart, Sue. (1985). "Toward Women's Political Resocialization: Patterns of Predisposition in the Learning of Feminist Attitudes." *Women & Politics* 5(4): 11–26.

———. (1987). "Maternal Health Care Policy: Britain and the United States." *Comparative Politics* 19: 193–211.

———. (1988). "Gender Differences and the Political Orientations of Southern College Students." *Women & Politics* 8(1): 69–86.

———. (1989). "The Life Course and Intergenerational Change." Paper presented to the Annual Meeting of the American Political Science Association. Atlanta.

Tolleson Rinehart, Sue, and Jerry Perkins. (1989). "The Intersection of Gender Politics and Religious Beliefs." *Political Behavior* 11 (March): 33–55.

Tomalin, Claire. (1974). *The Life and Death of Mary Wollstonecraft*. New York: Harcourt Brace Jovanovich.

Tucker, Robert C. (1978). *The Marx-Engels Reader*. 2d ed. New York: W. W. Norton.

Verba, Sidney. (1961). *Small Groups and Political Behavior: A Study of Leadership*. Princeton: Princeton University Press.

Verba, Sidney, and Norman Nie. (1972). *Participation in America*. New York: Harper & Row.

Von Martin, Alfred. (1944). *Sociology of the Renaissance*. New York: Oxford University Press.

Wald, Kenneth D. (1987). *Religion and Politics in the United States*. New York: St. Martin's Press.

Walker, Alice. (1982). *The Color Purple*. New York: Washington Square Press.

Ware, Susan. (1981). *Beyond Suffrage: Women in the New Deal*. Cambridge, Mass.: Harvard University Press.

———. (1984). "ER and Democratic Politics: Women in the Postsuffrage Era." In Joan Hoff-Wilson and Marjorie Lightman, eds., *Without Precedent: The Life and Career of Eleanor Roosevelt*. Bloomington: Indiana University Press.

Wattenberg, Ben J. (1987). *The Birth Dearth*. New York: Pharos Books.

Weissberg, Robert. (1974). *Political Learning, Political Choice, and Democratic Citizenship*. Englewood Cliff, N.J.: Prentice-Hall.

Welch, Susan. (1977). "Women as Political Animals? A Test of Some Explanations for Male-Female Political Differences." *American Journal of Political Science* 21 (November): 711–730.

Welch, Susan, and Lee Sigelman. (1988). "A Black Gender Gap?" Paper presented to the Annual Meeting of the Midwest Political Science Association. Chicago.

Wilcox, Clyde. (1989). "Feminism and Anti-Feminism among Evangelical Women." *Western Political Quarterly* 42 (March): 147–160.

———. (1990). "Race Differences in Abortion Attitudes: Some Additional Evidence." *Public Opinion Quarterly* 54 (Summer): 248–255.

Wilcox, Clyde, Lee Sigelman, and Elizabeth Cook. (1989). "Some Like It Hot: Individual Differences in Responses to Group Feeling Thermometers." *Public Opinion Quarterly* 53 (Summer): 246–257.

Wilson, Edward O. (1978). *On Human Nature*. Cambridge, Mass.: Harvard University Press.

Wollstonecraft, Mary. ([1792] 1975). *A Vindication of the Rights of Woman*. Edited by Miriam Brody Kramnick. London: Penguin Books.

AUTHOR INDEX

SUBJECT INDEX